THE PHILOSOPHY OF THOMAS REID

D1471045

To Selwyn Alfred Grave 1916–2002

THE PHILOSOPHY OF THOMAS REID

A Collection of Essays

Edited by

JOHN HALDANE

and

STEPHEN READ

First published as volume 52, number 209 of *The Philosophical Quarterly*, 2002
The essay 'Of Power' by Thomas Reid first published in volume 51, number 202 of
The Philosophical Quarterly, 2001

350 Main Street, Malden, MA 02148-5018, USA
108 Cowley Road, Oxford OX4 1JF, UK
550 Swanston Street, Carlton South, Melbourne, Victoria 3053, Australia
Kurfürstendamm 57, 10707 Berlin, Germany

First published 2003 by Blackwell Publishing Ltd

Library of Congress Cataloging-in-Publication Data has been applied for

ISBN 1-40510-905-X

A catalogue record for this title is available from the British Library

Set by Christopher Bryant
Printed and bound in the United Kingdom
by MPG Books Ltd, Bodmin, Cornwall

for further information on
Blackwell Publishing, visit our website:
http://www.blackwellpublishing.com

CONTENTS

1   Introduction   *John Haldane*   I

2   Of Power   *Thomas Reid*   14

3   Reid and Epistemic Naturalism   *Patrick Rysiew*   24

4   The Problem with Reid's Direct Realism   *J. Todd Buras*   44

5   Reid's Foundation for the
      Primary/Secondary Quality Distinction   *Jennifer McKitrick*   65

6   Reid, Kant and the Philosophy of Mind   *Etienne Brun-Rovet*   82

7   Reid and Priestley on Method and the Mind   *Alan Tapper*   98

8   Common Sense and the Theory of Human Behaviour   *Ferenc Huoranszki*   113

9   How to Reid Moore   *John Greco*   131

10 A Defence of Scottish Common Sense   *Michael Pakaluk*   151

11 Reid on Fictional Objects and the Way of Ideas   *Ryan Nichols*   169

12 Reconsidering Reid's Geometry of Visibles   *Gideon Yaffe*   189

    Index   208

I

INTRODUCTION

By John Haldane

I. THE LIFE AND WORK OF THOMAS REID

On 13 October 1797, a year to the week following Reid's death, Kant received a letter from a Swedish bishop sending the results of his (Lindblom's)
investigations into Kant's genealogy. In his reply, Kant wrote 'I have known
for quite some time that my grandfather ... came originally from Scotland,
that he was one of the many people who emigrated from there ... towards
the end of the last century'.[1] He also held that the family name was
originally spelt 'Cant'. Had he known more about Scotland, this might well
have encouraged him to suppose that he was a descendant of the Cant
family, one associated with the east of the country, a region that had long
traded with the northern European mainland. Recent research by Lord
Murray strongly suggests that Kant was wrong about his ancestry, but had
he been right, then his forebears would have been members of a family who
lived and owned land in Glen Dye, part of the heather uplands of Grampian
in the parish of Strachan, about twenty miles from Aberdeen.[2]

On 26 April 1710, almost fourteen years to the day before Kant's own
birth, there was born, in the manse of this parish, Thomas, second son of
the Rev. Lewis Reid. Like Kant, Thomas Reid was to be brought to life as a
critical philosopher by reflecting on the sceptical empiricism of David
Hume, which he sought to counter by placing human knowledge on a better
foundation than that of impressions and ideas. For these reasons Reid has
been described as 'the Scottish Kant', a characterization which, had his own

---

[1] A. Zweig (ed.), *Immanuel Kant: Correspondence* (Cambridge UP, 1999), p. 256.
[2] See Ronald King Murray, 'Immanuel Kant: Had He a Scottish Connection?', *Scots Philosophical Newsletter*, 12 (1995), p. 812.

genealogical beliefs been correct, might have applied to Kant himself. Such are the engaging ironies of (counterfactual) history.

If Kant's antecedents are in doubt, Reid's are well documented. On his father's side he could number six generations of clergymen dating back to the Reformation, and a Greek and Latin Secretary to King James VI of Scotland (I of England), whose name was also Thomas and whose brother Alexander was a physician to Charles I. Through his mother he was related to the Gregory family, which included several distinguished mathematicians. Three of his uncles were professors of mathematics at Edinburgh, Oxford and St Andrews, and two of his cousins held chairs of history and of mathematics, again at Oxford and at St Andrews. One of these uncles invented the reflecting telescope, was a friend of Newton, and introduced Newtonian science into the Scottish universities. Several of his scientific instruments remain in St Andrews to this day.

Against this intellectual family background, it is unsurprising that Thomas Reid showed an aptitude for study. Educated at home until the age of ten, he then enrolled at the local Kincardine School, and two years later in 1722 transferred to the Aberdeen Grammar School, where he remained for only a few months before entering Marischal College in the same city. The College, which in later years merged with the University of Aberdeen, operated the 'regent' system, in which each student cohort was taught natural, moral and metaphysical philosophy by the same teacher throughout the entire course of study. For the three years of Reid's time there he, together with some forty other students, was instructed by George Turnbull. Himself a son of a Presbyterian minister, Turnbull was an important figure in the development of Scottish moral philosophy, in which, as in other aspects of his thought, he cautioned against rationalist apriorism and argued in favour of a broad 'empiricalism'. I have coined this last term to distinguish general appeals to inner and outer experience from the specifically reductionist position later developed by Hume and others, and I believe it fits equally well Reid's own developed position.

Turnbull could not have failed to influence Reid, and there is reason to think that the influence was more than one of general encouragement. Turnbull's *Principles of Moral Philosophy*, published in 1740, is the text of lectures given during the period of his regency at Marischal from 1721 to 1727. In some respects its philosophy resembles the then fashionable idealism of Berkeley, from whom Turnbull quotes approvingly, but it also makes a number of particular claims which later find strong echoes in Reid's realist epistemology and metaphysics. At one point Turnbull writes about causation, and contends that the only 'active power' is the will. In and of itself, nature has no 'productive energy'; thus what we experience as causality is either our own agency, or that of another, operative in things. Elsewhere he maintains that our judgements and reasoned conclusions, particularly in the moral sphere, should be tested against the measure of 'common sense', which is fully adequate to determine their truth or falsity: 'Common sense is sufficient to teach those who think of the matter with seriousness and attention all the duties of common life ... all that is morally fit and binding'.[3]

Both notions recur in Reid's thought, though the idea and role of common sense is broadened and deepened. In *Essays on the Active Powers* (1788) and in later writings (particularly that reproduced here), Reid argues that power, strictly speaking, is not necessitation but the exercise of a capacity to produce or not to produce an effect: this, he contends, presupposes both will and understanding. While thus rejecting Hume's claim that we have no experience of causation as such, Reid agrees that when we ordinarily ascribe causality to natural events, 'we mean nothing more than a constant conjunction by the laws or rules of nature which experience discovers'.[4]

'Common sense' became a term of art in Reid's philosophy, and the set of ideas it represents has been associated predominantly with his name ever since the publication in 1764 of *An Inquiry into the Human Mind on the Principles of Common Sense*. Unlike the *sensus communis* of the scholastics, this is not a faculty of sense, nor a distinctive power of the intellect, nor yet the common consensus conceived as general opinion. Rather it is reason itself, as that is structured by, or necessarily grasps, a set of principles the negation of which is self-contradictory or self-refuting. Reid himself describes it as 'the first degree of reason [which] judges of things self-evident',[5] and goes on to illustrate various of these self-evident principles and to put them to use against Humean and other scepticisms.

It is a matter of scholarly debate just how many such principles Reid thought there might be, and what the different categories are to which they belong, but evidently he assumed that some were logical, some epistemological and others metaphysical. The question of their status is the most important one from the point of view of the rejection of sceptical empiricism and of anti-realism more generally. In Hume's account, all truth pertains either to matters of fact or to relations of ideas. In so far as the latter are merely definitional, be it explicitly or implicitly so, this category of truth is the domain of tautology, and contains no genuinely informative truths about

---

[3] George Turnbull, *The Principles of Moral Philosophy* (London: Millar, 1740; facsimile edn New York: Olms, 1976), p. 16.

[4] See 'Of Power', dated 13 March 1792, first published in *The Philosophical Quarterly*, 51 (2001), and reprinted below, pp. 14–24.

[5] Reid, *Essays on the Intellectual Powers of Man*, in *The Works of Thomas Reid*, ed. W. Hamilton (Edinburgh: Thin, 1895; facsimile edn Hildesheim: Olms, 1967), essay VI, 'Of Judgement', ch. 11, 'Of Common Sense', p. 425.

reality. With regard to the first, Hume's theory of impressions (conceived of as distinct mental items between which no necessary connections hold, but only those of psychological association) undermines the possibility of reasoning from one state of knowledge to another. According to Hume, what pass for such reasonings, be it from 'is' to 'ought', or from effect to cause, are habits of mind arising from experiences of conjunction and contiguity, assisted by propensities to project psychological dispositions onto the world.

Reid saw very clearly the meaning and implications of Hume's ideas, and was perhaps the first to do so. He was a careful reader of *A Treatise of Human Nature*, the work of which Hume complained that it 'fell deadborn from the press, without attaining such distinction as even to excite a murmur among the zealots'.[6] That stillbirth had been in January 1739, when Hume was twenty-seven and Reid exactly one year older. A decade later Hume published a more accessible and less boldly sceptical version of his views in the form of *An Enquiry Concerning Human Understanding*. It was this, and not the *Treatise*, that triggered Kant's awakening from 'dogmatic slumber'.

It was nearly a quarter of a century before Reid published his rejoinder to Hume's philosophy, but it is clear that the system presented in his *Inquiry into the Human Mind* had been worked on for many years before. In 1758 he delivered a paper to the Aberdeen Philosophical Society, 'On the Difficulty of Just Philosophy of the Human Mind', and various other papers and discourses on the themes of the *Inquiry* were given to the same society in the following years. By his own account, however, Reid had been exercised by Hume's scepticism for some twenty years prior to 1764. It seems likely that the long process of formulating his own account of human knowledge began with readings of Hume in the early 1740s, once Reid had become settled as minister of New Machar (a parish to the north-west of Aberdeen).

He had been appointed there in 1737, probably through the influence of his cousin John Gregory, who was then Professor of Medicine at King's College, Aberdeen. Reid had completed his four-year degree course at Marischal in 1726, and the following winter began a further four years of study, this time directed towards the Presbyterian ministry in which his father had also served. Having been elected a 'Clerk' in 1732, he was shortly thereafter appointed librarian of his old college. This provided him with an opportunity to resume philosophical and scientific reading. In 1736 Reid embarked upon a journey to England. There he visited Cambridge, London and Oxford, at the last of which he stayed with his cousin, the Professor of History, David Gregory. Sometime not long after he had returned to the library at Marischal came news of the appointment to New Machar.

[6] Hume, 'My Own Life', 18 April 1776, reprinted as Appendix A of E.C. Mossner, *The Life of David Hume* (Oxford: Clarendon Press, 1980), p. 612.

The years that followed saw marriage to his cousin Elizabeth (in 1740), and the start of a family that in due course involved the birth of six girls and three boys. Two daughters were born either side of the 1745 rebellion, and Reid recounts having made the acquaintance of a prominent Jacobite when that gentleman (Hepburn of Keith) stayed the night at New Machar while *en route* to Culloden, soon to be the site of the bloody defeat of Bonnie Prince Charlie's rebel army. The same year as the battle, 1746, his 22-year-old wife fell ill, and Reid wrote a petitionary prayer on her behalf:

> O God, I desire humbly to supplicate Thy Divine Majesty in behalf of my distressed wife, who is by Thy hand brought very low, and in imminent danger of death, if Thou, who alone doest wonders, do not in Thy mercy interpose Thy almighty arm, and bring her back from the gate of death.[7]

Elizabeth, who by that point had had four children, recovered, and lived on for almost half a century until 1792. Following her death Reid (who was by then 82) wrote to Dugald Stewart again in humble and moving terms:

> By the loss of my bosom friend, with whom I lived fifty-two years, I am brought into a new kind of world at a time of life when old habits are not easily forgot, or new ones acquired. But every world is God's world, and I am thankful for the comforts he has left me.[8]

Between times Reid's career had proceeded to distinction. He had begun publishing in 1748 with a short paper on 'Quantity' given to the Royal Society (a year after Kant's own first publication on a related topic). In 1751 he had been elected to a regent mastership at King's College, where he taught natural and physical science and moral philosophy and metaphysics. Seven years later he co-founded with his cousin John Gregory, the Professor of Medicine, the aforementioned Aberdeen Philosophical Society. Over the course of its fifteen-year existence the society, popularly known as the 'Wise Club', numbered among its members James Beattie, George Campbell, John Farquhar and Alexander Gerard, and served as forum for the development of the 'common sense' response to Humean scepticism. In 1762 Reid received an honorary Doctorate of Divinity from Marischal College, and the following year was appointed Professor of Moral Philosophy in the University of Glasgow, in succession to Adam Smith. At about the same point as he accepted the Glasgow chair he sold to a publisher the text of the *Inquiry*, the result of twenty years' reflection on Hume's sceptical empiricism.

In 1762, Reid's friend Hugh Blair, who was then minister of the High Kirk in St Giles' Church, Edinburgh, was appointed Regius Professor of

---

[7] As quoted in A. Campbell Fraser, *Thomas Reid* (Edinburgh: Oliphant, 1898), p. 345.

[8] D. Stewart, 'Account of the Life and Writings of Thomas Reid, D.D.', in Reid, *Works*, ed. Hamilton, p. 30.

Rhetoric and Belles-Lettres at Edinburgh University. Shortly thereafter, and probably at Reid's instigation, Blair delivered to Hume a partial draft of Reid's *Inquiry*, with the request that he provide a 'judgement of the argument and of the piece in general'. Hume replied to Blair, who evidently forwarded the letter to Reid himself. It offered several criticisms, but prefaced these with the observation that what Hume had been shown was only a small part. In response, Reid prepared an abstract of the whole *Inquiry*, and again had Blair relay this. The result was a direct one-round exchange between Reid and Hume. Although brief, this suggests mutual respect, with Reid the more admiring of the pair and Hume sending compliments to Campbell, Gerard and Gregory, his 'adversaries' in Aberdeen.[9] Those familiar with Kant's *Prolegomena* may recall his withering comment on Hume's domestic philosophical critics:

> It is positively painful to see how utterly his opponents, Reid, Oswald, Beattie, and lastly Priestley, missed the point of the problem [of causation] ... they so misconstrued his valuable suggestion that everything remained in its old condition, as if nothing had happened.[10]

It has already been noted that Kant's familiarity with Hume's work was through the later and avowedly less unsettling *Enquiry*, whereas Reid had encountered and engaged the ferocious scepticism of the *Treatise*. It should now be added that there is no direct evidence of Kant's ever having read any of Reid's work, as opposed to having read an account of the common sense philosophy.[11] I recommend, therefore that, so far as Reid himself is concerned, readers should take Kant's estimation *cum grano salis*.

Thomas Reid remained at Glasgow for thirty years. In 1773 he was visited by Boswell and Johnson, on their way back from the tour of the Western Highlands. At that time, mail coaches arriving at the Gallows' Gate, in the east of the city, would be met by waiters dressed in embroidered coats, red breeches and powdered hair, sent from the Saracen's Head Inn. There it was that the travellers entertained the distinguished and well known

---

[9] For an account of the exchange, see Paul Wood, 'David Hume on Reid's *An Inquiry into the Human Mind, on the Principles of Common Sense*: a New Letter to Hugh Blair from July 1762', *Mind*, 95 (1986), pp. 411–16. A transcription of the complete set of extant correspondence appears in Reid, *An Inquiry into the Human Mind on the Principles of Common Sense*, ed. D.R. Brookes (Edinburgh UP, 1997).

[10] Kant, *Prolegomena to Any Future Metaphysics*, tr. and ed. G. Hatfield (Cambridge UP, 1997), p. 89.

[11] Such as Joseph Priestley's *An Examination of Dr Reid's 'Inquiry', Dr Beattie's 'Essay on the Nature of Truth' and Dr Oswald's 'Appeal to Common Sense'* (London: Johnson, 1774), or James Beattie's *An Essay on the Nature and Immutability of Truth* (Edinburgh: Kincaid & Bell, 1770), the latter appearing in German translation in 1772. It should be noted, however, that in his illuminating book on *Scottish Common Sense Philosophy in Germany 1768–1800* (McGill-Queen's UP, 1987), Manfred Kuehn holds it very likely that Kant read Reid in a French translation.

professor, along with two (unnamed) university colleagues, to both breakfast and supper. Of the day's conversation, Boswell records nothing beyond remarking that 'the professors ... did not venture to expose themselves much to the battery of cannon which they knew might play upon them'.[12] Reid may have judged that this was not the occasion for philosophical discourse, or perhaps he engaged in it, and it passed Boswell by. Certainly Dr Johnson did not find it easy to absorb philosophical opinions that countered his own convictions. When being told three years later by Boswell that on his death-bed Hume had professed himself 'quite easy at the thought of Annihilation', Johnson retorted 'He lied; he had a vanity in being thought easy at the prospect.... And you are to consider that upon his own principle of Annihilation he had no motive not to lie.'[13] Certainly any suggestion that Reid might be lacking in communicative skills or intellectual resources is wholly countered by the record of his correspondence with Lord Kames (formerly Henry Home). This ranges widely over various subjects, and includes what I believe to be the first discussion of a 'brain/personal identity' thought-experiment. Reid writes (in ironic rejection of Priestley's materialism)

> I would be glad to know your Lordship's opinion whether ... if two or three such [intelligent] beings should be formed out of my brain, whether they will all be me, and consequently all be one and the same intelligent being.[14]

In 1774 Reid published *A Brief Account of Aristotle's Logic* as an appendix to Kames' *Sketches of the History of Man*. This was his only publication while he was teaching at Glasgow. A month after his seventieth birthday, Reid wrote to Kames to report that he found himself growing old, and had requested the College to appoint an assistant and successor. As was then the way, this gentleman (Archibald Arthur) delivered versions of Reid's own lectures to the students. Meanwhile Reid himself set about preparing the same material, amended and developed, for publication. This appeared in two stages: in 1785 as *Essays on the Intellectual Powers of Man*, and in 1788 as *Essays on the Active Powers of Man*. Four years later his dear wife Elizabeth died. The couple had nine children, but by that point only one, Martha, survived, and she had been widowed in the very same year as her mother passed away. Thereafter Martha cared for her father, accompanying him on occasional visits out of Glasgow, as when in the summer of 1796 they went to stay for a few weeks in Edinburgh with their cousin Dr James Gregory. This was the son of John Gregory with whom Reid had founded the Aberdeen Philosophical Society, and like his father he was a Professor of Medicine. He was

[12] Boswell's *Journal of a Tour to the Hebrides with Samuel Johnson*, ed. F.A. Pottle (New York: McGraw Hill, 1961), p. 365.

[13] Boswell, *Letters*, ed. C.B. Tinker (Oxford: Clarendon Press, 1924), Vol. 1, p. 264.

[14] Letter to Lord Kames of 1775: Reid, *Works*, ed. Hamilton, p. 53.

also the author of philosophical writings opposing the necessity of the will; and being appreciative of Reid's achievements as a philosopher, he commissioned Henry Raeburn to paint the old man's portrait during this summer stay. More often seen in reproduction, the painting hangs today in Fyvie Castle, a dozen miles on the road north from New Machar, and it is this image that appears on the cover of the present volume. James Gregory served history well, for within weeks of returning to Glasgow, Reid fell ill, and thereafter suffered a series of strokes that led to his death in October of that year.

Eight years later Kant also died. Thus, within a decade, there ended the lives of the two great anti-sceptical contemporaries of Hume. It would be idle to attempt to compare them in point of genius. Kant's influence has unquestionably been the greater, and his imaginative power was superior. Yet his writing is notoriously difficult, and usually most obscure where it is most important to be clear. Reid, by contrast, lays so great an emphasis upon clarity and brevity of expression that his prose is perhaps the most modern of any eighteenth-century philosophical writer. In the following century this stylistic rigour was congenial to those of empirical and pragmatic disposition, largely but not wholly confined to the literate peoples of Britain and North America. Later still, Reid was rediscovered by those in the British philosophical tradition for whom idealism and scepticism were philosophical diseases. G.E. Moore was in his debt, as, indirectly, were Wittgenstein, Austin and Ryle. In the next generation he was taken up in Britain by Anthony Woozley at the University of St Andrews, and in America by C.J. Ducasse and Roderick Chisholm at Brown University. Of the latter, Keith Lehrer tells the story that while Chisholm was chairman of the philosophy department he received a telephone call from a man of the world, who said that although he was busy, he had the time and the inclination to read just one serious philosophy book; and he asked for a recommendation. Chisholm took a day to respond, but then the reply was direct: read Reid.[15]

II. THE ESSAYS

This the reader may now do, for the first of the following essays is by Reid himself. 'Of Power' had not previously been published prior to its appearance as the opening article in the January 2001 number of *The Philosophical Quarterly*, some 209 years after the date of its writing. The subject of the essay bears upon the understanding of the operations of nature, and to that extent

[15] See K. Lehrer, *Thomas Reid* (London: Routledge, 1989), p. 1.

it belongs to the philosophy of science – though it also bears significantly on general metaphysics, the philosophy of mind, and even, in its later stages, upon the philosophy of religion. In it, Reid revisits themes explored in his *Essays on the Active Powers of Man* (especially essay I, 'Of Active Power in General', and essay IV, 'Of the Liberty of Moral Agents'), and in his private correspondence with Lord Kames and Dr James Gregory. As in those writings, Reid's style and methods are fresh and remarkably modern; and the interest of what he has to say about the concepts of natural power and voluntary agency is undiminished by the passage of the years.

The text is transcribed, with minimal editing, from the manuscript in the collection of the University of Aberdeen (MS 2131/2/II/2). This is in Reid's own hand and is dated 13 March 1792, when he was eighty-one years old and had retired from the Chair of Moral Philosophy in Glasgow. In his small but excellent study of Reid's life and work, A. Campbell Fraser quotes from this manuscript, and refers to it as '[Reid's] last expression of reflective thought'.[16] In 1795 Reid read a scientific paper on 'Muscular Motion' to the Glasgow Literary Society, and two years prior to that presented to the same society 'Observations on the Danger of Political Innovation'.[17] It appears, however, that 'Of Power' was indeed Reid's last piece of philosophical writing.

In editing the text for a philosophical readership I have judged it apt to convert Reid's frequent capitalizations into lower case and to insert quotation marks where he refers to a word such as 'power' or 'cause'. I have also modernized spelling which might otherwise have proved distracting (e.g., in 'physick' and 'conjoyned'), though I have retained the original where it is still familiar (e.g., 'shewed' and 'connexion'). At several points Reid mentions figures whose work is not well known to present-day readers, or refers to still famous persons by what are now unfamiliar styles, e.g., 'L. Bacon' (i.e., Lord [Francis] Bacon). The latter issue I have dealt with by adopting current conventions, the former by providing footnotes to the text. No notes appear in Reid's manuscript. The punctuation, by contrast, is almost entirely Reid's own, the exceptions being instances where sense was at risk from evidently eccentric or erroneous breaks or continuations. There are one or two places where I have inserted words for the sake of sense or fluency. These additions are indicated by square brackets. It is hoped that readers will engage this piece of writing as they might the work of any

[16] A.C. Fraser, *Thomas Reid* (Edinburgh: Oliphant, 1898), p. 119. I am indebted to Fraser's 'life', and also to Dugald Stewart's earlier account. Fine as the former is, however, the time is long overdue for a new biography of one of Scotland's greatest and most enduring thinkers.

[17] The paper 'Of Muscular Motion in the Human Body' has recently been published in *Thomas Reid on the Animate Creation: Papers Relating to the Life Sciences*, ed. P. Wood (Edinburgh UP, 1995), pp. 103–24.

contemporary philosopher. Happily, the clarity of Reid's prose is liable to assist with this.

The same issue of the *Quarterly* as first published 'Of Power' announced the subject of its 2001 essay competition as 'Thomas Reid, Scottish Philosophy and the Common Sense Tradition'. In setting this topic, it was hoped that essayists would pursue the possibilities suggested by Reid's work, as well as provide critical assessments of it, and explore other aspects of Scottish philosophy and of the common sense tradition. That hope was not disappointed. The field was one of the largest drawn by the annual competition, and happily it contained a large number of publishable essays, several from younger scholars. Unsurprisingly, the primary focus of most of the papers, and that of all of those republished here, is Reid's philosophy. They divide into three broad groupings: first, those examining Reid's account of knowledge, second, papers concerning issues at the interface of philosophy of mind and metaphysics; and third, essays dealing with Reid in relation to the thought of others, in particular Joseph Priestley and Kant (a further essay, not drawn from the competition entries, addresses the relation between Reid and G.E. Moore). Whatever their particular focus, they all testify to the continuing philosophical interest of Reid's thought.

Sixty years ago Anthony Woozley published an edited volume of Reid's *Essays on the Intellectual Powers of Man* (1941). Prior to that the printings of Reid's main writings were in the nineteenth century. Given the ease of his prose, anyone who had access to these issuings of the 1846 Sir William Hamilton edition was in a position to assess the interest of the text. This was, however, long out of print and not readily obtainable, even in university libraries; so Reid's readership was small, and in consequence the modern secondary literature was tiny. Even so, a paper such as Peter Winch's 'The Notion of "Suggestion" in Thomas Reid's Theory of Perception', published in *The Philosophical Quarterly* fifty years ago in 1953, and those by Richard Taylor and Timothy Duggan, 'On Seeing Double' (*PQ* 1958), by David Blumenfeld 'On Not Seeing Double' (*PQ* 1959), and by Duggan alone on 'The Scottish Philosophy of Common Sense' (*PQ* 1961), indicated to non-historians that the work under discussion was likely to be relevant to contemporary concerns in the areas of philosophy of perception and epistemology. With the publication of S.A. Grave's study *The Scottish Philosophy of Common Sense* (1960, a version of a PhD thesis completed at St Andrews under Woozley's supervision), and with the appearance of Reid's main writings in paperback editions edited by Baruch Brody (1969), Timothy Duggan (1970), and by Keith Lehrer and Ronald Beanblossom (1975), it became possible for others to see Reid's importance and to begin to study his work both in its historical context and as a contribution to present-day philosophical interests. Grave's contribution was especially important in providing secondary literature during a period when the field was largely neglected, and it was with sadness that news of his death was received as this volume was going to press. In honour of his work it is dedicated to him.

Over the last twenty years the scale and pace of Reid studies have increased significantly. This is due in no small part to the publication of Keith Lehrer's *Thomas Reid* (1989) and to Lehrer's many related essays; to the appearance of a number of groups of papers, published as books or as thematic issues of journals; and to the developing critical edition of Reid's own writings, including those that had not previously been published. (Details of these are given in the short bibliography appended below.) With new monographs now appearing at the rate of one every two or three years, a second *Companion to Reid* in press, the Reid Project progressing at the University of Aberdeen, and a Reid Society recently established in the United States, it is possible to say that the inspirer of the 'Scottish Common Sense School' is now among the most frequently discussed of eighteenth-century British philosophers.

The following new essays are further testimony to the level of interest in the field, and to the fact that it is drawing new generations of philosophers. With the tricentenary of Reid's birth falling in 2010, the prospect of celebratory conferences, symposia, further papers and books is in view. By publishing the essay 'On Power' and the special issue on *The Philosophy of Thomas Reid*, and now supporting the publication of this related volume, *The Philosophical Quarterly* is pleased to renew its association with the renaissance of Reid scholarship and of critical engagement with his philosophy.[18]

[18] 'Of Power' is published by kind permission of the University of Aberdeen, which owns the manuscript. Thanks are due to the staff of Historic Collections there and to the Department of Philosophy's Reid Project, in particular Gordon Graham; and to Stephen Read, the Editorial Chairman of *The Philosophical Quarterly*, for supporting the idea of its original publication. I am also grateful to these named for assistance in connection with matters bearing upon the special issue of *The Philosophical Quarterly* on *The Philosophy of Thomas Reid*, Vol. 52 No. 209 (October 2002), in which the other ten essays were also published. Part I of the present introduction draws extensively from 'Thomas Reid: Life and Work', in John Haldane (ed.), *Thomas Reid*, in *American Catholic Philosophical Quarterly*, 74 (2000), and I am grateful to the American Catholic Philosophical Association for permission to re-use that material here. Work on the present volume was done while I held the Royden Davis Chair of Humanities at Georgetown University.

III. SELECTED BIBLIOGRAPHY OF WRITINGS
BY AND ABOUT REID

(i) Works by Reid in the new critical editions

1. *Practical Ethics, Being Lectures and Papers on Natural Religion, Self Government, Natural Jurisprudence, and the Law of Nations*, edited by Knud Haakonssen (Princeton UP, 1990).

2. *Thomas Reid on the Animate Creation: Papers Relating to the Life Sciences*, edited by Paul Wood (Edinburgh UP, 1995).

3. *An Inquiry into the Human Mind on the Principles of Common Sense*, edited by Derek R. Brookes (Edinburgh UP, 1997).

4. *Essays on the Intellectual Powers of Man*, edited by Derek R. Brookes (Edinburgh UP, 2002).

5. *The Correspondence of Thomas Reid*, edited by Paul Wood (Edinburgh UP, in press).

6. *Lectures and Papers in Logic, Rhetoric and the Fine Arts*, edited by Alexander Broadie (Edinburgh UP, in press).

(ii) Monographs

1. *Thomas Reid's Inquiry: the Geometry of the Visibles and the Case for Realism*, by Norman Daniels (New York: Franklin, 1974; 2nd edn Stanford UP, 1989).

2. *Thomas Reid's Newtonian Realism*, by William Ellos (Univ. Press of America, 1981).

3. *Claude Buffier and Thomas Reid: Two Common Sense Philosophers*, by Louise Marcile-Lacoste (McGill-Queen's UP, 1982).

4. *Thomas Reid and the Way of Ideas*, by Roger Gallie (Dordrecht: Kluwer, 1989).

5. *Thomas Reid*, by Keith Lehrer (London: Routledge, 1989).

6. *Thomas Reid on Freedom and Morality*, by William Rowe (Cornell UP, 1991).

7. *Reid and his French Disciples: Aesthetics and Music*, by James Manns (Leiden: Brill, 1994).

8. *Common Sense and Improvement: Thomas Reid as Social Theorist*, by Peter Diamond (New York: Peter Lang, 1998).

9. *Thomas Reid: Ethics, Aesthetics and the Anatomy of the Self*, by Roger Gallie (Dordrecht: Kluwer, 1998).

10. *Companion to the Works of Thomas Reid*, by John Christian-Smith (Lampeter: Edwin Mellen Press, 2000).

11. *Thomas Reid and the Story of Epistemology*, by Nicholas Wolterstorff (Cambridge UP, 2001).

12. *Thomas Reid and Scepticism: his Reliabilist Response*, by Philip de Bary (London: Routledge, 2002).

(iii) Collections of essays

1. *Thomas Reid: Critical Interpretations*, edited by Stephen Barker and Tom Beauchamp (Temple UP, 1976).

2. *The Philosophy of Thomas Reid*, edited by Lewis White Beck, *The Monist*, 61 (1978).

3. *Thomas Reid and his Contemporaries*, edited by William Alston, *The Monist*, 70 (1987).

4. *The Philosophy of Thomas Reid*, edited by Melvin Dalgarno and Eric Matthews (Dordrecht: Kluwer, 1989).

5. *Thomas Reid*, edited by John Haldane, *American Catholic Philosophical Quarterly*, 74 (2000).

6. *The Cambridge Companion to Thomas Reid*, edited by Rene van Woudenberg and Terence Cuneo (Cambridge UP, in press).

2

OF POWER

By Thomas Reid

How men get the conception of power is a question of some difficulty. It is not an object either of sense or of consciousness. Locke rashly determined that we get this idea [in] both these ways. Hume shewed that it can be got in neither of them and thence rashly concluded that there is no such conception in the human mind.

Every voluntary exertion to produce an event seems to imply a persuasion in the agent that he has power to produce the event. A deliberate exertion to produce an event implies a conception of the event, and some belief or hope that his exertion will be followed by it. This I think cannot be denied. The consequence is that a conception of power is antecedent to every deliberate exertion of will to produce an event. We have reason to think that voluntary exertions are as early as any other operation of the thinking being, and if they be all deliberate, that is, intended to produce an event which we believe to be in our power, we should be led to think a conception of power, and even a belief that such and such events are in our power, are innate, [or] at least antecedent to every act of volition. But I am rather inclined to think that our first exertions are instinctive, without any distinct conception of the event that is to follow, consequently without will to produce that event. And that finding by experience that such exertions are followed by such events, we learn to make the exertion voluntarily and deliberately, as often as we desire to produce the event. And when we know or believe that the event depends upon our exertion, we have the conception of power in ourselves to produce that event.

This account of the origin of our conception of power, makes it to be the fruit of experience and not innate; though it must be as early as any deliberate voluntary exertion to produce a certain event. This account likewise supposes that an exertion is something different from a deliberate will to produce the event by that exertion, and that there may be exertion without will. It must be acknowledged that these two are so conjoined, when we have got some knowledge of the extent of our power, that we find it very difficult to distinguish them. As this distinction is supposed in the account we have given of the origin of our conception of power, it may be proper to give some other instances which confirm it.

When I will to rise and walk immediately, the exertion seems inseparably conjoined with the volition, and both appear as one and the same act of mind: but I resolve to rise and walk an hour hence. This is a deliberate act of will, as well as the will to do it immediately; but no exertion follows for an hour. Here the will is disjoined from the exertion therefore they are different.

Again I will to walk for half an hour. The exertion immediately succeeds. During my walk, my thought is wholly occupied, on some other subject than the walk, so that there is not a thought of it or will concerning it at present in my mind; yet the exertion of walking continues. In this instance there is exertion without will, as in the last there was will without exertion.

Volition, I think does not admit of degrees. It is complete in itself and incapable of more and less. Exertion on the other hand may be great or small or middling. Therefore volition and exertion are not the same. If so, there may be exertion without deliberate will; and experience of the consequence of such exertions may at the same time give us the conception of power and teach us that the events known to be consequent upon such exertions are in our power.

Supposing we were unable to give any account how we first got the conception of power, this would be no good reason for denying that we have it. One might as well prove that he had no eyes in his head for this reason[:] that neither he nor any other person could tell how they came there.

That certain events are produced when we will to produce them is a matter of every day and every hour's experience. This may give us a conception of power in ourselves, as early as we have occasion for it. And I see no other way we can possibly acquire it.

It is easy and natural to think that other men have such a power as we find in ourselves. We judge of things unknown by what we know, and as we first know by consciousness that we think and act and feel pain and pleasure, we are by analogy rather than by reasoning led to think the same of other men; and indeed not only of other men but of other things. It is a discovery made by degrees, and by observation and instruction, that many of the things about us, are so very unlike to us as to be perfectly inanimate and unthinking. It is a just observation of the Abbé Raynal[1] that savages, whenever they perceive motion which they cannot account for, there they

[1] Reid is here referring to Abbé Guillaume-Thomas Raynal (1713–96), author of *Histoire philosophique et politique des établissements et du commerce des Européens dans les deux Indes* (1770).

Of Power

How Men get the Conception of Power is a question of some Difficulty. It is not an Object either of Sense or of Consciousness. Locke rashly determined that we get this Idea both these ways. Hume shewed that it can be got in neither of them & thence rashly concluded that there is no such conception in the human Mind.

Every voluntary exertion to produce an Event seems to imply a perswasion in the Agent that he has power to produce the Event. A deliberate Exertion to produce an Event, implies a conception of the Event, and some belief or Hope that his Exertion will be followed by it. This I think cannot be denied. The consequence is that a conception of Power is antecedent to every deliberate Exertion of Will to produce an Event. We have reason to think that voluntary Exertions are as early as any other operation of the thinking Beings and if they be all deliberate, that is intended to produce an Event which we believe to be in our Power, we should be led to think a Conception of Power, & even a belief that such and such Events are in our power, are innate, at least antecedent to every Act of Volition. But I am rather inclined to think that our first Exertions are instinctive, without any distinct conception of the Event that is to follow, consequently without will to produce that Event. And that finding by Experience that such exertions are followed by such Events, we learn to make the exertion voluntarily & deliberately, as often as we desire to produce the event, & when we know or believe that the Event depends upon our Exertion, we have the conception of power in ourselves to produce that Event.

This account of the origin of our conception of Power, makes it to be the fruit of Experience and not innate; though it must be as early as any deliberate voluntary exertion to produce a certain Event. This Account likewise supposes that an Exertion is something different from a deliberate will to produce the Event by Exertion without Will. It must be acknowledged that Exertion, & that there may be Exertion without Will. It must be acknowledged that these two are so conjoyned, when we have got some knowledge of the extent of our Power, that we find it very difficult to distinguish them. As this distinction is supposed in the account we have given of the origin of our conception of Power, it may be proper to give some other instances which confirm it.

When I will to rise & walk immediately, the Exertion seems inseparably conjoyned with the volition & both appear as one & the same Act of Mind. But I resolve to rise and walk an hour hence. This is a deliberate act of Will, as well as the will to do it immediately; but no exertion follows for an hour. Here the Will is disjoyned from the Exertion therefore they are different. Again I will to walk for half an hour. The Exertion immediately succeeds.

During

Facsimile (1:4 scale) of the first page of Reid's manuscript, reproduced by kind permission of Aberdeen University Library. The margin (not shown) bears the date, March 19 1792.

conceive a soul. And I think the structure of all languages, in the genders of nouns, and the voices of verbs affords a strong proof of this. 'There is' says Mr Hume (*Nat[ural] History of Religion* Sect. 3) 'an universal tendency among mankind to conceive all beings like themselves, and to transfer to every object, those qualities, with which they are familiarly acquainted, and of which they are intimately conscious'.

I apprehend that most (if not all) ambiguous words had at first one meaning, and in process of time have been used in other meanings, which were conceived to have some similitude, analogy, or some other relation to their first meaning. And it may happen that the original meaning from which the others were derived, may become less common than some of the others. Dr Johnston [*sic*] gives thirteen meanings of the word *power* and some of these he expresses by three or four different words which are not perfectly synonymous. And he certainly does not enumerate all the meanings in which it is used.

So far indeed is this word extended, that we ascribe power, not only to thinking beings who may produce some effect by will and exertion, but to beings believed to be perfectly inanimate and passive, and not only to beings or substances, but to qualities, relations and even to mere privations, such as darkness, ignorance, [and] want.

If the observations of Raynal and Hume, mentioned above, be just, we may the more easily account for the ascribing of power to things which are now believed to be inanimate, though perhaps in the first stages of society they were considered as animated beings.

Although it were granted that all the different meanings of the word 'power' have been derived from its original meaning before mentioned, (which indeed I take to be the case) it does not follow from this, that all those meanings are *species* of one and the same *genus*, and that there is one general nature in them all joined with some specific difference. It is perhaps impossible to give a reason why the word 'power' has been applied to what are called the powers of numbers, such as the square, cube, etc. Yet this singular meaning of 'power' is a *genus* of which there are innumerable *species* well known and distinctly conceived by mathematicians.

The origin I have above assigned to our first and most proper conception of power, is, I think, admitted by philosophers, if we except Mr Hume, who maintains that we have no notion of power at all, and that it is a word without any meaning.

The word 'cause' is not only as ambiguous as the word 'power' but has a very near relation to it. And perhaps, if we were to give a general definition of it, we might say that a cause is that which has power to produce the effect. If in this definition the word 'power' be taken in all its latitude, I apprehend the definition may apply to every thing that is called a cause as well as the τὸ ἐξ οὗ, or *the principle of change.*

I think however that there is an original and most proper conception of a cause from which all its other meanings have been deduced, and that this is very nearly allied to the original and proper conception of power.

When we attend to objects without us we see innumerable changes or events, some constantly conjoined with a certain effect which succeeds; but we perceive no real connexion between them. Antecedent to experience we should see no ground to think that heat will turn ice into water any more than that it will turn water into ice. Mr Hume's reasoning on this subject in [the] Essay on Necessary Connexions[2] would have convinced me if I had not been convinced before by Sir Isaac Newton. That author resolves the whole science of physics into two problems. The first, from the phenomena of nature to discover by induction the laws of nature. The second, from the laws of nature to explain or account for the phenomena of nature. Newton indeed is the first author in whom I have found this idea of the science of physics. Former authors ancient and modern not excepting Francis Bacon, have conceived it to be the province of physics to discover the causes of the phenomena of nature. Physics according to Bacon is either contemplative or operative. The first is *inquisitio causarum*, which he also divides into two parts, the first enquires into the efficient and material causes, the second into the formal and final. According to Newton, when physics shall be carried to the utmost perfection, there would not be found in the whole science such a conception as that of a cause; nothing but laws of nature, which are general facts grounded on experience, and phenomena which are particular facts, included in the more general, and consequent upon them. Some indeed call the laws of nature, 'causes'. But surely no man that thinks can believe that laws of nature can produce any phenomenon unless there be some agent that puts the law in execution.

Since therefore there is nothing external to us from which we can draw the conception of an efficient or productive cause, it must be deduced from something in our own mind.

We are conscious that we have power to produce certain events by our will and exertion. The conviction of this power is implied in the very voluntariness of exertion, for no man makes an exertion to do what he does not think to be in his power. In our own voluntary actions, therefore, we have a conviction and consequently a conception of efficient or productive power in ourselves. And this conception we had so early that it must be the work of nature.

[2] See Hume, *An Enquiry Concerning the Human Understanding*, §7, 'Of the Idea of Necessary Connexion'.

To this account of the origin of our conception of productive power or efficiency Mr Hume objects, that though we find a constant conjunction between our volitions and certain events, we discover this only by experience, and see no necessary connexion between our will and the motion of our body which follows it, any more than we see between heat and the melting of ice, and therefore as the last gives us no conception of productive power, but solely of constant conjunction, so neither can the first.

To this I answer that if a man believed that in heat there was a will to melt ice, he would undoubtedly believe that there is in heat a real efficient power to produce that effect, though he were ignorant how or by what latent process the effect is produced. So we, knowing that certain effects depend on our will, impute to ourselves the power of producing them, though there may be some latent process between the volition and the production which we do not know. So a child may know that a bell is rung by pulling a certain peg, though he does not yet know how that operation is connected with the ringing of the bell, and when he can move that peg he has a perfect conviction that he has power to ring the bell.

I apprehend, that our belief, that things which have always been found to be conjoined in time past, will continue to be conjoined in time to come, is not grounded on reasoning, but may rather be called instinctive, like our belief in testimony. We believe in both these cases before we have the power of reasoning. And I can perceive no premises from which the conclusion believed can be logically inferred when reason is ripe. Our instinctive belief of what is to happen would often and does often lead us into mistakes, though highly necessary before we have the use of reason, and when we learn to reason we regulate this belief by just rules of induction. But the rules of induction, or of reasoning from experience, do not produce the belief of what is to come, they serve only to regulate and restrain it. In like manner our reasoning about testimony serves only to restrain and regulate the unlimited belief which we have in it by nature.

Thus I think it appears that, from our own active exertions, we very early get the conception of active power, and of an efficient cause. But it is a very different question how we come to be persuaded that every event and every thing that has a beginning must have an efficient cause. This belief cannot be got from experience, because we perceive no efficient cause in one tenth part of the events that fall under our view. Besides no necessary truth can derive its evidence from experience. This has been received as a necessary truth by all men learned and unlearned from the beginning of the world, till Mr Hume called it in question, because he could not perceive a necessary agreement of the ideas of the proposition. I have said what occurred to me to prove it to be a first principle (*Essays* Vol. 1. Chap[ter] on the first

Principles of Necessary Truth).[3] But let it be observed that by a cause I mean only an efficient cause which by its active power produces the effect. It is still another question whether active or productive power can, or cannot be in an inanimate subject.

With regard to this question there have been different opinions among philosophers. It is not easy to determine what kind of being it was which the Peripatetics called 'Nature', to whose operation they ascribed all that we call the *phenomena of nature*. It is certain that Cudworth, a very acute metaphysician, thought that the Deity in the government of the material world, employed certain immaterial beings which he called 'plastic natures', who are endowed with active power but without wisdom or intelligence who are the proper efficient causes of generation and other natural phenomena.[4] The famous J. Le Clerc defended this notion of Cudworth and Bayle attacked it.[5] And after many replies and duplies[6] neither was able to convince the other. To me Bayle seems to have much the advantage in the argument. I conceive it to be a first principle, that a complex work which in all its parts is admirably adapted to a certain purpose, must have been contrived by an intelligent being who had that purpose in view and knew how [to] adapt the means to the end. Nor do I see how a regular well contrived work, may not be produced by a dance of atoms as well [as] by a being who has active power without intelligence. And it seems to me very strange that philosophers who thought the system of Epicurus too ridiculous to deserve refutation, should yet ascribe the phenomena of nature to unintelligent causes.

I believe, not the Peripatetics only but the vulgar in all ages have been prone to attribute real efficiency or productive power to unintelligent and even to inanimate things, and that when they say that heat melts ice, and that cold freezes water, they conceive the heat and the cold as really efficient causes, though inanimate. This belief of the vulgar seems to be as general, as that the earth is at rest and that all the heavenly bodies go round it in twenty-four hours.

[3] See Reid, *Essays on the Intellectual Powers*, essay VI, ch. 6, 'First Principles of Necessary Truth'.

[4] Reid is here alluding to the spiritualist interpretation of nature advanced by Ralph Cudworth in *The True Intellectual System of the Universe* (1678). Given what Reid says earlier, it is interesting to find Cudworth writing that 'we are certain of the existence of our own souls, partly from an inward consciousness of our own cogitations, and partly from that principle of reason that nothing cannot act. And the existence of other souls is manifest to us, from their effects upon their respective bodies, their motions, actions, and discourse' (tr. and ed. J. Harrison, London: 1845, Vol. II, p. 515).

[5] Jean Le Clerc (1657–1737) publicized Cudworth's ideas in a series of journals he established, including *Bibliothèque universelle* and *Bibliothèque ancienne et moderne*.

[6] Obsolete term in Scots law meaning a reply to a reply (answered in turn by a 'triply').

Leibniz taught that the whole creation, bodies as well as minds, consist of monads, or individual substances, each of which was so made at first by the creator that, like a watch wound up, it has within itself the cause of all the changes it shall ever undergo. And though no one substance or monad acts upon another yet all keep time to one another, by a pre-established harmony, so as to produce the phenomena of the universe. In this system no cause whatsoever (excepting the Deity the first cause of all) produces any effect, but upon itself. Even the Deity has no occasion to interpose in the government of the world after he once made it except in the case of miracles. He made it at first so perfect as to go on of itself without needing his helping hand. No one part of it does in reality receive either benefit or harm from any other part. Every man from the time of his creation to eternity would have done and suffered all that he really does and suffers, although there had not been another being in the Universe. He would have enjoyed the vicissitude of day and night though there had been no sun nor moon. But the sun and moon rise and set, by a pre-established harmony, in perfect correspondence with that day and night which succeed each other in his mind, from its own internal frame, without being influenced in the least by anything external to him.

In this system, there may be causes in the sense of David Hume. But proper and efficient causes there are none in the universe but one, I mean the Deity. Nor was there ever any power exerted but in the act of creation, or in miracles.

The modern system of necessity advanced by some of the disciples of Dr Priestley, which makes every action of the Deity to be necessary, although I take it to be a very natural consequence of denying all liberty in human actions, excludes all power out of the universe. For power and necessity are contradictory. And according to this system power is an attribute which cannot possibly exist in any subject.

To return to the question whether active or productive power can be in an inanimate subject.

If the account before given of the origins of our notion of power be just, it seems to follow that will is necessarily implied in the notion of power. Volition and what follows upon our volitions is all that we conceive to be in our power. What a man never willed cannot be imputed to him as his action. A man's power is measured by what he can do if he will. This is the measure of power when we speak of power in any intelligent or animated being. In this sense, which I take to be the only proper sense of the word, it is evident that a being which has no will can have no power. And when we impute power to dead matter it must be understood in some popular or analogical, and not in the proper sense. Power in the proper sense is under the command of him who has the power, and we cannot infer the act from the power because there is no necessary connection between them. It is otherwise with regard to the powers we ascribe to inanimate beings. Even when our volitions are compelled by an irresistible motive, such as the fear of immediate death, or the violence of torture, the action is not imputed to the man or considered as an exertion of his power, but as a necessary consequence of fear or torture, necessity and power being incompatible.

The powers therefore which in a vague and popular sense we ascribe to inanimate things differ from power taken in the proper sense in two things [respects]; the last implies volition and cannot exist without it, but the first is not accompanied with any volition but is in beings which have neither understanding nor will. Another difference between the power that is properly so called and that which is not, is that the first implies no necessary connection with the act. Because a man has the power of walking it does not follow that he walks at this moment; on the contrary a power to walk implies a power not to walk. If a man has the distemper called 'St Vitus Dance' we don't say that he has the power of moving, but that he moves necessarily, or that he has not the power to be at rest. For power properly so called is inconsistent with necessity. On the contrary the powers which we ascribe to inanimate things are always conjoined with necessity, and must, without a miracle, be exerted to their utmost whenever the circumstances concur which by the laws of nature are necessary to their exertion.

Hence it appears that power when ascribed to an intelligent being is a thing essentially different from the powers ascribed to inanimated beings. And their definition is as different as their nature. When an event depends upon the will of an intelligent being, we say it is in his power. And though he have no will nor inclination to produce the event, [and] though it should never be produced, it is not the less in his power upon that account. His power is exerted only according to his will, and when he does not will to exert it, it is dormant and produces no effect.

When we ascribe power to inanimate things, we mean nothing more than a constant conjunction by the laws of nature which experience discovers between the event which we call the effect and something which goes before it. Thus we say the sun has power to retain the planets in their orbits, heat has power to melt lead, and cold to freeze water. If the ignorant be led by the ambiguity of the word, to conceive any efficient power in the sun, the heat, or the cold to produce the effects ascribed to them, this is a vulgar error which philosophy corrects. By what agent those effects are really produced we know not, but we have good reason to believe that they cannot be produced by inanimate matter.

This distinction of the proper, and the vague or popular meaning of the word 'power' is important in the intricate question about liberty and necessity. The defenders of necessity must maintain either that there is no such distinction, and that 'power' can have no meaning but that of a constant conjunction of that which we call the cause with the effect, which is David Hume's opinion; or if they admit that we can conceive a power which is really efficient, they must say that there neither is, nor can be any such power in the universe.

3

REID AND EPISTEMIC NATURALISM

By Patrick Rysiew

Central to the contemporary dispute over 'naturalizing epistemology' is the question of the continuity of epistemology with science, i.e., how far purely descriptive, psychological matters can or should inform the traditional evaluative epistemological enterprise. Thus all parties tend to agree that the distinction between psychology and epistemology corresponds to a firm fact/value distinction. This is something Reid denies with respect to the first principles of common sense: while insisting on the continuity of epistemology with the rest of science, he does not wish to derive an 'ought' from an 'is', nor to reduce the epistemological to the psychological. His view is that the first principles are constitutive principles, hence that they are simultaneously descriptive and prescriptive, and thus that with regard to them there is in this sense simply no fact/value gap to be bridged.

I. INTRODUCTION

According to James Maffie, the debate over 'naturalized epistemology' centres on the question of the continuity of epistemology and science:

> Naturalists are united by a shared commitment to the continuity of epistemology and science. Naturalist and non-naturalist divide over whether or not the continuity exists.[1]

But if we take the dispute between epistemic naturalists and non-naturalists in this way (not that we should do so, as will emerge later), it seems clear that Reid would see himself as falling into the former camp. After all, among other things, Reid professes a staunch Newtonianism:

> Let us, therefore, lay down this as a fundamental principle in our inquiries into the structure of the human mind and its operations – that no regard is due to the conjectures and hypotheses of philosophers.... Let us accustom ourselves to try every opinion by the touchstone of fact and experience.[2]

[1] J. Maffie, 'Recent Work on Naturalized Epistemology', *American Philosophical Quarterly*, 27 (1990), pp. 281–93, at p. 281.

[2] Reid, *Essays on the Intellectual Powers* (henceforward *IP*) I iii, in *Thomas Reid: Philosophical Works*, ed. W. Hamilton, 8th edn (Berlin: Georg Olms, 1885), p. 236a.

Indeed, as Norman Daniels, for example, sees it, Reid's 'experimentalist orientation' in carrying out his 'analysis of the human faculties'[3] shows that he is quite good about practising what he preaches; in fact Daniels thinks that Reid's work should be seen as 'a precursor to recent work in cognitive psychology and "naturalized epistemology"'.[4]

Yet Daniels himself in the very same book also claims that Reid attempts to establish the reliability of our faculties by means of a dogmatic appeal to God's providence: 'Reid's only defence against the sceptical outcome of his own nativism – namely, that our constitutions might lead us to systematically false beliefs – is his belief that God would not deceive us.... Reid justifies natively given "common sense" beliefs through a dogmatic appeal to God as a non-deceiver' (Daniels, 1st edn, pp. 117, 119–20). As Daniels later realized (afterword to his 2nd edn, esp. pp. 132–3), this hardly sits well with the portrayal of Reid as a staunchly naturalistic 'scientist of the mind' (p. 133). But Daniels is not alone in thinking that Reid's epistemology is somehow essentially theistic. According to Derek Brookes and others, while perhaps naturalistic enough in its methodology, Reid's epistemology contains and/or requires commitment to the existence and providence of God.[5] This makes one wonder whether, on this reading, Reid's epistemology really is naturalistic after all. I am not convinced that he endorses a *providentialist* epistemology: as I read him, he makes no essential appeal to God in his epistemology, for instance, in defending the rationality of our common sense beliefs. This is not to say, however, that I see Reid as fitting comfortably with contemporary epistemic naturalisms – not because he is obviously a non-naturalist, but because he appears to reject an assumption shared by many on each side in the contemporary epistemological debate between naturalists, non-naturalists and anti-naturalists. Just what this assumption is, and why Reid rejects it, will be taken up below. But first I shall briefly address the matter of Reid and 'providential naturalism'.

II. CARTESIAN APPEALS AND PLANTINGA'S CHALLENGE

Reid was well aware of the question-begging character of appealing to God in defending the reliability of our faculties. Indeed, he takes Descartes to task on just this count.

[3] Reid, *Inquiry into the Human Mind* (hereafter *Inq*), ed. Hamilton, I ii, p. 99a.
[4] N. Daniels, *Thomas Reid's 'Inquiry': the Geometry of Visibles and the Case for Realism*, 2nd edn (Stanford UP, 1989), pp. xi, 133.
[5] D.R. Brookes, in his edition of Reid's *Inquiry* (Pennsylvania State UP, 1997). The claim has also been recently endorsed by K. Haakonssen (ed.), *Practical Ethics* (Princeton UP, 1990), and P.B. Wood (ed.), *Thomas Reid on the Animate Creation* (Pennsylvania State UP, 1996).

> Des Cartes certainly made a false step in this matter, for having suggested this doubt among others – that whatever evidence he might have from his consciousness, his senses, his memory, or his reason, yet possibly some malignant being had given him those faculties on purpose to impose upon him; and, therefore, that they are not to be trusted without a proper voucher. To remove this doubt, he endeavours to prove the being of a Deity who is no deceiver; whence he concludes, that the faculties he had given him are true and worthy to be trusted.
>
> It is strange that so acute a reasoner did not perceive that in this reasoning there is evidently a begging of the question.
>
> For, if our faculties be fallacious, why may they not deceive us in this reasoning as well as in others?[6]

Still, according to Brookes (p. xiv), Reid did endorse 'providential naturalism', a view comprised of the following four tenets:

1. Adherence to Newton's *regulae philosophandi*
2. Belief that the ultimate explanation of the laws of nature is to be found in God's providence
3. A teleological orientation in discovering those laws
4. Belief that the end/purpose of our cognitive processes is (among other things) to furnish us with true beliefs.

As Brookes sees it, while Reid makes no Cartesian-style appeal to God's providence in *arguing for* the reliability of our faculties, it is Reid's view that 'the *rationality* of [our belief in the general reliability of our faculties] is best sustained within the context of providential naturalism' (p. xxii) – that is, by (among other things) belief in God. Brookes continues:

> For on this account, there is no reason to believe that scepticism about the external world is a live possibility. Providential naturalism is a philosophical system, a set of beliefs of which no member either affirms or leads to the denial of the reliability of our faculties – a feature, Reid argued, that could not be claimed of a system such as David Hume's.

It is hardly clear to me that Reid was a 'providential naturalist' in quite the way Brookes here suggests. Why the qualification? Because, strictly speaking, even if Brookes is right in portraying Reid as an adherent of providential naturalism as described above, i.e., of the view comprised of tenets (1)–(4), that would at most have Reid giving God's providence an *explanatory* role in accounting for the source of (among other things) our faculties and our belief in their basic reliability. But from that nothing whatever follows about whether providentialist considerations play any *justificatory* role in Reid's defence of the rationality of such beliefs. What is more, the passage

---

[6] *IP* VI v, p. 447b; cf. K. DeRose, 'Reid's Anti-Sensationalism and his Realism', *Philosophical Review*, 98 (1989), pp. 313–48, at pp. 327–8.

just cited ('For on this account … ') is a very close paraphrase not of anything in Reid, but of Alvin Plantinga's recent claims to a similar effect:

> [If] you find yourself with the doubt that our cognitive faculties produce truth … you can't quell that doubt by producing an argument about God and his veracity, or indeed any argument at all; for the argument, of course, will be under as much suspicion as its source. Here no argument will help you; here salvation will have to be by grace, not by works. But the theist has nothing impelling him in the direction of such scepticism in the first place; no element of his noetic system points in that direction; there are no propositions he already accepts just by way of being a theist, which together with forms of reasoning … lead to the rejection of the belief that our cognitive faculties have the apprehension of truth as their purpose and for the most part fulfil that purpose.[7]

Ergo, according to Plantinga, 'naturalistic epistemology flourishes best in the garden of supernaturalistic metaphysics' (*WPF*, p. 237); 'The right way to be a naturalist in epistemology is to be a supernaturalist in metaphysics' (p. 211).

What is the thinking behind these claims? In a nutshell, Plantinga's view is that knowledge requires warrant, warrant being that normative/evaluative element which, when added (in sufficient degree) to true belief, gives the bearer knowledge.[8] But warrant involves proper functioning, Plantinga argues; and there is simply no plausible naturalistic account of proper functioning in the offing, nor therefore of the normative dimension of knowing. In fact, he claims, in opposition to 'Darwinian optimists' such as Quine, Fodor, Dennett, Goldman, Lycan and Millikan,[9] natural selection actually makes it *very unlikely* that most of our beliefs are true, or that our faculties are generally reliable. So the naturalist who believes that we are the products of natural selection ought for that very reason to regard this belief as suspect.[10] In this way a thoroughgoing naturalism destroys itself, engendering as it does, Plantinga thinks, this sort of irrationality and incoherence: 'Naturalistic epistemology conjoined with naturalistic metaphysics leads via evolution to scepticism or to violations of canons of rationality' (*WPF*, p. 237).

Again this is Plantinga's view. But Brookes implies that the only difference Reid saw between his system of belief and Hume's – that what Reid thought gave Hume's 'system', but not his own, a natural impulse towards scepticism – was that he, Reid, was a theist; and this is just false. Most

[7] Plantinga, *Warrant and Proper Function* (Oxford UP, 1993, hereafter *WPF*), p. 105.

[8] See Plantinga, *Warrant: the Current Debate* (Oxford UP, 1993), p. 3.

[9] For a sample of the relevant claims, see S. Stich, *The Fragmentation of Reason* (MIT Press, 1990), pp. 55ff. Here are a couple: 'Natural selection guarantees that organisms either know the elements of logic or become posthumous' (Fodor); 'Natural selection guarantees that *most* of an organism's beliefs will be true, *most* of its strategies rational' (Dennett).

[10] See *WPF*, pp. 218–19, for Patricia Churchland's and Darwin's own worries to this effect.

centrally, Reid rejects, while Hume accepts, what the former described as 'the ideal theory', the view that all the mind is immediately acquainted with are its own 'perceptions' ('ideas', 'impressions', etc.). And it is 'the ideal theory', and that alone, which Reid regards as the principle upon which 'Hume's sceptical system' is built (see esp. 'Dedication' to *Inq*, p. 96a). Whereas to say that Reid held that the rationality of our belief in the reliability of our faculties is 'best sustained' by (among other things) a belief in God is most naturally taken as implying that Reid thought that without the help of theism, believing one's faculties not to be fallacious is less than fully rational. But that seems to me not to be Reid's view at all; and taking it to be such underrates the strength and intended force of his response to the sceptic. (Of which, more presently.) So, as a purely interpretative question, whether or not Reid accepted providential naturalism in the sense of theses (1)–(4), above, and thus whatever explanatory role Reid accorded to God, I doubt very much that Reid's is a 'providentialist epistemology' in the way in which Plantinga's ultimately is. (I say 'ultimately' because, as Plantinga says, up to the final discussion of naturalism in *Warrant and Proper Function* his account of proper functionalism is thoroughly naturalistic: his claim that 'The right way to be a naturalist in epistemology is to be a supernaturalist in metaphysics' comes after that.)[11]

But that leaves Plantinga's challenge: how might *thoroughgoing* epistemic naturalists introduce into their picture epistemic normativity and the rationality of, e.g., belief in the reliability of our faculties? Here I shall present what I take to be Reid's proposed way of responding to this challenge. Still, quite apart from the role God does or, as I see it, does not play in Reid's epistemology, as already mentioned, I think that his epistemological views sit ill with contemporary discussions of epistemic naturalism. But to make this clear I shall need first to review briefly some of the central features of Reid's position.

III. REID ON COMMON SENSE AND THE FIRST PRINCIPLES

According to Reid, 'sense' is closely connected with, or connotes, judgement and cogitation: 'in common language, sense always implies judgement. A man of sense is a man of judgement. Good sense is good judgement' (*IP* VI ii, p. 421b). This is not to say that, as Reid would have it, 'common sense'

---

[11] For rejections of Brookes' reading of Reid, see D.D. Todd, 'An Inquiry into Thomas Reid', *Dialogue*, 39 (2000), pp. 381–8; Daniels; DeRose; K. Lehrer, 'Reid on Primary and Secondary Qualities', *Monist*, 61 (1978), pp. 184–91, and 'Reid, God and Epistemology', co-authored with B. Warner, *American Catholic Philosophical Quarterly*, 74 (2000), pp. 357–72.

and 'reason' are co-extensive terms. The relation between reason and common sense, rather, is as follows: 'We ascribe to reason two offices, or two degrees. The first is to judge of things self-evident; the second to draw conclusions that are not self-evident from those that are. The first of these is the province, and the sole province, of common sense' (*IP* VI ii, p. 425b). Thus, for Reid, common sense is a *degree* of reason; specifically, it is that degree of reason which is requisite for judging 'of things self-evident', and which entitles humans 'to the denomination of reasonable creatures' (*ibid.*).

For Reid, then, 'common sense' itself is not a purely descriptive notion (it suggests reasonableness, for instance).[12] Also worth noting is the fact that it is not Reid's view that common sense operates only at the level of ratiocination or 'intellection' – it is not, in effect, that an individual must be capable of sophisticated or extended reason*ing* in order to be called 'a reasonable creature'. (Non-logicians can be reasonable creatures.) A reasonable person, rather, is one who is 'capable of managing his own affairs, and answerable for his conduct towards others' (*ibid.*). So, on Reid's account, common sense is just as operative at the practical level as it is at the level of reasoning or ratiocination: 'Common sense is that degree of judgement which is common to men with whom we can converse and transact business' (*IP* VI ii, p. 421b). For Reid, common sense straddles – indeed, it *unifies* – the theory/practice distinction: 'The same degree of understanding which makes a man capable of acting with common prudence in the conduct of life, makes him capable of discovering what is true and what is false in matters that are self-evident, and which he distinctly apprehends' (*IP* VI ii, p. 422b).

As Nicolas Wolterstorff has recently argued, it is not always easy to reconcile all of the various things Reid says about common sense.[13] Thus, for instance, from the passages just cited, it appears that Reid conceives of common sense as an instinctive faculty with which we are naturally endowed. In his later writings, however, Reid more often speaks of common sense as though it were a set of epistemically basic propositions. But perhaps we can go some way towards bringing into line these two conceptions of common sense if we think of the matter as follows: we can think of common sense as the faculty which gives rise to a set of basic propositions or beliefs. In any case, in considering Reid's epistemology, it is appropriate for us to focus on that feature of common sense (or that way of conceiving of common sense) which Reid himself stresses in his mature work, i.e., common sense as a set of basic beliefs or fundamental propositions which

[12] Similarly, the German '*gesunder Menschenverstand*', often rendered as 'common sense', literally translated means 'healthy human understanding'.
[13] N. Wolterstorff, *Thomas Reid and the Story of Epistemology* (Cambridge UP, 2001), pp. 218–27.

serve as the foundation for all human thought, action and knowledge (cf. *IP* VI iv, p. 435a).

Reid divides these first principles of common sense into two groups: the first principles of necessary truths, and those of contingent truths. Since it is the epistemic status of the latter (i.e., the contingent ones) that is called into question by the sceptic, I shall focus my discussion on them.

Among the first principles of contingent truths are the following: (1) that the things of which I am conscious do exist; (3) that those things did really happen which I distinctly remember; (5) that those things do really exist which we distinctly perceive by our senses, and are what we perceive them to be; and (7) that the natural faculties, by which we distinguish truth from error, are not fallacious (*IP* VI v, pp. 441a–52a).

Like Hume, Reid holds that one cannot help assenting to these propositions. He writes, for example, that 'Philosophy was never able to conquer that natural belief which men have in their senses' (*IP* II iv, p. 259b); '[a] man may as soon, by reasoning, pull the moon out of her orbit, as destroy the belief of the objects of sense' (*IP* IV x, p. 328a). Or again: a person 'may struggle hard to disbelieve the information of his senses, as a man does to swim against the torrent; but ah! it is in vain.... For, after all, when his strength is spent in the fruitless attempt, he will be carried down the torrent with the common herd of believers' (*Inq* VI xx, p. 184a).

Citing such passages, Wolterstorff has remarked that these words of Reid's are 'so far from contradicting Hume's position as to do nicely as a statement of it'.[14] And having noted that this last metaphorical description of the irresistibility of our common sense beliefs 'could in its entirety have been written by Hume', he goes on to quote approvingly, as Galen Strawson has recently done,[15] the famous (1812) exchange in which James Mackintosh

... remarked to Thomas Brown that on the question of the existence of the external world Reid and Hume 'differed more in words than in opinion'. 'Yes,' answered Brown. 'Reid bawled out, We must believe an outward world; but added in a whisper, We can give no reason for our belief. Hume cries out, We can give no reason for such a notion; and whispers, I own we cannot get rid of it.'

Though Wolterstorff (like Strawson) is certainly correct that both Hume and Reid hold that our common sense beliefs are irresistible, and though it is true that Reid and Hume each subscribes to *some* sort of nativist view, Wolterstorff and Strawson are both too quick in concluding from this that Reid and Hume 'differed more in words than in opinion'. Here Paul Vernier provides a more accurate assessment of the situation:

[14] Wolterstorff, 'Hume and Reid', *Monist*, 70 (1987), pp. 398–417, at p. 400.
[15] G. Strawson, 'What's so Good about Reid?', *London Review of Books*, Vol. 12 No. 4, 22 February 1990, pp. 14–15.

There is no disagreement on the irresistibility of [for example] our everyday belief in objective reality between Hume and Reid, only about whether there are philosophical grounds for it.... The real issue is this: although we are compelled in practical circumstances to accept these [common sense] beliefs, have we any justificatory grounds for them?[16]

It is over *this* question that Reid and Hume differ.

Like Hume, Reid fully accepts that the contingent basic beliefs of common sense cannot without circularity be given demonstrative proof. After all, it is 'contrary to the nature of first principles to admit of direct or *apodictical* proof' (*IP* VI iv, p. 439a); the idea of demonstration from something *more* basic is quite simply in conflict with the rock-bottom status of our basic beliefs (cf. *IP* I ii, p. 231a). In addition to thus ruling out any deductive arguments for the first principles, Reid also discounts the relevance of inductive support, and hence the prospect of appealing to probabilistic reasoning (*IP* VI iv, pp. 434a–5b). And yet, while Hume takes it to be an epistemological defect of our common sense beliefs that they can neither be given demonstrative proof nor be the product of empirical generalization – though this is not necessarily a bad thing, all things considered – Reid maintains that the impossibility of *directly* arguing for the contingent first principles of common sense is no barrier to justification of a sort that is satisfactory to reason. (Nothing I say here commits me to reading Hume as an out-and-out sceptic. For my purposes, it may well be true that his intent is to 'put reason in its place' – to show that belief is more properly a part of the 'sensitive' rather than the cogitative part of our nature.)

Of first principles, Reid writes 'Their evidence is not demonstrative, but intuitive. They require not proof, but to be placed in a proper point of view' (*IP* I ii, p. 231b); 'they may admit of illustration, yet being self-evident, do not admit of proof' (p. 231a); 'there are certain ways of reasoning even about them, by which those that are just and solid may be confirmed, and those that are false may be detected' (*IP* VI iv, p. 439a). By 'confirmation' here, Reid cannot and does not mean proof by appeal to external evidence; for first principles are supposed to be *self*-evident. What Reid is claiming, rather, is that it is possible to confirm that certain principles *are first principles*. As the appeal to external evidence has already been ruled out, the confirmation cannot take the form of direct justification, and must instead consist in the indirect justification of a first principle.

According to Reid, so long as one's judgement has not been 'perverted, by education, by authority, by party zeal, or by some other of the common

---

[16] P. Vernier, 'Thomas Reid on the Foundations of Knowledge and his Answer to Skepticism', in S. Barker and T.L. Beauchamp (eds), *Thomas Reid: Critical Interpretations* (Temple UP, 1976), pp. 14–24, at p. 19.

causes of error' (*IP* VI iv, p. 438a), there are (at least) five types of argument which can be used in non-evidence-based confirmations of first
principles. These strategies are: (1) an 'argument *ad hominem*', showing some
inconsistency in the denial of one first principle on the basis of another
which is on the same epistemic footing; (2) an informal *reductio ad absurdum*,
whereby denial of the first principle in question is shown to lead to
absurdity; (3) an argument from the consent of the learned and unlearned
across time; (3a) an argument from the common structure of all languages;
(4) an argument from the *prima facie* primitiveness of some first principles;
and (5) an argument from the practical indispensability of a first principle (*IP* VI iv, pp. 439a–41b).

To repeat, these are strategies for defending first principles as first
principles, and are not intended as arguments for their truth. Reid himself
admits at several points that it is (logically) possible that our foundational
beliefs are false. Of the idea that our sensations suggest something external,
for example, he writes 'The belief of it, and the very conception of it, are
equally parts of our constitution. If we are deceived in it, we are deceived by
Him that made us, and there is no remedy' (*Inq* V vii, p. 130b); 'we must
[trust the testimony of our faculties] implicitly, until God gives us new
faculties to sit in judgement upon the old' (*IP* VI v, p. 447b; cf. VII iv,
pp. 488b, 486a). Here, though, the point is not that we should despair of our
inability to demonstrate the truth of our first principles; it is rather that it is a
mistake to seek the impossibility of error with regard to them.

There is, for Reid, a presumption in favour of the truth of our first principles – they are, so to speak, innocent until proved guilty. Keith DeRose
(pp. 326–32) has proposed that we should understand Reid's argument here
thus. With respect to our native belief-forming faculties, we have three
choices: (1) beginning with an attitude of trust towards them all; (2) regarding them all as suspect (until they can be proved innocent); and (3) beginning
by regarding only some of them as trustworthy, and going on from there. Of
these, in Reid's view, only the first option (trusting them all) makes sense.[17]
The second (distrusting them all) is not only psychologically impossible; *of
necessity* it is pointless, for why should we distrust them all, unless we take
ourselves to have some reason for doing so? How could we take ourselves to
have such a reason unless we were trusting at least some of them? And
the third (trusting only some) is of necessity arbitrary: why trust only one
– reason, say – when the others are equally a part of our constitution,

---

[17] Reid distinguishes between 'thorough and consistent' sceptics and 'semi-sceptics' – the
former being those who adopt (2), the latter (3). Were we ever to encounter a total sceptic,
Reid says, we would have to '[leave him] to enjoy his scepticism' (*IP* VI v, p. 447b; cf. *Inq*
V vii, p. 130a).

and when any argument for the trustworthiness of reason would have to assume what is at issue?

> Why, sir, should I believe the faculty of reason more than that of perception? – they came both out of the same shop, and were made by the same artist; if he puts one piece of false ware into my hands, what should hinder him from putting another? (*Inq* VI xx, p. 183b)

The only reasonable strategy is to begin by placing trust in *all* of the first principles, in all of one's natural (truth-orientated) faculties. First principle (7) speaks to the reliability of the natural faculties 'by which we distinguish truth from error'.

Of course it is, once again, (logically) possible that all of our basic beliefs are mistaken – this is a trivial point that applies to all contingent propositions; but it is equally (and just as trivially, logically) possible that our basic common sense beliefs are entirely correct. So logical possibilities do not tell us anything here: in effect, they cancel each other out, and we are left with the question of whether we have any *reasonable* grounds – not whether we have any *possible* grounds – for doubting the veracity of the first principles of common sense.

But for Reid, reasonable or rational doubt is evidence-based doubt, and the 'mere logical possibility that some contingent propositions are false (that there are other minds, that there is an external world etc.) is not only not good evidence that such propositions are false, or even might be: it is no evidence at all'.[18] So it is only if we take infallibility to be a necessary condition for certainty that we shall be led to suppose that certainty about the truth of our common sense beliefs cannot be had. For Reid, though, 'logical certainty' – certainty where it is impossible that one might be mistaken – attaches only to necessary truths; with respect to contingent propositions, including, of course, the contingent first principles of common sense, the best we could possibly hope for is 'epistemic certainty', or the complete absence of any reasonable doubt as to their truth.[19] And this, Reid thinks, is exactly what we do have: in the absence of any reasonable (i.e., evidence-based) doubt as to their truth, we have no reasonable alternative to the dictates of common sense. And since any evidence as to the fallaciousness of one or all of our faculties would have to presume the veracity of at least one of them, given that the first principles 'all come out of the same shop' (*Inq* VI xx, p. 183b, cf. strategy (1) above), that evidence would in fact undermine the attempted argument. In this sense, there *could not be* any reasonable

[18] D.D. Todd, 'A Reply to Strawson's "What's so Good about Reid?"', *London Review of Books*, Vol. 12 No. 7, 5 April 1990, p. 4.

[19] Here I am drawing especially on what Reid says in *IP* VII iii, 'Of Probable Reasoning' (pp. 481b–4a).

(evidence-based) doubt as to the truth of the first principles. So since it is perfectly rational to act on and believe that to which there is no reasonable alternative (never mind *could not* be any), it is perfectly rational for us to hold to the first principles of common sense. Indeed, when to the fact that we (do or could) have no *reasonable* alternative to our basic beliefs we add the further observation that they are irresistible, it becomes clear that we have no alternative to them *whatsoever*.

Thus I do not see that scepticism is a 'live possibility' (Brookes, p. xxii) for Reid, or that he thinks that the rationality of belief in the veracity of our faculties requires metaphysical supernaturalism: ' ... the unjust *live by faith*, as well as the *just*' ('Dedication' to *Inq*, p. 95b), Reid says; rejecting or 'accepting God's goodness as a reason for trusting in one's faculties presupposes, if nothing else, one's faculty of reason' (Wolterstorff, p. 212; cf. Lehrer, pp. 367–72). '*Every* kind of reasoning for the veracity of our faculties, amounts to no more than taking their own testimony for veracity' (*IP* VI v, p. 447b; my italics). Until we are given new faculties to sit in judgement on the old, we all not only must, but ought to, trust the ones we have. If Reid is correct in holding that common sense is a degree of reason, then the first principles of common sense are *ipso facto* dictates of reason.

IV. THE FIRST PRINCIPLES AS CONSTITUTIVE PRINCIPLES

I have spent the last several pages reconstructing Reid's defence of the first principles of contingent truths; and it should go without saying that I believe that in doing so I have remained faithful to Reid's views. None the less it is also my view that we have yet to get at the heart of Reid's defence of common sense. So I shall consider again DeRose's reconstruction of Reid's argument (Wolterstorff, ch. 8, presents Reid's response to the sceptic in very similar terms). What he takes it to be is as follows. With respect to our native belief-forming faculties, we have three choices: we can trust them all, trust none, or trust only some; the second is of necessity pointless, and the third is arbitrary; only the first seems viable; hence we ought to accept all of the first principles.

I believe that, taken on its own terms, this reconstruction of (a portion of) Reid's response to the sceptic is accurate enough. But if we are to understand the real character of his defence of the first principles, we must be cautious about how exactly we regard arguments such as this. Specifically, we must guard against thinking that the foregoing argument (or something like it) *just is* 'Reid's argument for the rationality of our common sense beliefs'. For one thing, the preceding argument seems to be an attempt to derive an 'ought' from an 'is', amounting to 'Unlike the first option, the second and third options are each untenable; hence we ought to trust all of our natural faculties'. Not that this feature would be universally regarded as sufficient reason to reject it.[20] But it cannot be the sort of argument that Reid intends. This is shown by what he says in response to Hume's challenge that some reason be given for 'how this new relation [i.e., an "ought"] can be a deduction from others which are entirely different from it [i.e., some set of purely descriptive statements]':

> This is to demand a reason for what does not exist. The first principles ... are not deductions. They are self-evident; and their truth, like that of other axioms, is perceived without reasoning or deduction.[21]

Reid is here addressing Hume's challenge as applied to the case of the first principles of morals ('of morals' are the words I have omitted). But it is obvious enough that what he says about these involves pointing to their status *as first principles*, and what is entailed thereby. In other words, there is every reason to think that what Reid says here about the first principles of morals – their axiomatic character; their not being deductions, or the product of reasoning – he regards as features of first principles in general. And indeed elsewhere he does speak of first principles in general as 'axioms' (e.g., *Inq* V viii, p. 130a, *IP* I ii, p. 230b).

So, for Reid, whatever the status of the attempt to derive an 'ought' from an 'is', a defence of the first principles could not take the form of such a (putative) derivation, if for no other reason than that first principles, *qua* first principles, cannot be derived from anything. Hence it cannot be the whole story to say that Reid's defence of the first principles (or certain portions thereof) can be reconstructed along the lines DeRose describes. Such arguments may serve, as it were, to display the normative character of our basic beliefs; but they cannot be the *source* of the authority these principles enjoy. (Reid, of course, did not think that the authority of the first principles hung on *any* argument that he or anyone else might give.) As I have emphasized, the first principles, Reid tells us, 'may admit of illustration, yet being self-evident, do not admit of proof' (*IP* I ii, p. 231a); they 'require not proof, but to be placed in a proper point of view' (p. 231b).

What then is 'the proper point of view' from which to regard the first principles? And what exactly is supposed to be the source of their authority, of their being things which we not only do abide by but ought to abide by, if

---

[20] John Searle, notably, in his *Speech Acts* (Cambridge UP, 1969), argues that a set of descriptive statements can entail an evaluative conclusion – that one can (in certain cases) derive an 'ought' from an 'is' (pp. 175ff.). Searle (p. 132) calls the denial that this is possible 'the naturalistic fallacy fallacy'.

[21] *Essay on the Active Powers*, V vii, p. 675b.

this source is not and cannot be any sort of argument? That the principles are apt descriptions of our credal lives is something nobody denies; but whence derives the prescriptive character which Reid so clearly takes these principles to have?

Reid does have an answer to these questions; and it is actually, as I see it, rather straightforward. Before presenting that answer, however, I shall suggest what I think is behind whatever difficulty we are having in making sense of Reid's position on this matter. The difficulty, I suggest, is due to our assuming that any account of what makes these principles not just descriptive but *prescriptive* – things we not only do but ought to believe – must be in terms of something other than the principles themselves. In so far as we ought to believe these things, we are tempted to think that this is because there exists some further consideration(s) or argument(s) for their justifiedness; and what we want is for those considerations to be made explicit, those arguments to be clearly stated. It seems to me, however, that Reid's whole point is that the first principles of common sense are their own source of authority. So how could that be the case?

Here, I think, we need first to take seriously Reid's calling the principles '*axioms*' (as in the quotation from *Active Powers* V vii above), axioms being (my edition of *Webster's* tells me) fundamental or universal principles or rules. Next, we must follow Searle (*Speech Acts*, pp. 33–4) in distinguishing between what he calls 'regulative' and 'constitutive' rules:

> ... we might say that regulative rules regulate antecedently or independently existing forms of behaviour; for example, many rules of etiquette regulate inter-personal relationships that exist independently of rules. But constitutive rules do not merely regulate, they create or define new forms of behaviour. The rules of football or chess, for example, do not merely regulate playing football or chess, but as it were they create the very possibility of playing such games. The activities of playing football or chess are constituted by acting in accordance with (at least a large subset of) the appropriate rules.

My suggestion is that Reid regards the first principles of common sense as constitutive principles – they are constitutive (for us, given our nature) of cognizing at all. If nothing else, though there are other things, it is Reid's recognition of the contingency of the first principles, and of the fact that our constitution (and so our view of what is essential to cognition as such) might have been very different from what it is, that separates him from Kant.[22]

And because (for us, given our constitution) the first principles create the very possibility of cognizing at all, there is a real sense in which (given our nature) we literally cannot imagine creatures for whom those principles are

---

[22] Cf. Wolterstorff, p. 231.

nothing – creatures who do not take their truth-orientated faculties to be reliable on the whole; who do not see life and intelligence in each other; who do not think that the things which they clearly and distinctly perceive really exist; and so on. It is, of course, easy to *speak* of such creatures – I have just done so. But it is significant that when actually confronted by (human) beings who seem to approximate to this, to the extent that they do resemble such creatures, we find ourselves unable to share, even imaginatively, their 'perspective' of the world. How, we wonder, could they even get around in the world if they did not trust their senses (etc.)? Hence our tendency to say, with Reid, that one who professes not to believe the first principles, but who acts as though he does believe them, 'either acts the hypocrite, or imposes upon himself' (*Inq* VI xx, p. 184a). In terms of Searle's distinction, the sceptic's mistake consists in wanting us to regard the first principles as merely regulative – as though it were perfectly clear to us that the whole business of cognition could exist independently of such things as taking one's faculties not to be fallacious.

Of course the constitutive rules of football and chess are both 'local' and 'optional' – the activities they help to define are just a couple of activities among many possible others; and it is up to you whether you engage in either. Even so, it is in the nature of constitutive rules that in so far as one is engaged in the relevant sort of activity, one not only will but ought to act in accordance with them. For instance, it is (so to speak) a 'logical' point that in so far as one is playing chess, one must not try to move one's rook on the diagonal – conversely, that one ought to move one's rook only vertically or horizontally. (Past a certain point, a failure to abide by the constitutive rules of an activity in which one is engaged means not just – or not even – that censure is due, but that one is no longer 'playing the game' at all. Hence in the case of concern to us here, gross failure to accept the first principles of common sense is, as Reid is constantly reminding us, just plain lunacy.) Thus constitutive rules have both a descriptive and a prescriptive aspect: they describe the behaviour (at least within certain limits) of one engaged in the activity in question; but for one who is so engaged, these rules also prescribe (and prohibit) certain ways of acting.

In the case of the first principles of common sense, of course, the relevant activity, namely, cognizing, is both global and mandatory: it is an activity one cannot help engaging in (what, after all, is the alternative?); and it is an activity that one engages in whenever one is engaged in any (other) activity at all. Some might object that prescriptions are apt only when the activity in question is voluntary.[23] It seems to me, however, that this objection rests on

---

[23] This appears, e.g., to be Dretske's view; see his 'Norms, History, and the Constitution of the Mental', in *Perception, Knowledge and Belief* (Cambridge UP, 2000), pp. 242–58, esp. p. 251.

an undefended conception of norms – one that Reid would have rejected as too narrow. As he, following Aristotle, might put it: if one is a carpenter, there are certain rules which one ought to follow *qua* carpenter, whether or not one is a carpenter voluntarily, and whether or not one can avoid performing the activity in the prescribed manner: it is the nature of the activity itself, and not the fact that one freely engages in it, which makes the performance of certain actions right or wrong (cf., e.g., *Nicomachean Ethics* I vii). In this way too, the suggestion would be that (*pace* Plantinga) norms can be given by nature itself – by the nature of the activity, thing or creature at issue. Hence the first principles are, for us, and in our view, the 'fixed point' upon which the business of cognizing rests (cf. *IP* VI iv, p. 435a). And precisely because they play this constitutive role, so long as we are engaged in the activity of cognizing, we not only must but *ought to* abide by them. As I see it, Reid's anti-sceptical arguments, like the discussion of the previous section, are best viewed not as attempts to *establish* either the truth of the first principles or the rationality of belief therein, but as attempts to place the first principles '*in a proper point of view*' (*IP* I ii, p. 231b; my italics): in so far as the arguments are effective, that is because they are successful 'illustrations' (p. 231a) of the constitutive role those principles play in our cognitive lives.

I think we can now see how Reid would want to answer Plantinga's challenge, as described earlier. Plantinga assumes that in defending the rationality of our belief in the reliability of our natural faculties, thoroughgoing naturalists will have to put their money on Darwinian theory and argue (in effect) that this belief is rational because, after all, we would not be here wondering whether our faculties were reliable unless they were! But that is not Reid's strategy. Whatever the probability that natural selection would give organisms a preponderance of true beliefs, Reid would say, arguments on either side are beside the point, because any such argument would presuppose that our faculties are reliable (cf. *IP* VI v, p. 447b; also Lehrer and Warner, esp. pp. 367ff.). Which points us back towards what Reid regards as the right place to look for the justification of our basic beliefs: in the axiomatic, foundational or constitutive role they enjoy in all of our reasoning, thought and action.

But even though Reid himself no more appeals to natural selection than to the providence of God in defending the first principles, has Plantinga not shown that Reid's naturalism and the attendant belief in the reliability of our natural faculties, *if combined with* Darwinian theory, leads to irrationality? That is contentious, at best. Plantinga himself allows that his arguments might provide good grounds only for 'simple agnosticism' on the question of the probability that our faculties are reliable, given natural selection (and metaphysical naturalism) (*WPF*, p. 229). But an attitude of agnosticism *vis à vis* the first principles would follow from that only if this probability were the sole determinant of the reasonability of that belief. (As though the first principles constituted a theory, and we were deciding what sort of credal attitude to adopt towards it.) And of course Reid would insist that it is not.

None of this is to say that Reid – or I, for that matter – would endorse 'Darwinian optimism' of the sort voiced by the likes of, e.g., Fodor and Dennett (cf. fn. 9 above). A defence of the first principles does not commit one to thinking that humans *come anywhere close* to approximating to 'the system of thought prescribed by the very best systems of deductive and inductive logic and decision theory'.[24] In effect, there is a confusion in Fodor and Dennett between reliability of the sort Reid claims for our natural faculties, on the one hand, and rationality (in the sense just indicated), on the other. (In my view, this confusion permeates much of the literature on 'evolutionary epistemology'.) The first principles speak to the reliability of some pretty homely beliefs – those issuing from the 'natural' faculties (e.g., that the table which I distinctly perceive does exist, that I had such and such for breakfast this morning); no mention is made of 'rationality' of the sort just described (a good portion of which is arguably not natural at all, but learnt, or otherwise acquired).

Moreover, Reid's point is that we must trust the natural *faculties* – not, in the end, every deliverance thereof: with regard to such homely beliefs as those just mentioned, even at its strongest, the claim (in effect) is that we are *prima facie* (not *ultima facie*) warranted in accepting them as true. Thus, e.g., that 'there is a certain regard to human testimony in matters of fact' (*IP* VI v, p. 450b), another first principle, does not mean that mature humans should not *often* withhold belief in particular cases of testimony. (Though Reid would also point out that defeaters of such beliefs, where they exist, will themselves presume the reliability of our natural faculties.)

Finally, even if certain false beliefs (e.g., an inflated self-conception) and unreliable or 'illogical' belief-forming 'heuristics' (e.g., biased sampling techniques in inductive reasoning) are, for us, 'instinctive' or 'automatic', that in itself does not commit Reid to regarding them as reliable or rational. To qualify as a first principle a belief, or a belief-forming mechanism, must be such that it cannot be explained away as the product of one or another 'prejudice' (*IP* I ii, p. 231a), such as, say, its utility in furthering certain social ends; or its being a way of coping with uncertain situations, or with other contingent local circumstances. To take a central example, however, our

---

[24] M. Matthen, 'Human Rationality and the Unique Origin Constraint', in R. Cummins, A. Ariew and M. Perlman (eds), *Functions: New Readings in the Philosophy of Psychology and Biology* (Oxford UP, 2002), pp. 341–72, at p. 364.

belief in the non-fallaciousness of our natural faculties cannot be explained away in this manner, if for no other reason than that the attempt to do so would require our taking that belief *not* to be subject to such treatment. So not everything that is 'natural' counts as a first principle for Reid; and whereas it is, typically, the unreliability of just such beliefs and heuristics as *can* be explained away in the manner just described which leads people to pessimistic views about human cognitive functioning, I have been suggesting here only that with regard to the first principles, Reid holds to what we might call 'the normativity of the natural'.[25]

All of which is to say that Reid is committed to a lot less optimism about human cognition than is evinced by the likes of Fodor and Dennett. And again, this is probably just as well; Darwinian or 'Panglossian' optimism (as Stich calls it) does not fit well with a lot of empirical findings – including everyday observations of our not so occasional irrationality. In all likelihood, it stems from an implausible adaptationist picture (cf. Matthen). But so far as I can see, there is – unsurprisingly! – nothing in Reid that commits him to that.[26]

V. NORMS AND FACTS: THE CURRENT DEBATE OVER EPISTEMIC NATURALISM

As Goldman, Maffie and Haack, for example, have documented, there are a great variety of positions that have been or might be termed forms of 'naturalism' in epistemology.[27] And I shall not even try here to present a comprehensive survey of the relevant literature, much less attempt to render it a coherent whole. Rather, in closing, I shall focus on one prominent thread running through it – the one which seems to me to sit least well with Reid's epistemological views. As I read him, Reid rejects an assumption shared by the majority of (epistemic) naturalists and non-naturalists or anti-naturalists alike.

[25] This phrase is Todd's: 'Plantinga and the Naturalized Epistemology of Thomas Reid', *Dialogue*, 35 (1996), pp. 93–107, at p. 99.

[26] Plantinga's challenge might be posed in another form, of course, *viz* that the naturalist must produce a viable account of proper functioning (cf. *WPF*, pp. 199–215). To which Reid's reply would be that *qua* cognitive-epistemic subject, a properly functioning human is, at minimum, one operating in accordance with the constitutive first principles of common sense. On this last point, cf. E. Sosa and J. Van Cleve, 'Thomas Reid', in S. Emmanuel (ed.), *The Blackwell Guide to the Modern Philosophers: From Descartes to Nietzsche* (Oxford: Blackwell, 2001), pp. 179–200, at pp. 198–9.

[27] See A. Goldman, 'Naturalistic Epistemology and Reliabilism', in P.A. French *et al.* (eds), *Midwest Studies in Philosophy*, Vol. XIX: *Philosophical Naturalism* (Univ. of Notre Dame Press, 1994), pp. 301–20; J. Maffie, 'Recent Work on Naturalized Epistemology'; S. Haack, *Evidence and Inquiry* (Oxford: Blackwell, 1993), ch. 6.

Previously, I noted that the naturalism/non-naturalism debate has to do with whether epistemology is continuous with the rest of science. And I believe that this question, in turn, is understood by most as having to do with whether and how the results of science – that is, purely descriptive findings concerning how we reason, about the causes of belief, about our predispositions to form beliefs in various ways, etc. – can bear upon the normative epistemological enterprise of evaluating our reasonings, beliefs and so forth, and the articulation of evaluative notions such as justification ('warrant') and knowledge. Thus the current debate over 'naturalized epistemology' centrally involves a debate over the relation, if any, between the descriptive and the evaluative (normative), between facts and values, in the epistemic domain. This is clear enough, I think, in some of the things that have been said in connection with the subject:

> ... a mix of philosophy and psychology is needed to produce acceptable principles of justifiedness (Goldman).

> ... any epistemologist who rejects scepticism ought to be influenced in his ... philosophical work by descriptive work in psychology (Kornblith).

> ... the results from the sciences of cognition may be relevant to, and may be legitimately used in the resolution of, traditional epistemological problems (Haack).

> ... it is hard to come up with convincing normative principles except by considering how people actually do reason, which is the province of descriptive theory (Harman).[28]

As it happens, each of the parties just quoted is more or less friendly to naturalizing epistemology. But that the issue has to do with negotiating the relation between prescriptions and descriptions, between the normative and the natural, is a belief that is just as evident in what opponents of naturalized epistemology have said. Just one example is provided by Lehrer's dismissal of Goldman's 'naturalistic' account of justification:

> ... the reliabilist [is] in error when he claims that it is what originates a belief that converts it into a justified belief and knowledge. This is, in effect, to confuse the *reason* a person has for believing something with the *cause* of his believing it.[29]

More generally, Hilary Kornblith has described the typical reaction among epistemologists to Quine's original suggestion[30] that, once naturalized, 'Epistemology, or something like it, simply falls into place as a chapter of psychology and hence of natural science':

[28] These quotations are taken from R. Feldman, 'Methodological Naturalism in Epistemology', in J. Greco and E. Sosa (eds), *The Blackwell Guide to Epistemology* (Oxford: Blackwell, 1999), pp. 170–86, at pp. 170–1.
[29] K. Lehrer, *Theory of Knowledge* (Boulder: Westview, 1990), pp. 168–9.
[30] W.V.O. Quine, 'Epistemology Naturalized', in *Ontological Relativity and Other Essays* (Columbia UP, 1969), pp. 69–90, at p. 82.

For many, [Quine's approach] seem[s] to involve rejecting the normative dimension in epistemological theorizing, and, in so doing, abdicating at least one central role which epistemology has generally played.... If epistemology is to become no more than a chapter of psychology, then on one straightforward account of what psychology is all about, the resulting discipline will become merely descriptive, and thereby lose all normative force.[31]

VI. REID'S RELATION TO THE CURRENT DEBATE

Even among those who are friendly to 'naturalizing epistemology' in one or another way, for instance, the theorists cited just previously, there are few who would follow Quine in recommending the *replacement* of epistemology by psychology: their view is that descriptive findings ought to inform epistemology considered as a normative enterprise. Why? Because, e.g., they seek a 'psychologically realistic' epistemology to which we can at least approximate, or because they are interested in the 'meliorative' project of helping us to improve ourselves, epistemically speaking.[32] So in the naturalism/non-naturalism debate, in arguing whether epistemology is continuous with science, the issue really is how far (if at all) the descriptive can or should inform the prescriptive; however, just about everybody is agreed that there is a reasonably clear-cut fact/value distinction to be drawn in the epistemic domain.

As Keith Lehrer has observed in his discussion of attempts to locate Reid with respect to another currently popular way of dividing up epistemologies (namely, as foundationalist or coherentist), 'Contemporary taxonomy recapitulates contemporary prejudices'.[33] And, as I have presented him above, this is precisely what Reid would say of the contemporary dispute between epistemic naturalists and non-naturalists – that the widely shared assumption of a reasonably clear-cut fact/value distinction with regard to all epistemic matters is a mere prejudice. At any rate, it is an assumption which Reid denies in the case of the first principles: as I have portrayed him, it is not that Reid thinks that we can derive an 'ought' from an 'is'; rather he holds that common sense is itself a normative notion, and that first

---

[31] Kornblith, 'Epistemic Normativity', *Synthese*, 94 (1993), pp. 357–76, at p. 357.

[32] Cf., e.g., Harman's arguments against certain forms of foundationalism and coherentism, and Goldman: 'Only cognitive science can tell us which [cognitive] processes belong to the human repertoire; and cognitive science is needed to help ascertain which processes in this repertoire possess the epistemically relevant properties': 'Précis and Update of *Epistemology and Cognition*', in K. Lehrer and M. Clay (eds), *Knowledge and Scepticism* (Boulder: Westview, 1989), pp. 69–87, at p. 73.

[33] Lehrer, 'Chisholm, Reid, and the Problem of the Epistemic Surd', *Philosophical Studies*, 60 (1990), pp. 39–45, at p. 43.

principles of common sense have a 'mixed' character, in the sense that they are simultaneously descriptive and prescriptive. The first principles are constitutive principles: they are beliefs that do and ought to guide the rest of our belief-forming and belief-revising practices; for, given our constitution, they really are, at least for us, the axioms or laws underlying any activity of forming and revising beliefs at all.[34] Or so I read Reid.[35]

Of course there is more to epistemology than first principles. And even if the first principles have the sort of 'mixed' character I think Reid takes them to have, that hardly implies that he rejects the fact/value distinction whole-sale, or that he thinks that the whole of epistemology will be like this. So I am not sure where this leaves Reid *vis à vis* 'naturalizing epistemology'. That he holds to something like 'the normativity of the natural' with regard to the first principles might seem a pretty radical form of naturalism. Then again, it is not quite right to say that Reid thinks (with Quine) that epistemology is to be *replaced* by psychology (either wholesale or with respect to the first principles), or that (in the case of the latter) we can reduce the normative to the natural. For either of these ways of putting things suggests that there is a real gap there to be bridged – which, as I read him, is precisely what Reid denies.

I do not myself think that the question 'Is Reid's epistemology naturalistic or not?' is in itself all that interesting. The question strikes me as largely terminological: what is the 'right' answer to it will depend upon what we mean by 'naturalism'. To my mind, the two interesting questions we are left with are (a) is the interpretation of Reid's epistemology I have been develop-ing and defending here (as against a providentialist interpretation, say) correct? And if so, (b) is the resulting view plausible? I hope that if I have done nothing else, I have managed to make it seem that neither of these questions should obviously be answered in the negative.[36]

University of British Columbia

---

[34] Cf. Todd's introduction to his edition of *The Philosophical Orations of Thomas Reid* (Southern Illinois UP, 1989), pp. 1–28, at pp. 10–11.

[35] As also do Todd, and William Alston, 'A "Doxastic Practice" Approach to Epi-stemology', in Lehrer and Clay (eds), *Knowledge and Scepticism*, pp. 1–29. Sosa and Van Cleve (pp. 198–9) come close to endorsing such a reading as well.

[36] This paper began during an NEH Summer Seminar, *Thomas Reid on Perception, Knowledge, and Action*, directed by James Van Cleve (July–August, 2000), in which I was very fortunate to take part. Other ancestors of the paper were presented at the APA Pacific Division Meeting and the University of British Columbia Philosophy Department. Thanks to all those whose comments forced improvements, and special thanks to Jonathan Cohen, Cindy Holder, Jack Lyons, D.D. Todd and James Van Cleve.

4

THE PROBLEM WITH REID'S DIRECT REALISM

BY J. TODD BURAS

There is a problem about the compatibility of Reid's commitment to both a sign theory of sensations and also direct realism. I show that Reid is committed to three different senses of the claim that mind independent bodies and their qualities are among the immediate objects of perception, and I then argue that Reid's sign theory conflicts with one of these. I conclude by advocating one proposal for reconciling Reid's claims, deferring a thorough development and defence of the proposal to another paper.

INTRODUCTION

In this paper I develop and defend the thesis that there is a problem with Reid's direct realism. I also think there is a solution to Reid's problem, and that in one passage Reid has the solution in mind, though he never develops it in detail. But defending Reid's solution to the problem is the task of a second paper. The task of this one is to show that Reid is committed to the *direct realist thesis*

DRT. Mind-independent bodily qualities are among the immediate objects of perception

and that this thesis proves incompatible with Reid's *sign theory of sensations*

STS. Sensations function as natural signs of bodily qualities in perception.

My thesis bears argument because of the persistence of a dispute among commentators on Reid as to whether he endorsed (DRT), and if so whether it is indeed at odds with (STS). Some argue that Reid endorsed both theses, but that they are not at odds; others argue that the theses are at odds, but that Reid did not endorse both; and, most recently, some have argued that Reid rejects (DRT), but not because it conflicts with (STS). My claim that he endorsed both theses, and that they are at odds with each other, is itself at odds with each of these interpretative camps.[1]

The crux of the problem with Reid's commitment to (DRT) and (STS), as I see it, is his official definition of sensation. Sensation, says Reid, is 'an act of mind which may be distinguished from all others by this, that it hath no object distinct from the act itself'.[2] After explaining how Reid understands (STS) and (DRT), and why I think he is committed to each, I shall then explain how this definition of sensation sets (STS) and (DRT) at odds. I conclude with a brief discussion of the lesson I think direct realists should learn from the problem Reid faces. Before beginning, however, I shall try to head off objections from one quarter with a few comments about Reid's definition of sensation, which, if I am right, is the root of the problem.

First, I acknowledge from the outset that the claim that sensations are acts of the mind that have no objects distinct from themselves has two plausible interpretations, and that the problem I describe below clearly arises only on one. The stronger interpretation takes the definition to claim that sensations have objects, but that the objects of sensations are not distinct from the sensations themselves. On this interpretation, sensations are reflexive mental acts, acts that take only themselves as objects. This is the interpretation that generates the problem I describe. The weaker interpretation takes the definition to claim simply that sensations are not to be numbered among the acts of the mind that have objects distinct from themselves. On this interpretation the definition is silent on the question of whether sensations have themselves as objects; it neither affirms or denies this, and so it may or may

[1] The controversy in the secondary literature first led me to believe that Reid has a problem; that the controversy persists is itself an argument of sorts for my thesis. Space allows me only to note here some parties to the dispute. The following fall into the first camp: P. Cummins, 'Reid's Realism', *Journal of the History of Philosophy*, 12 (1974), pp. 317–40; N. Daniels, *Thomas Reid's Inquiry: the Geometry of Visibles and the Case for Realism* (New York: Franklin, 1974); E.H. Madden, 'Was Reid a Natural Realist?', *Philosophy and Phenomenological Research*, 47 (1986), pp. 255–76; K. DeRose, 'Reid's Anti-Sensationalism and his Realism', *Philosophical Review*, 98 (1989), pp. 313–48; G.S. Pappas, 'Sensation and Perception in Reid', *Noûs*, 23 (1989), pp. 155–67; J.J. Haldane, 'Reid, Scholasticism and Current Philosophy of Mind', in M. Dalgarno and E. Matthews (eds), *The Philosophy of Thomas Reid* (Dordrecht: Kluwer, 1989), pp. 285–384; R. Copenhaver, 'Thomas Reid's Direct Realism', *Reid Studies*, 4 (2000), pp. 17–34. They believe Reid endorsed (DRT), but do not see (or at least discuss) any conflict between (DRT) and (STS). Examples of the second camp, which holds that Reid's theses conflict, but that he was not ultimately committed to both, include Hamilton and Mill (cf. Madden, pp. 256–9); S.A. Grave, *The Scottish Philosophy of Common Sense* (Oxford: Clarendon Press, 1960), pp. 151–89; J. Immerwahr, 'The Development of Reid's Realism', *Monist*, 61 (1978), pp. 245–56. The third camp encompasses W. Alston, 'Reid on Perception and Conception', in Dalgarno and Matthews, pp. 35–48; N. Wolterstorff, *Thomas Reid and the Story of Epistemology* (Cambridge UP, 2001). They do not think (DRT) conflicts with (STS), but do think there is at least one important sense in which Reid is not a direct realist.

[2] Reid, *Essays on the Intellectual Powers of Man* (hereafter *IP*), ed. A.D. Woozley (London: Macmillan, 1941), I i, p. 18, also II xvi, p. 151.

not lead to the problem I describe. On neither interpretation, however, does the definition claim that sensations have no objects at all, that sensations are referentially empty; and it is this claim that is required to keep the problem I describe from arising at all. The stronger interpretation rules this possibility out altogether. The weaker is compatible with sensations having no objects at all, but it does not claim as much. Some might find a reason to take it in this direction in Reid's claim that 'there is no difference between a sensation and the feeling of it'. But Reid himself takes this claim as a reason to maintain only that 'in sensation, there is no object distinct from the act of the mind by which it is felt' (*IP* II xvi, pp. 150–1). Since this simply restates the ambiguous claim, Reid's claim that sensations are nothing but feelings does not settle the issue for or against the strong reading.

Secondly, I take it that the burden of proof is on those who would defend either the weaker reading or the referentially empty view of sensations. My reason for thinking the presumption is against the referentially empty view of sensations is that this is the one thing Reid's definition clearly does not say. The claim that sensations are referentially empty would have to be supported from other texts in Reid, and I know of none. My reasons for thinking the burden of proof is against the weak reading of the definition are threefold. The first is the context of the ambiguous sentence. The sentence is Reid's official (and mature) definition of sensations. In a context such as this, I do not think it is charitable to interpret Reid as claiming only that sensations do not have one sort of objects (objects distinct from the sensations themselves), while remaining silent on the question of whether they have another (objects identical to the sensations themselves). For if this were his intention, his official definition of sensation would be incomplete at best, and the definition would be clumsily worded, to say the least. Secondly, infinite regress concerns (discussed in §III) suggest that the stronger interpretation is philosophically plausible, especially for Reid. Given Reid's views of such faculties as consciousness and reflection (discussed in §II), I see no room for a non-regressive explanation of how sensations become objects of thought apart from the reflexive view of sensations. Finally, the reflexive view of sensation is a necessary condition of the problem for Reid's realism which I describe below. The fact that he explicitly owns up to the problem I describe (in a passage discussed in §III) is therefore very strong evidence indeed for the strong reading of his definition.

Those unconvinced by these considerations may want to conditionalize the thesis I defend as follows: *if* sensations are reflexive mental acts, *then* Reid faces a problem with the compatibility of (DRT) and (STS). In the discussion below I shall assume that the antecedent of this conditional is true, and bracket further disputes on this point for another occasion.

I. REID'S THESES

Reid unequivocally and frequently endorses (STS), as well as the realist element of (DRT), i.e., the claim that there are mind-independent bodily qualities. However, his commitment to the direct element of (DRT), i.e., the claim that mind-independent bodily qualities are among the immediate objects of perception, is rarely formulated explicitly. Consequently I shall concentrate the discussion in this section on establishing that Reid is committed to the direct element of (DRT) in at least three senses, confining my discussion of the less controversial points to a few brief comments.

Reid's realism. Throughout his mature philosophical career, Reid was an unflinching substance dualist. He believed the world to be populated by individuals of two metaphysically independent sorts of substances, one mental, one material.[3] Individuals of both sorts are subject to a range of modifications (or exemplify certain qualities), and are endowed with a range of powers (or exemplify capacities to enter into certain relations with others). Among the modes of material substances, Reid listed the standard primary and secondary qualities. Among the modes of mental substances, he included the basic operations of thinking and willing, as well as more complex mental operations like sensing, perceiving, remembering, imagining and reasoning. For Reid, then, there are material substances with determinate qualities and powers that are metaphysically independent of mental substances and their qualities and powers.

Reid's account of perception. In perception the ontological barrier between thought and extension is crossed. The qualities of otherwise independent substances interact and reflect dependencies. Smell a pine; taste a pear; hear a piccolo; touch a pebble; see a penguin. In all such cases, the modifications of a thinking substance (e.g., sensations and perceptions) parallel modifications of a material substance (e.g., scent, flavour, timbre, texture or colour). The task of a realistic theory of perception is to account for this correlation of mental and material modes, of sensory ideas and sensible qualities (Reid owns the realist's task at *IP* II vii, p. 86). To do this, realists are compelled, on the one hand, to allow the powers of material substances[4] to reach across

---

[3] Reid's dualism is affirmed unequivocally in *An Inquiry into the Human Mind on the Principles of Common Sense* (*Inq*), ed. D.R. Brookes (Edinburgh UP, 1977), V vii, pp. 67–8, 72; II vi, pp. 32–3; VII, p. 210.

[4] The power by which bodies determine the mind to think was the subject of debate among early modern philosophers, as were more global concerns about the nature of any causal powers. For a survey of the main options see S. Nadler, *Causation in Early Modern Philosophy* (Pennsylvania State UP, 1993). See *Inq* VI xxiv, esp. pp. 198–9, and *IP* II iv, p. 69 for Reid's most complete discussion of causation; and Wolterstorff, pp. 54–63, for discussion.

the ontological barrier and cause modifications of thinking substances. On the other hand, they endow the mental operations involved in perception with the power to reach across the ontological barrier and refer to the qualities of material substances, or take bodily qualities as their objects.

According to Reid, the general structure of the process by which physical events occasion the mental acts constitutive of perception is as follows.[5] The perceptual process begins with a physical impression made upon our sense organs by material objects, either by means of direct contact or through some appropriate medium. This impression generates a series of events in the nervous system that culminate in an impression on the brain. The impression on the brain is the last physical event in the process, and it occasions the first mental operation, a sensation. The sensation is followed by the mental act of perception, which Reid analyses in terms of two simpler operations: conception and belief (*IP* II v, p. 79).[6] The sort of belief involved in perception is a judgement (an affirmation or denial) that a material object presently exists and exemplifies a certain quality. As Wolterstorff (pp. 4–9) has recently explained, Reid takes perception to involve conception as well as belief, because to have beliefs about bodies and their qualities we must have objects in mind in such a way as to take them and their qualities as the objects of mental operations. 'Conception' is Reid's term for the simple act of apprehension involved in (and required for) any such belief (perceptual or not) about an object. By itself, conception implies no judgement about the object conceived. It is simply a thought about (a mental grip on) the object (*IP* I i, p. 9, IV i, p. 229).

Thus, for Reid, perception is conception and belief about the present existence of bodily qualities formed by means of the senses. (STS) and (DRT) fill out the details of this account of perception by explaining the nature of sensations and the relation of sensations to perception.

The sign theory. 'The external senses have a double province', says Reid: they 'make us feel' and 'they make us perceive'. In the former role they yield a variety of sensations; in the latter they yield conception and beliefs. Both results are equally 'the work of nature'; and 'in our experience we never find them disjoined' (*IP* II xvii, pp. 164–5).[7] According to the sign theory, sensations are 'natural signs' of perceived qualities. Since space does not

---

[5] The structure summarized here is described in greater detail at *Inq* VI xxi, pp. 174–5, 177, and in still greater detail at *IP* II i–v, pp. 52–78.

[6] In two places (*IP* II xvii, pp. 163, 165) Reid says that the operations of sensation and perception are simultaneous. I am not inclined to make much of this locution; see Immerwahr, 'The Development of Reid's Realism', for someone who is.

[7] Even in the case of our perception of visible figure, which is the closest we get to a perception unaccompanied by a sensation, Reid grants that there are some sensations present, just not sensations unique to visible figure. See *Inq* VI iii–viii, pp. 82–103, for Reid's vexing discussion of this topic; and Wolterstorff, pp. 136–43, and Daniels, pp. 3–20, for comment.

permit me to defend a thorough interpretation of Reid's sign theory, I shall simply indicate the points that are crucial for present purposes.

Reid wants the claim that a sensation, say, of hardness is a natural sign of a hard body to be understood as 'other words' for the claim that 'by an original principle of our constitution, a certain sensation of touch both suggests to the mind the conception of hardness, and creates the belief of it' (*Inq* V ii, p. 58, V viii, p. 74). I take him to be analysing the relation of natural signification in terms of the suggestion relation. Reid is saying, then, that a relation of natural signification holds between a sensation and a material object iff a relation of suggestion holds between the sensation and the conception of and belief about that object. He is not claiming that sensations take bodily qualities as their objects (sensations have no object distinct from themselves); but that sensations suggest mental acts that do take bodily qualities as their objects.

In his discussion of Berkeley's famous coach example, Reid says that 'we all know, that a certain kind of sound [i.e., an auditory sensation] suggests immediately to the mind, a coach passing in the street', and indicates that by 'suggests' he means 'produces' (*Inq* II vii, p. 38). Suggestion is a transition from one mode of thought (e.g., clip-clop and clattery auditory sensations) to another (conception of and belief in the coach), where the first is 'got by means of' the second, and if the first had not occurred then the second would not have occurred (*Inq* V iii, p. 61). Thus I take Reid to be analysing the suggestion relation between two modes of thought in terms of a causal relation between these modes of thought.

So, in the final analysis, a sensation is a natural sign of a bodily quality iff the sensation caused by the influence of a bodily quality on our sense organs in turn causes the conception of and belief about the bodily quality.

The directness of Reid's realism: three senses distinguished. I follow Jackson in defining the mediate/immediate distinction in terms of the 'by virtue of' relation. Jackson defines this relation as follows: if 'Fa' may be analysed in terms of b being F, where $a \neq b$, and 'aRb' may be analysed in terms of c bearing R to d, where $a \neq c$ and/or $b \neq d$; then 'Fa' is true in virtue of b being F, and 'aRb' is true in virtue of c bearing R to d. Thus x is a mediate object of (visual) perception for S at t iff S perceives x at t, and there is a y such that $x \neq y$ and S perceives x by virtue of perceiving y.[8] I think this fairly represents the content of the terms in the early modern debate, though I know of no careful account of the distinction in Reid or his contemporaries.

Realists fall into two warring factions when it comes to accounting for the aboutness of perceptual modes of thought. Both sides agree, on pain of

[8] F. Jackson, *Perception: a Representative Theory* (Cambridge UP, 1977), pp. 15, 20.

infinite regress, that there must be some things perceptual beliefs take as their objects immediately, that is, not by virtue of taking other things as their objects. The two sides disagree as to whether the qualities of bodies are among the immediate objects of perception, or whether the immediate objects of perception are only the sensations which bodily qualities cause in us ('sensory ideas', 'sense impressions' or 'sense-data'). Direct realists take the first option; representative realists take the second.

The battle between these camps is spread out over three fronts, each of which specifies one of the senses in which a bodily quality may be an immediate object of perception.

First, if beliefs about bodily qualities are not inferred from (and/or justified by) beliefs about something else, bodily qualities may be immediate objects of perception in an *epistemic* sense. If so, bodily qualities are the only things we must bear a belief attitude towards in order to have perceptual beliefs. If not, then we must bear some belief relation to something else, since perceptual beliefs about the qualities of bodies must be inferred from (and/or supported by) other beliefs. Those who opt for epistemic mediacy typically claim that beliefs about bodily qualities must be inferred from beliefs about the sensations these qualities cause in us. In that case beliefs about bodily qualities would be mediated *epistemically* by beliefs about sensation, since the attitude of belief towards bodily qualities would be achieved by virtue of a belief relation to sensations.

A second sense of immediacy concerns the *presentational content* of perceptual beliefs. The presentational content of a belief is given by the concept (or description) under which the object of perception is apprehended, or, more formally, by the value of 'F' in the belief-statement form 'S believes of the b such that Fb that b is G'. If through perception you come to believe of a body you conceive of as hard that it is brown, you apprehend the body under the concept HARD; the body is presented to the mind under this concept. If the content of HARD is absolute or non-relative (i.e., the firm adhesion of the parts of a body), then the presentational content of the perceptual belief is immediate. We need not think of the body in relation to anything else, and therefore need not think of anything else, in order to present the body to ourselves in the way we do in perception. If on the other hand the presentational content of HARD is given by a relative or sensational description (i.e., the quality that causes such and such sensations in me), then the presentational content of the perceptual belief is mediate. It is by virtue of thinking of our sensations that we think of the body in the way we do when we perceive it. We could not present bodily qualities to ourselves in terms of the sensations they generate in us without taking sensations themselves as objects of thought.

A third sense of immediacy concerns the *referential content* of perceptual belief. The referential content of perceptual beliefs is what these beliefs are about; or, more formally, the value of '*b*' in the belief-statement form above. The referent of perceptual belief is, for Reid, the object apprehended by the act of conception required for perceptual belief. If bodily qualities may be apprehended directly, without first apprehending anything else, then perceptual beliefs would be referentially immediate. If not – if, say, we must apprehend bodily qualities by virtue of apprehending sensations – then perceptual beliefs are referentially mediated by sensations. They are about bodily qualities by virtue of being about sensations. In this case the mind would be thinking about bodily qualities by proxy, using sensations to represent them. Presumably sensations bear a relation to bodily qualities that makes them natural facilitators of mediated thought about bodies. Representative realists of Reid's day identified this relation as similarity (*IP* II xiv, p. 135). If all perceptual beliefs are about bodily qualities by virtue of being about sensations that are similar to them, Reid and his opponents agree that the mind 'hath no immediate intercourse' (*Inq* VI vi, p. 91) with bodily qualities, that bodily qualities are not 'present to the mind' (*IP* II xiv, p. 143).

The directness of Reid's realism: arguments for each sort. By Reid's own lights, his chief philosophical contribution was to have questioned, and ultimately to have rejected, representative realism, which he took to be virtually universal among his predecessors.[9] 'All philosophers, from Plato to Mr Hume', he says in a characteristically incautious moment of historical reflection, 'agree in this, That we do not perceive external objects immediately, and that the immediate object of perception must be some image present to the mind' (*IP* II vii, p. 86). Unfortunately neither Reid nor his opponents distinguished the different senses in which perceptual beliefs may take bodily qualities as their immediate objects. While it is possible to mix and match epistemic, presentational and referential mediacy and immediacy in a variety of combinations, Reid took his opponents to be occupying one extreme: mediacy on all fronts.[10] His endorsement of (DRT) is meant to nail down the other extreme: immediacy on all fronts. My purposes are best served by keeping the varieties of immediacy distinct, since, as I shall show, (STS) comes into conflict with (DRT) only over the referential sense of immediacy.

---

[9] Reid's most detailed effort to defend his frequent and liberal attribution of representative realism to his predecessors is *IP* II vii–xv, pp. 86–134; *Inq* VII, pp. 203–18, and I iii–vii, pp. 16–23, present briefer versions of the same claims.

[10] For Reid's own characterization of the fundamental commitments of his opponents' system see *IP* II viii, p. 100, and II x, p. 114, *Abstract* of *Inq*, p. 259, and *Inq* II vi, p. 33; for discussion of the system Reid is characterizing and attacking see Wolterstorff, pp. 23–44, and Grave, 'The "Theory of Ideas"', in S. Barker and T. Beauchamp (eds), *Thomas Reid: Critical Interpretations* (Temple UP, 1976), pp. 55–61.

In general Reid had three complaints against representative realism. It was counter-intuitive, since it denied the common opinion that the sun, moon and stars, penguins, pears and pebbles, are the immediate objects of perception.[11] It was typically assumed without argument, and what argumentative support it received was paltry indeed.[12] Worst of all, it led inexorably to scepticism (*Inq* I iii–vii, pp. 16–23, esp. p. 23). Waxing eloquent, Reid says (*Inq* V viii, pp. 75–6) that representative realism 'like the Trojan horse, had a specious appearance both of innocence and beauty; but ... carried in its belly death and destruction to all science and common sense'.

The sceptical consequences of representative realism figure prominently in Reid's argument against epistemic and referential mediacy, and for epistemic and referential immediacy.[13] As Reid saw it, representational realism blithely wagered all our perceptual beliefs about material objects, and with them, 'all science and common sense', on a bet which it was sure to lose to the sceptic. For given epistemic and referential mediacy, the sceptic does not have to do much to prove that the following are true:

C. None of our perceptual beliefs about material objects is justified

C′. None of our perceptual beliefs is about material objects.

The sceptic only has to show that

P1. We cannot infer perceptual beliefs about material objects from beliefs about sensations

P1′. We cannot apprehend material objects by virtue of apprehending sensations that resemble them.

For the representational realist has already granted the conditional premises by which (C) follows from (P1), and (C′) follows from (P1′):

P2. If we cannot infer perceptual beliefs about material objects from beliefs about sensations, then none of our beliefs about material objects is justified

P2′. If we cannot apprehend material objects by virtue of apprehending sensations that resemble them, then none of our perceptual beliefs is about material objects.[14]

---

[11] This point is made at *IP* II xiv, pp. 135–7. See DeRose, pp. 317–20, for discussion of Reid's view of the 'vulgar' belief in bodies in comparison with Berkeley and Hume.

[12] This point is made best at *IP* II xiv, p. 137–46. Constraints of space prevent a detailed analysis of the arguments offered in support of representative realism and Reid's objections.

[13] Reid's strategy of arguing the anti-sceptical 'facts' of perception against the representative realist's 'hypothesis' is clearest at *Inq* V vii–viii, pp. 67–76. I owe the explication of Reid's strategy in this paragraph to lectures on Reid by Keith DeRose.

[14] Reid took Berkeley and Hume to be arguing in both these ways: see *Inq* V iii, p. 61, and V vii, p. 75. See DeRose, pp. 313–17, for a further discussion of their arguments for (C′); for a discussion of Reid's understanding of the argument for (C), see Wolterstorff, pp. 185–92.

Representational realists were sure to lose their wager with the sceptic, because they granted what Reid considered the only controversial premises of the sceptic's arguments. Reid thought the truth of (P1) to be demonstrated by the arguments of Berkeley's *Principles*, §§18–21, and Hume's *Treatise*, I iv 2. 'I think it is evident', Reid says, 'that we cannot, by reasoning from our sensations, collect the existence of bodies at all, far less any of their qualities. This hath been proved by unanswerable arguments by the Bishop of Cloyne, and by the author of the *Treatise of Human Nature*' (*Inq* V iii, p. 61). Reid held that the truth of (P1') is demonstrated simply by attending carefully to one's sensations (say, of touch) and comparing them to the qualities of bodies (say, hardness). 'Total dissimilitude' is Reid's oft-repeated verdict (*Abstract*, p. 259; also *Inq* V ii, p. 57). Given the truth of (P1) and (P1'), the sceptic's conclusions were, as Reid so colourfully put it, 'carried in the belly' of the representative realist's endorsement of (P2) and (P2').

Of course Reid was just as convinced of the falsity of (C) and (C') as he was of the truth of (P1) and (P1'), since he considered scepticism of either form obviously contrary to the principles of common sense. The falsity of (C) and (C'), together with the truth of (P1) and (P1'), entails the falsity of (P2) and (P2'). If (P2) is false, then we have justified perceptual beliefs that are not inferred from beliefs about sensations. If (P2') is false, then in perception we apprehend material objects, but not by virtue of apprehending sensations that resemble them. How, then, does Reid think we apprehend material objects and get our beliefs about them?

The path from Reid's rejection of epistemic and referential mediacy to his endorsement of epistemic and referential immediacy runs by way of the lack of alternatives (*Inq* V ii, pp. 57–8):

> Here then is a phaenomenon of human nature, which comes to be resolved. Hardness of bodies is a thing that we conceive as distinctly, and believe as firmly, as anything in nature. We have no way of coming at this conception and belief, but by means of a certain sensation of touch, to which hardness hath not the least similitude; nor can we, by any rules of reasoning, infer the one from the other. The question is, How we come by this conception and belief?
>
> ... I see nothing left, but to conclude, that, by an original principle of our constitution, a certain sensation of touch both suggests to the mind the conception of hardness, and creates the belief of it.

Reid's appeal to 'original principles of our constitution' at this point implies that human beings are simply set up, by contingent laws of nature, with the capacity to apprehend and hold beliefs about the qualities of bodies when they affect our sense organs. The power to think of and hold beliefs about objects is thus among the 'simple and original, and therefore inexplicable, acts of the mind' (*Inq* II iii, p. 28). Negatively, this means that the power to

apprehend and hold beliefs about bodily qualities cannot be explained by
anything else; positively, that such powers are primitive facts about the constitution of our cognitive equipment. Whatever else having conceptions and
beliefs by original principles of our constitution means, Reid is clear that it
means having them immediately. In the clearest statements I have found to
this effect, Reid says that perceptual beliefs are 'immediate and not the
effect of reasoning' (*IP* II vi, p. 79; also *Inq* V viii, p. 76); and 'something
which is extended and solid, which may be measured and weighed, is the
immediate object [i.e., referent] of my touch and sight. And this object I
take to be matter, and not an idea' (*IP* II xi, p. 123; also II xiv, p. 143).

Reid's case for presentational immediacy depends not on his anti-
scepticism but his anti-sensationalism about the content of perceptual
beliefs.[15] Like his anti-scepticism, his anti-sensationalism depends crucially
on his anti-similarity arguments. According to Reid, the radical dissimilarity
of our sensations and bodily qualities does not only show that we cannot
think of bodily qualities by virtue of thinking about any sensations similar to
them. It also shows that our concept of a bodily quality is not, as representative realism requires, 'copied from' sensations (as Hume would have it);
nor even 'derived from' sensations by means of operations like abstraction,
combination and division (as Berkeley says). Reid thus offers absolute concepts of bodily qualities as an argument against presentational mediacy.

So confident was Reid that 'from sensation alone' we cannot 'collect any
notion of extension, figure, motion' that he was willing to wager all our
thoughts about the material world on this issue (*Inq* V vii, p. 70):

> This I would, therefore, humbly propose, as an *experimentum crucis*, by which the ideal
> system must stand or fall; and it brings the matter to a short issue: Extension, figure,
> motion, may, any one, or all of them, be taken for the subject of this experiment.
> Either they are ideas of sensation, or they are not. If any one of them can be shewn to
> be an idea of sensation, or to have the least resemblance to any sensation, I lay my
> hand upon my mouth, and give up all pretence to reconcile reason to common sense
> in this matter, and must suffer the ideal scepticism to triumph. But if, on the other
> hand, they are not ideas of sensation, nor like to any sensation, then the ideal system
> is a rope of sand, and all the laboured arguments of the sceptical philosophy against a
> material world, and against the existence of every thing but impressions and ideas,
> proceed upon a false hypothesis.

Reid's point, I take it, is this: if presentational mediacy holds, then all our
concepts of all bodily qualities are 'ideas of sensation', i.e., sensational concepts, or concepts of bodily qualities in terms of the sort of sensations they
produce in us. On the other hand, if we have concepts of bodily qualities
that are not 'ideas of sensations', then presentational mediacy is false. Reid

[15] See DeRose, and Daniels, pp. 97–113, for more on Reid's anti-sensationalism.

argued at length that we have no sensational concepts at all of certain primary qualities (e.g., extension) because they generate no special sensation in us, no sensation over and above the sensations produced by qualities (e.g. figure, motion) that presuppose them. Other primary qualities (e.g., hardness) generate special sensations in us, but our concept of them is absolute none the less, because we can think of these qualities without thinking of them in terms of the sensations they generate in us.[16] Thus the presentational content of (at least some of) our concepts of bodily qualities is not mediated by sensations. Indeed, since the presentational content of absolute concepts involves no reference to anything else, the content of (at least some of) our concepts of bodily qualities is presentationally immediate.

II. THE CONFLICT BETWEEN REID'S THESES

I have now shown what (DRT) and (STS) mean to Reid, and that he en-dorses each claim. The next task is to show that (DRT) and (STS) conflict, that there is something about the claim that sensations are signs of perceived qualities that spoils, in one sense or another, the claim that bodily qualities are among the immediate objects of perception.

Certainly (STS) entails that sensations are *causally necessary* for perception. This is the core of what it means for sensations to suggest perceptions, and thus to be signs of bodily qualities. So (STS) entails that sensations mediate perception in at least the way physical impressions on our sense organs and brains mediate perceptual beliefs. But this does not yet entail that sensations mediate perception in the epistemic, the presentational or the referential sense. After all, countless things are causally necessary for the formation of perceptual beliefs, *viz* all the physical events which 'intervene between the object and our perception of it' (*Inq* VI xxi, p. 174). But we need not take any of these as an object of thought in order to have our perceptual beliefs, with their presentational and referential content.

Are there significant enough differences between sensations and the neural events that causally mediate our perception to entail that the former but not the latter mediate perception in one of the three relevant senses? There certainly are, at least for a dualist like Reid. Sensations are mental acts, indeed reflexively mental acts; neural events are not. The mentalness of sensations has implications that threaten each of the three senses of the claim that bodily qualities are the immediate objects of perception; and in the referential case it succeeds in undermining the claim.

[16] Reid argues for these points via thought-experiment at *Inq* V vi, pp. 65–7; see DeRose, pp. 332–48, and Daniels, pp. 73–96, for a discussion of Reid's line of argument.

Does (STS) entail epistemic mediacy? No; because suggestion is not inference.

Because sensations are mental, it is true that a mode of thought intervenes between objects and our perception of them. Given (STS), the mind must pass through a sensation on its way to an apprehension of and belief about bodily qualities. But, as we have seen, this movement of thought is not an inference, and indeed could not be made by inference. Nor is a sensation even the sort of thing to which a belief about bodies could be related by inference. Inference is a relation between beliefs; sensations are feelings. So it is not the case that we have perceptual beliefs by virtue of having other beliefs. Nor is it the case that the intervening sensational mode of thought is the evidence that justifies or warrants perceptual belief, for Reid. Such beliefs have all the epistemic merit they need because they are the result of original principles of our constitution. Further, if we are unsure of the epistemic merits of the beliefs our constitution determines us to have, then no evidential support makes much difference: as Reid puts it, 'we are deceived by Him that made us, and there is no remedy' (*Inq* V vii, p. 72).

A more subtle worry[17] arises from Reid's claim that sensations are 'natural principles of belief', by which he means that when we have a sensation, we are 'necessarily determined to believe that the sensation really exists' (*Inq* II iii, p. 27). Reid is claiming that whenever there is a true material-object belief-statement of the form 'S believes of the b such that Fb that b is G', there is not only a true statement to the effect that 'S feels sensation e'; but also a true sensational belief-statement 'S believes there is an e such that Fe'. But this does not mean that it is by virtue of believing there is an e such that Fe that we believe there is an b such that Fb. For the belief about sensations has only half of what it takes to be that by virtue of which we have a belief about bodies. Not only must there be a one-to-one correlation of sensational belief-statements and material-object belief-statements, it must also be the case that the former analyses the latter (see above, p. 462). But there is no reason to think sensational belief-statements analyse material-object belief-statements for Reid. There is no asymmetrical dependence between these beliefs: neither of them is metaphysically or explanatorily more fundamental than the other. The sensational belief neither constitutes nor causes the material-object belief. The beliefs are independent effects of the fact that S feels e. So it is not by virtue of having beliefs about anything else that we have our perceptual beliefs about bodily qualities.

Does (STS) entail presentational mediacy? No; because sensational and absolute concepts are not convertible.

---

[17] The argument of this paragraph has been greatly improved by the comments of Michael Della Rocca and Keith DeRose.

Reid is right that perception of bodily qualities under absolute concepts refutes presentational mediacy. But he is certainly not right about how absolute concepts accomplish so much. In the *experimentum crucis* passage, Reid seems to think that absolute concepts of bodily qualities do not convert with sensational concepts because the two sorts of concepts are not one-to-one. He argues that there are some absolute concepts of bodily qualities that have no sensational counterpart: he lists extension, figure and motion in the passage quoted above, and later adds hardness and roughness to the list (*Abstract*, p. 260). If the experiment is simply a matter of determining whether sensationalists can account for the presentational content of such concepts, then there is reason to think Reid must, as he says, 'lay my hand upon my mouth ... and suffer the ideal scepticism to triumph'.

As DeRose notes (pp. 338–43), a sufficiently subtle sensationalist (e.g., Berkeley) will have a perfectly good account of the content of these concepts. Even when there is no unique sensation associated with the perception of a bodily quality, (STS) entails that there is some sensation or set of sensations associated. The sensationalist will identify the presentational content of thoughts involving absolute concepts in terms of the sensations (or set of sensations) one would have if one were to perceive a body with that quality. For example, the subtle sensationalist will accept Reid's account of hardness$_{absolute}$, i.e., the firm adhesion of the parts of a body, by identifying the content of this concept with hardness$_{sensational}$, the sensations I would have were I to attempt to alter the relative positions of the parts of a body. By repeating this manœuvre, the subtle sensationalist can give an account of any putatively absolute concept.

What is more, the sensationalist account has a notable advantage over Reid's own. As DeRose explains, the sensationalist account of the presentational content of sensations has considerable explanatory power. For the sensationalist account explains why we need repeated experience, even scientific research, in order to arrive at an 'absolute' concept of a bodily quality. To think of hardness in terms of the sensations I would have if I tried to alter the relative position of the parts of a body, I must form and test hypotheses about the set of sensations that accompany the perception of hard things. But Reid's account of the origin of the content of such concepts as hardness is that the sensations that generate perception of hard bodies 'conjure up' their presentational content 'by a natural kind of magic'; they give us the conception of hardness all 'at once' (*Inq* V iii, p. 60). Yet even Reid grants that the perception of bodily qualities 'unfold[s] ... by degrees'; so that 'sensations of touch do not from the very first suggest the same notions of body and its qualities, which they do when we are grown up' (*Inq* V vii, p. 72). Reid's account of the content of absolute concepts has no explanation of this fact. All Reid says (*ibid.*) is 'Perhaps Nature is frugal in this, as in her other operations'.

So if the point of the *experimentum* passage is that representative realists cannot account for absolute concepts (or even that Reid offers a better account of them), then it seems that Reid's case for presentational immediacy is in trouble. If the presentational content of all absolute concepts is identified with the presentational content of a sensational concept, then the thoughts we judge in perception have their presentational content by virtue of taking sensations as their object. For in that case, what it is to think about bodily qualities (even under absolute concepts) is to think of them in terms of the sensations they cause in us.

But this misses what is perhaps the crucial point of Reid's challenge to the representative realist, to show that our ideas of qualities like hardness are 'ideas of sensations'. For even if there is a sensational concept for every absolute concept of bodily qualities, it does not follow that they are equivalent. It follows only that every absolute concept is *extensionally* equivalent to a sensational concept, i.e., that for every absolute concept there is a sensational concept that picks out all and only the same things. But (certainly with respect to concepts) extensional equivalence is not equivalence *simpliciter*. Something about my thought that one and the same billiard ball is hard$_a$ and hard$_s$ is not the same. In the former case, I am thinking about the ball in terms of the relation of its parts; in the latter case, I am thinking about it in terms of its relation to something that happens in my head. What I am thinking about may be the same; but the way I am thinking about it certainly is not.

This is difference enough to show that the presentational content of hardness$_a$ cannot be identified with the presentational content of hardness$_s$. So even if there is a sensational concept for every bodily quality, it does not follow that the thoughts we form about bodies in perception have their presentational content by virtue of taking sensations as their object. Nor does it matter whether Reid or the sensationalist is right about how we come by our absolute concepts. The point is simply that we have them; having them is not a matter of having a sensational substitute; and they constitute the content of at least some perceptual beliefs.

Does (STS) entail referential mediacy? Yes; because, as Reid says, sensations are necessarily felt, and are feelings that have 'no object distinct from that act of the mind by which it is felt' (*IP* II xvi, p. 151).

Because sensations are necessarily felt, it is not possible to have but not feel the mode of thought which according to (STS) intervenes between objects and the perception of them. The intervening mode of thought, says Reid, 'can be nothing else than it is felt to be. Its very essence consists in being felt; and, when it is not felt, it is not. There is no difference between the sensation and the feeling of it – they are one and the same thing' (pp. 150–1). Given the nature of sensations, (STS) entails not only that we must *have* a sensation, but also that we must *feel* a sensation, in order to perceive bodily qualities.

Furthermore, these intervening feelings are not non-intentional mental states, (referentially) empty buzzes that are not about anything at all. For reasons discussed in the introduction, I am assuming that they are reflexive mental acts, which are about themselves or take themselves as their objects. A sensation, then, is a mode of thought which is about a sensation; and feeling a sensation is (or at least involves) having a mode of thought about a sensation. Thus because a sensation intervenes between objects and the perception of them, a mode of thought about something other than bodily qualities intervenes. More importantly, because it is by virtue of having/ feeling a sensation that we have a perceptual belief about an object; and because having/feeling a sensation is (or involves) having a mode of thought about a sensation, it is by virtue of having a mode of thought about a sensation that we have a perceptual belief about an object.

In sum: the thoughts involved in perception cannot be about bodily qualities without first being about the sensation-signs of bodily qualities – and this is so whether or not our thoughts about sensations figure in the presentational content of our thoughts about bodies, or in the epistemic basis of our thoughts about bodies. For we must have a thought about our sensations in order to have a sensation; and we must have a sensation in order to apprehend and hold beliefs about bodies; and we must apprehend and hold beliefs about bodies in order to perceive bodies. It is therefore by virtue of thinking about the sensations which signify bodily qualities that we have beliefs about bodily qualities in perception. So if sensations function as signs of bodily qualities in perception, then bodily qualities are not among the (referentially) immediate objects of perception. (STS) $\rightarrow \neg$(DRT$_{referential}$). This is the problem with Reid's direct realism.

No relief is to be found from the problem in Reid's claim that, more often than not, sensations are 'fugitives', hiding 'in the shadows' of the bodily qualities they bring to mind (*Inq* V ii, p. 56). The point of these metaphorical remarks is not that sensations usually fail to intervene between bodily qualities and our perception of them. Rather the point is that we are not in the habit of attending to our sensations. 'We are accustomed to use the sensation as a sign, and to pass immediately to the thing signified' (*ibid.*). Nor should we think inattentiveness amounts to unconsciousness. If it did, some might seek relief from our problem by burying the suggestive work of sensations beneath the level of conscious thought. But Reid assumes that 'we are conscious of many things to which we give little or no attention'. Attention, he explains, is an act of reflection, an inward parallel of outward perception which takes mental operations as its objects (*IP* I ii, p. 25). He offers (*IP* I v, p. 42) this analogy by way of elaboration:

> The difference between consciousness and reflection, is like to the difference between a superficial view of an object which presents itself to the eye while we are engaged about something else, and that attentive examination which we give to an object when we are wholly employed in surveying it.

This analogy also makes it clear that the difference between the sensations we attend to and those of which we are merely conscious is not a difference between *actually* having thoughts about our sensations and only *potentially* having the thoughts. The difference is rather between involuntary mental operations (which usually remain tacit) and voluntary mental operations (which are always explicit). In short, by granting that sensations are typically unattended, Reid is not granting anything that mitigates the problem.

In the absence of relief from some other quarter, it is worth noting that the battle between Reid and representative realists collapses into an internal squabble. For if the sign theory shows that our mental grip on bodily qualities is mediated by our mental grip on our sensations, then Reid's break with representative realism is merely over the nature of that mediation. The issue is not, as (DRT) advertised, whether any such mediation is involved in perception, but whether it is a matter of resemblance or signification. Where the representative realist holds that sensations mediate our apprehension of bodily qualities by virtue of their intrinsic properties, i.e., their similarity to bodily qualities, Reid's sign theory would be implying that sensation-signs mediate apprehension of bodily qualities by virtue of their extrinsic properties, i.e., their causal relations (in one direction) to brain states and (in the other direction) to the mental acts constitutive of perception.

III. THE LESSON FOR DIRECT REALISTS

If, as I have now argued, (STS) and (DRT) are at odds over the immediate objects of perception, then there are two ways to reconcile them: one way revises (STS) to accommodate (DRT)'s claim on the immediate objects of perception, the other adapts (DRT) to suit (STS)'s claim about the immediate objects. In the one passage I know of (*IP* II ix, p. 108) where Reid himself faces squarely the problem I have pressed, he hints at a solution of the second sort.

> There is a sense in which a thing may be said to be perceived by a medium. Thus any kind of sign may be said to be the medium by which I perceive or understand the

thing signified. The sign by custom, or compact, or perhaps by nature, introduces the thought of the thing signified. But here the thing signified, when it is introduced to the thought, is an object of thought no less immediate than the sign was before. And there are here two objects of thought, one succeeding another.

Reid's strategy here is to deny what has so far been taken for granted, the biconditional which (at p. 462 above) I offered as a working definition of mediate objects of perception: x is a mediate object of perception for S at t iff S perceives x at t, and there is a y such that $x \neq y$ and S perceives x in virtue of perceiving y. Specifically, Reid sees that he must deny the right-to-left implication. In the passage just quoted his suggestion is that although we get bodily qualities in mind by virtue of getting sensations in mind, we still get bodily qualities in mind immediately. I take this to be denying that if S perceives x at t, and there is a y such that $x \neq y$ and S perceives x in virtue of perceiving y, then x is a mediate object of perception for S at t. As I read him, Reid is claiming that having a sensation accounts for the fact that we have a perceptual belief, but not for the fact that the perceptual belief takes a body (or any body) as its object. The aboutness of perceptual belief remains a primitive feature of the mental states involved in perception.

As I warned at the outset, defending Reid's solution to his problem is the task of another paper. It is admittedly not at all clear what the immediacy of immediate perception is supposed to consist in, if not the absence of something by virtue of which we perceive bodily qualities. It is also unclear whether denying the right-to-left implication above makes direct realism hard enough to come by, or at any rate an interesting classification of theories of perception. Finally, it remains to be seen whether a solution to Reid's problem developed from the passage above can be defended as an overall interpretation of his theory of perception. These issues cannot be settled here.

However, I can note why Reid's problem requires a revision of (DRT) of the sort he proposes, rather than a revision of (STS). Certainly solutions that stretch (STS) to suit (DRT) are open to direct realists, but they come at quite a cost. An assessment of the cost of such solutions serves not only to show why Reid proposes what he does, but also to show that Reid's problem reflects a deep-seated problem for direct realists about the role of sensation in perception.

Suppose a direct realist claimed sensations were not natural signs of bodily qualities in the sense that they suggest (or cause) the perception of such qualities. Then either (a) sensations are not signs of bodily qualities at all, or (b) they are signs in some other sense.

If (a) sensations are not signs of bodily qualities at all, then what should a direct realist say about their relation to perception? The only alternative I know of is David Armstrong's. According to Armstrong, perception is nothing but acquiring immediate beliefs about (or dispositions to believe immediately) particular facts concerning the physical world by means of the senses.[18] The sensations (he calls them 'sense-impressions') that accompany perception are nothing but an immediate belief (or dispositions to believe immediately) that we are perceiving something (pp. 87–93, 127–32). This is a purely doxastic account not only of perception but also of sensation. The beliefs that constitute both are independent, but regularly correlated, causal results of events in the central nervous system.

The problem with such an account is not that it fails to distinguish hearing a coach pass from other ways of acquiring the belief that a coach is passing, say, by being told as much. For being told that a coach is passing is not regularly accompanied by a belief that one is perceiving the coach (p. 114). The problem is that there is more to the sensations that accompany perception than merely the belief that one is perceiving something, or even the belief that one is perceiving something by hearing it. There is a qualitative aspect to the sensory experience involved in hearing a coach – something that it is like to hear the clip-clop and clatter – which is distinct from the belief that one perceives a coach. If we say that the perceptual belief about the coach is not caused by the sensory experience, but is none the less accompanied by it, Armstrong (p. 89) contends that the qualitative aspect of sensation is not important to the analysis of perception: 'We could pay such sense-impressions our phenomenological respects, and pass them by'.

I doubt that passing by the qualitative aspects of perception is a good idea for the direct realist, or anyone else. The main reason is that the content of many perceptual beliefs is explicitly about the qualitative aspects of sense experience, *viz* 'the sky now looks purple to me'; 'this pear tastes ripe'; 'the piccolos sounded especially shrill at the last rehearsal'. More importantly, such statements about the phenomenal character of perceptual experience may be true when the corresponding belief-statement – 'I believe that I am perceiving the sky now to be purple' – is false. When I see a blue sky through rose-coloured glasses, the sky looks purple; but I neither believe (nor am disposed to believe) that I am perceiving a purple sky.[19]

A direct realist who wanted to reject Reid's account of the natural signification relation may thus opt for the claim (b) that sensations are signs of bodily qualities in some sense other than Reid's. But if sensations are not

---

[18] D.M. Armstrong, *Perception in the Physical World* (London: Routledge & Kegan Paul, 1961), p. 105.

[19] The argument presented here is developed in greater detail by Jackson (*Perception*, pp. 38–48). He argues that the analysis of such 'looks'-locutions in terms of beliefs fails, not only because 'looks'-statements do not entail belief-statements, but also because belief-statements do not entail 'looks'-statements.

signs of bodily qualities in the sense that they suggest (or cause) the perception of bodily qualities, then in what sense are they signs? Though I know of
no alternative, perhaps a proposal could be mustered here from Reid's
remark in two passages that sensations are produced by impressions on the
brain *at the same time* as perceptions are (*IP* II xvii, pp. 163, 165). Taking a cue
from these passages, one could reject Reid's view that sensations are modes
of thought one passes through on the way to perception, claiming instead
that sensations are modes of thought that occur together with perception.
One could revise Reid's notion of natural signification accordingly: sensations signify bodily qualities not by being constantly conjoined to perception
as cause is conjoined to effect, but by being constantly conjoined as
simultaneous effects are conjoined to a common cause. Just as a change in
wind direction is, in this sense, a natural sign of a change in barometric
pressure, because both events are simultaneous effects of frontal passage; so
this peculiar clip-clop and clattery auditory experience is a sign of a passing
coach, because the auditory sensation and the perception of the coach are
simultaneous effects of the brain events caused by the coach.

This attempt to reconcile direct realism to the role of sensation in perception *misplaces* the qualitative aspect of sense experience which Armstrong
leaves out, and it does so at the expense of its plausibility. It is not plausible
to think that the perceptual belief in a passing coach is related to the clip-
clop and clattery auditory experience in the same way as a change in wind
direction is related to changes in barometric pressure. For there is an
asymmetrical relation between the two mental events (sensation and perception) caused by the brain event, and there is none between the two
events caused by frontal passage. The change in wind direction does not
explain the change in barometric pressure, but (as Reid notes) the clip-clop
and clattery auditory experience does explain the perception of a passing
coach. This is why the sensory experience is a sign of the perception, but not
vice versa, whereas the change in wind direction is a sign of the change in
barometric pressure only if a change in barometric pressure is a sign of a
change in wind direction. If only causes explain, then the asymmetrical
explanatory relation between sensory experience and perception reflects an
asymmetrical causal relation. If not, the difference between the perceptual
and barometric 'sign' relations is still not compromised. For the explanatory
relation present in the former but not in the latter case is presumably
grounded in some fact about the cases. Any difference in the facts about the
two cases is sufficient to prove the proposed account of the signification of
sensations implausible.

In the absence of any other proposals, then, the claim that sensations are
not signs of bodily qualities is too costly, and the claim that they are signs in

some other sense is not plausible. The only recourse left for a direct realist is to deny Reid's claim that sensations are reflexive mental acts which take themselves as objects, and opt instead for a thoroughly non-intentional (referentially empty) view of sensations. The trouble here is that no clear alternative proposal is available. Certainly it is open to the direct realist to claim that sensations are non-intentional in the sense that neither their intrinsic nor extrinsic features make them about other things. But this does not yet deny Reid's claim that sensations merely *signify* (suggest modes of thought about) bodily qualities, while *being about* themselves. Can direct realists claim that sensations are even more non-intentional, that they are not even about themselves? Surely no theory of sensations should deny that sensations are (at least sometimes) objects of modes of thought. But if it is not by virtue of having a sensation that we have a mode of thought about a sensation, then by virtue of what are sensations thought of? One cannot argue that to have a mode of thought about a sensation, we must have a second mode of thought by virtue of which our thought is about a sensation, since that leads to an infinite regress. This second mode of thought is gratuitous unless it too is (at least sometimes) an object of thought. But if, for some reason, the sensation cannot be an object of thought except by virtue of a second thought, then by parity of reasoning the second cannot be an object of thought except by virtue of a third; and so on, *ad infinitum.* Of course, if the second mode of thought can be thought of without a third, then I ask why the first cannot be thought of without a second. If it is not by virtue of having a second mode of thought that sensations are thought of, then it must be by virtue of the features of sensations themselves that they are thought of. Which is to say that sensations must be about themselves, if they are ever to be an object of thought.

For better or worse, then, direct realists appear stuck with something like Reid's understanding of the claim that sensations are natural signs of bodily qualities. Since attempts to reconcile the conflict between (STS) and (DRT) by modifying (STS) appear to be a dead end, what direct realists need is, as Reid suggested, an account of the immediacy of immediate perception that accommodates better the function of sensations in perception. This is the (philosophical) lesson which my defence of the (historical) thesis that there is a problem with Reid's direct realism offers to direct realists.[20]

Yale University

[20] I thank Keith DeRose, Nicholas Wolterstorff, Robert Adams, Michael Della Rocca, Andrew Dole and Andrew Chignell for helpful discussions of earlier drafts of this paper.

5

REID'S FOUNDATION FOR THE PRIMARY/SECONDARY QUALITY DISTINCTION

By Jennifer McKitrick

Reid offers an under-appreciated account of the primary/secondary quality distinction. He gives sound reasons for rejecting the views of Locke, Boyle, Galileo and others, and presents a better alternative, according to which the distinction is epistemic rather than metaphysical. Primary qualities, for Reid, are qualities whose intrinsic natures can be known through sensation. Secondary qualities, on the other hand, are unknown causes of sensations. Some may object that Reid's view is internally inconsistent, or unacceptably relativistic. However, a deeper understanding shows that it is consistent, and relative only to normal humans. To acquire this deeper understanding, one must also explore the nature of dispositions, Reid's rejection of the theory of ideas, his distinction between sensation and perception, and his distinction between natural and acquired perceptions.

The distinction betwixt primary and secondary qualities hath had several revolutions. Democritus and Epicurus, and their followers, maintained it. Aristotle and the Peripatetics abolished it. Des Cartes, Malebranche, and Locke, revived it, and were thought to have put it in a very clear light. But Bishop Berkeley again discarded this distinction, by such proofs as must be convincing to those that hold the received doctrine of ideas. Yet, after all, there appears to be a real foundation for it in the principles of our nature.[1]

And so Reid summarizes the history of thought on sensible qualities, inviting the following questions. Where did these earlier accounts go wrong? What, according to Reid, is the real foundation of the primary/secondary quality distinction? How is it to be found in the 'principles of our nature'? Does Reid offer a viable alternative to the views of Locke and others? These are the questions I aim to answer in this paper.

Traditionally, the distinction is roughly that primary qualities such as shape, size and motion are in some sense observer-independent features of the world, while secondary qualities, such as colour, smell, taste and sound are more closely tied to our particular (human) perceptual perspective.

---

[1] Thomas Reid, *An Inquiry into the Human Mind on the Principles of Common Sense* (hereafter *Inq*), ed. Derek R. Brookes (Edinburgh UP, 1997), V iv, p. 62.

Beyond this rough characterization, there is little consensus. Many have noted that primary and secondary qualities somehow 'involve' dispositions.[2] I think that disagreement about the nature of primary and secondary qualities is in large part a disagreement about the nature of this involvement. Consequently some understanding of the nature of dispositions is important to understanding the debate.

In §I, I sketch a few accounts of dispositions to serve as a framework for subsequent discussion. In §II, I explore competing accounts of primary and secondary qualities. In §III, I explain why Reid rejects the Lockean accounts. In §IV, I present Reid's alternative, according to which the distinction is epistemic rather than metaphysical. In §V, I defend the coherence of Reid's view. In §§VI–VII, I defend Reid against the charge that his distinction collapses upon scrutiny. This defence further explicates the nature of Reid's distinction.

I. DISPOSITIONS

When 'the vulgar' talk of dispositions, they usually think of character traits, such as cowardice, shyness, irritability, etc. But people also talk of physical objects as being 'disposed to do so and so'. The fragile glass is disposed to break. The water-soluble tablet is disposed to dissolve in water. Contemporary philosophers point to properties like fragility, elasticity and solubility as paradigm examples of dispositions. Reid speaks of dispositions in terms of 'occult' or 'latent' qualities:

> ... are there not numberless qualities of bodies, which are known only by their effects, to which, notwithstanding, we find it necessary to give names? Medicine alone might furnish us with a hundred instances of this kind. Do not the words *astringent, narcotic, epispastic, caustic*, and innumerable others, signify qualities of bodies, which are known only by their effects upon animal bodies?[3]

> ... the notions which our senses give us of secondary qualities, of the disorders we feel in our own bodies, and of the various powers of bodies ... are all obscure and relative notions, being a conception of some unknown cause of a known effect. Their names are, for the most part, common to the effect, and to its cause; and they are a proper subject of philosophical disquisition. They might therefore, I think, not improperly be called *occult* qualities.[4]

[2] For example, see N. Wolterstorff, *Thomas Reid and the Story of Epistemology* (Cambridge UP, 2001), p. 110.
[3] *Inq* VI v, p. 88. I take 'qualities' to be synonymous with 'properties'.
[4] Reid, *Essays on the Intellectual Powers of Man* (hereafter *IP*), ed. Baruch A. Brody (MIT Press, 1969), II xviii, p. 274. See also pp. 306–8 for 'latent' qualities.

Reid says that there are three types of occult qualities: bodily disorders (unknown causes of certain symptoms), powers in objects to affect other objects (mechanical, chemical, medical, etc.), and secondary qualities (*IP* II xviii, p. 275). The secondary qualities are distinguished from other occult qualities by the fact that their common effects are sensations in humans. In order to say more about qualities, primary, secondary and occult, the following terms are helpful:

Manifestation – a type of event that occurs when a disposition is triggered. The manifestation of fragility is breaking.

Circumstances of manifestation – conditions which trigger the occurrence of the manifestation. The fragile glass breaks when struck.

Causal basis – a property 'in virtue of which' the disposed object has the disposition. When the disposition is triggered, the causal basis is part of the cause of the manifestation, the other part being the circumstances of manifestation. (If we are reluctant to say that properties are causes, or parts of causes, we can say that the event, or the fact that the object has the property, is part of the cause. Or we could say that the property is a causally relevant property of the cause.) The glass is fragile in virtue of some microstructural property of the glass.

An obvious approach to understanding dispositional concepts is in terms of conditionals.[5] On this view, to say something is fragile is just to say that if it were struck, it would break, or something on those lines. In general, to have a disposition is to be such that if you were in the circumstances of manifestation, you would exhibit the manifestation. In other words,

X has disposition D to exhibit M in C iff if X were in C, X would exhibit M.

This analysis is too simple, and is unlikely to withstand scrutiny. However, it is possible that modern philosophers have something like the conditional view in mind when speaking of powers or latent qualities.

An alternative approach to analysing dispositional concepts is in terms of second-order properties.[6] A *second-order property* is a property of having a property that satisfies a certain condition. For example, suppose that I like squareness and roundness. X is square. Y is round. X and Y both have the

[5] Views along these lines can be attributed to Hume, *Treatise of Human Nature*, ed. P.H. Nidditch (Oxford UP, 1978), I iii 14, II i 10; R. Carnap, 'Testability and Meaning', *Philosophy of Science*, 3 (1936), pp. 420–71, at p. 444; G. Ryle, *The Concept of Mind* (London: Hutchinson, 1949), p. 125; M. Dummett, *Truth and Other Enigmas* (London: Duckworth, 1978), p. 150.

[6] Accounts along these lines have been defended by Mark Johnston, 'How to Speak of the Colors', *Philosophical Studies*, 68 (1992), pp. 221–63; and David Lewis, 'Finkish Dispositions', *The Philosophical Quarterly*, 47 (1997), pp. 143–58.

second-order property of having a property that I like. (A second-order property should not be confused with a secondary quality.) According to a second-order property account of dispositions, a disposition is a second-order property of having a property that causes a certain type of event – the manifestation. In other words, a disposition is the property of having a causal basis. This can be formulated as follows:

> X has disposition D to produce manifestation M in circumstances C iff there is some property P such that (X has P & P would cause M in C).

This does not entail that D is the same property as P. P is a first-order property, the causal basis of D. D is the second-order property of having P – more accurately, the property of having some property *or other* that plays a certain causal role. Dispositions are, typically, multiply realizable. Crystal glasses and eggshells are both fragile, but presumably they have different microphysical structures that account for this.

According to the two views above, a disposition and its causal basis are two distinct properties. Yet a third view of dispositional concepts, David Armstrong's, claims that the distinction between a disposition and its causal basis is 'a verbal distinction that cuts no ontological ice'.[7] I shall call this 'the identity view'. 'The fragility of the glass' and 'the crystalline structure of the glass' are but two ways of referring to the same property of the glass. We use the former for pragmatic purposes, or out of ignorance. While such disposition ascriptions may be true, that is not to say that the glass has some property over and above its crystalline structure. Armstrong espouses this view in the following passage (p. 15):

> If dispositions are states of the disposed object, they are marked off from (many) other states by the way they are *identified*. When we speak of the brittleness of an object we are identifying a state of the object by reference to what the thing which is in that state is capable of bringing about (in conjunction with some active, triggering cause), instead of identifying the state by its intrinsic nature. And this in turn is connected with the role that dispositional concepts play in our thinking. We introduce such a concept where, for example, it is found that an object of a certain sort, acted upon in a certain way, behaves in certain further ways of a relatively unusual sort. We assign responsibility for this behaviour to some relatively unusual state of the object. But since we normally do not know, prior to painful and extensive scientific investigation, what the nature of the state is, we name it from its effects.

This passage is remarkably reminiscent of Reid's discussion of occult qualities (*Inq* VI v, p. 88; *IP* II xviii, p. 274):

> ... are there not numberless qualities of bodies, which are known only by their effects, to which, notwithstanding, we find it necessary to give names?

[7] D.M. Armstrong, *Belief, Truth, and Knowledge* (Cambridge UP, 1973), p. 15.

... Their names are, for the most part, common to the effect ... they are a proper subject of philosophical disquisition.

I understand 'philosophical disquisition' to include natural philosophy, that is, scientific investigation. Reid is not reverting to mediaeval Aristotelianism in his appeal to occult qualities, but is merely allowing that we refer to some properties whose intrinsic natures are unknown to us. According to Reid, a property conceived of as an occult quality is conceived of as an unknown cause of a known effect. Once we learn more about the cause, we can conceive of the same property in terms of its intrinsic nature. According to Reid, an expression like 'narcotic' does not merely refer to the power of opium to relieve pain. It also refers to some (as yet) unknown intrinsic property, in virtue of which opium has this power.

Dispositional ascriptions, on this view, are placeholders or promissory notes, offered until we learn more. We use a disposition term to pick out a property by reference to its typical effect. The effect is a semantic constituent of the disposition term. A disposition term is a kind of *relational specification* of a property. Something is relationally specified if we pick it out by its relation to something else.[8] In this case, the relation is to the typical effect of the property. To say that a disposition term is a relational specification of a causal basis is to say that the disposition and the causal basis are one and the same property.[9] Hence relational specification goes hand in hand with the identity view. (These views are typically held in conjunction. They could, in principle, come apart. For example, someone could hold that dispositions are identical to their causal bases, but that disposition terms are not relational specifications of those bases.)

So dispositional concepts can be analysed in terms of conditionals, second-order properties, or relational specifications of causal bases. Which approach should we employ to understand Reid's talk of 'occult' and 'latent' qualities? Perhaps the answer to this question is underdetermined by the texts, but Reid's discussion suggests that he holds the identity view. I shall

[8] Whether something is relationally specified varies according to how we refer to it. Bob is relationally specified if we pick him out by saying 'the guy standing next to Harry'. Properties can be relationally specified as well. 'Bob's favourite property' is relationally specified by reference to Bob. A relationally specified property is not necessarily an extrinsic property. I could pick out squareness as 'Bob's favourite property'. This is consistent with squareness being intrinsic to the square thing. I disagree with Gideon Yaffe, who takes Reid's relational specification of secondary qualities to show that they are not intrinsic: 'Thomas Reid', E.N. Zalta (ed.), *The Stanford Encyclopedia of Philosophy*, URL http://plato.stanford.edu.

[9] Multiple realizability is an apparent problem for the identity theorist. It seems that a disposition cannot be identical with two distinct causal bases. As with identity theories in philosophy of mind, there are a number of ways in which an identity theorist might reply, such as appealing to token–token identity, rather than type–type identity. See, e.g., Armstrong, *The Mind/Body Problem* (Boulder: Westview, 1999), p. 101.

now explore the ways in which dispositions may be involved with secondary qualities.

II. COMPETING VIEWS OF PRIMARY AND SECONDARY QUALITIES

According to Frank Jackson,

> There is an important sense in which we know the live possibilities as far as colour is concerned. We know that objects have dispositions to look one or another colour, that they have dispositions to modify incident and transmitted light in ways that underlie their dispositions to look one or another colour, that they have physical properties that are responsible for both these dispositions, and that their subjects have experiences as of things looking one or another colour. We also know that this list includes all the possibly relevant properties.[10]

Jackson's statement about colour can be generalized. Physical objects have dispositions to cause mental events, or instantiations of mental properties. The causal basis for such a disposition is to be found among the intrinsic physical properties of the object. In short, the properties which are candidates for being primary or secondary qualities are mental properties, dispositions in objects to cause mental properties, and the causal bases of those dispositions. Most philosophers who talk about primary qualities identify them with the base properties, but there is less of a consensus about the secondary qualities.

Some have identified secondary qualities with certain mental properties, or something in the mind of the perceiver – an idea, a sensation, an impression, an appearance, an experience. This view is attributed to the Greek Atomists and to Galileo.[11] Many attribute this view to Locke, and to early modern philosophers in general. Berkeley's Hylas credits 'philosophers' with the view that secondary qualities 'are only so many sensations or ideas existing nowhere but in the mind' (Berkeley, *Three Dialogues*, p. 23). Hume calls the view that secondary qualities are 'nothing but impressions in the mind' a 'fundamental principle' of modern philosophy (*Treatise*, p. 226). Reid says 'Des Cartes, Malebranche, and Locke, revived the distinction between primary and secondary qualities. But they made the secondary qualities mere sensations' (*Inq* V viii, p. 73). In more recent times, Graham

[10] F. Jackson, 'The Primary Quality View of Colour', in *From Metaphysics to Ethics* (Oxford UP, 2000), p. 87.

[11] R.M. Adams, 'Editor's Introduction' to Berkeley's *Three Dialogues between Hylas and Philonous* (Indianapolis, Hackett, 1979), p. xv; Galileo Galilei, *The Assayer*, in R.H. Poplin (ed.), *The Philosophy of the Sixteenth and Seventeenth Centuries* (New York: Free Press, 1966), §48, p. 65.

Priest says 'I shall use the term "secondary property" solely as referring to the appearance'.[12]

Others have identified secondary qualities with dispositions of objects to produce mental events. Robert Boyle (who is credited with coining the terms 'primary' and 'secondary' qualities) held this view.[13] Contemporary proponents include J.J.C. Smart (in his early work), Colin McGinn and John McDowell.[14] This view is also attributed to Locke.[15] The following passage from Locke seems to support this interpretation:

> Secondly, such qualities, which in truth are nothing in the objects themselves, but powers to produce various sensations in us by their primary qualities, i.e., by the bulk, figure, texture, and motion of their sensible parts, as colours, sounds, tastes, etc., these I call *secondary* qualities.[16]

According to Locke, objects have configurations of primary qualities that produce various ideas in the minds of sentient beings. Some of these ideas resemble the qualities in the object that produced them. These are ideas of primary qualities. The idea of roundness resembles a quality of the object that produces it. However, other ideas, such as ideas of redness or sweetness, do not resemble any quality in the object. These are ideas of secondary qualities. If we think that there is something in the object that resembles the idea, we are mistaken. However, there is something in the object that we may call the secondary quality, and this is the disposition to cause the idea. The causal basis of this disposition is a configuration of primary qualities.

III. REID'S REJECTION OF SOME LOCKEAN VIEWS

Reid rejects the view that secondary qualities are sensations in the mind, because it conflicts with common sense and linguistic practices.

[12] G. Priest, 'Primary Qualities are Secondary Qualities Too', *British Journal for the Philosophy of Science*, 40 (1989), pp. 29–37, at p. 32.

[13] R. Boyle, 'The Origin of Forms and Qualities', in *The Works of the Honourable Robert Boyle* (London, 1772), pp. 18–27.

[14] D.M. Armstrong, 'Smart and the Secondary Qualities', in P. Pettit (ed.), *Metaphysics and Morality* (Oxford: Blackwell, 1987), pp. 1–15, and 'Values and Secondary Qualities', in T. Honderich (ed.), *Morality and Objectivity* (London: Routledge, 1985), pp. 110–29; C. McGinn, *The Subjective View* (Oxford: Clarendon Press, 1983), p. 8.

[15] My interpretation of Locke follows J.L. Mackie, *Problems from Locke* (Oxford: Clarendon Press, 1976), pp. 7–36.

[16] Locke, *An Essay Concerning Human Understanding* (London: Everyman, 1990), II xxiii 9, p. 136. This passage is perhaps not conclusive support. Mackie (p. 12) notes 'In this often-quoted remark "nothing ... , but" means (despite the comma) "nothing except"; but many students and some commentators have read it as if "but" were the conjunction, and so have taken the first part of the remark as saying that secondary qualities are not in objects at all'.

The vulgar say, that fire is hot, and snow cold, and sugar sweet; and that to deny this is a gross absurdity, and contradicts the testimony of our senses (*IP* II xvii, p. 258).

... to deny that there can be heat and cold when they are not felt, is an absurdity too gross to merit confutation. For what could be more absurd, than to say, that the thermometer cannot rise or fall, unless some person be present, or that the coast of Guinea would be as cold as Nova Zembla, if it had no inhabitants? (*Inq* V i, p. 54)

Reid notes that there is an ambiguity in many property terms, and this causes some confusion. Words like 'red', 'sweet' and 'hot' are usually used to refer to qualities in bodies, but sometimes they are used to refer to the sensations those qualities cause (*Inq* V i, p. 54; *IP* I xvi, pp. 242–3). While there are a number of linguistic options for clarifying this ambiguity, Reid says that philosophers abuse language when they say things like 'Colours exist nowhere but in the mind'.

Reid's disagreement with the Lockean view, however, is more than terminological. The basis of Locke's distinction is that primary qualities resemble the ideas they cause, while secondary qualities do not. Reid baulks, for this account presupposes the maligned 'theory of ideas', the view that the immediate objects of perception are mental entities which sometimes represent and resemble objects in the world.[17] If there are no ideas to resemble or fail to resemble qualities in the world, they cannot serve as the basis for the distinction. Even if one granted the theory of ideas, Locke's account would still fall prey to Berkeley's criticisms. Reid credits Berkeley for exposing 'the absurdity of a resemblance between our sensations and any quality, primary or secondary, of a substance that is supposed to be insentient' (*IP* II xvii, p. 264). There is nothing about an unconscious object like a table that resembles the cool sensation one gets by stroking its surface, *nor* the sensation of hardness one gets by pressing against it. Since no qualities in bodies resemble sensations, resemblance cannot serve to distinguish primary qualities from secondary qualities. According to Berkeley (*Three Dialogues*, pp. 24–5), whatever reasons we have to believe that secondary qualities are only in the mind are equally reasons to believe primary qualities are only in the mind. Noting this, Reid concludes (*IP*, p. 264) that if you hold the theory of ideas, you lose not only the distinction between primary and secondary qualities, but also knowledge of the material world.

IV. REID'S ACCOUNT OF THE DISTINCTION

Despite Reid's rejection of the above accounts, he still thinks that some distinction can be maintained. But how?

---

[17] See *IP* II xiv, 'Reflections on the Common Theory of Ideas', p. 211.

First of all, he replaces Lockean ideas with 'sensations'. Reid's account of sensation is roughly as follows.[18] Suppose I come into contact with an apple. The apple impinges upon my sense organs, giving rise to a sensation in my mind. The sensation is a sign of a quality in the apple. The sensation suggests to me a conception of the quality in the apple, and I come to believe that this quality really exists. That is to say, I *perceive* the quality signified. Reid is perhaps the first to note the important distinction between sensation and perception. Speaking of the primary/secondary quality distinction, Reid says 'all the darkness and intricacy that thinking men have found in this subject, and the errors they have fallen into, have been owing to the difficulty of distinguishing clearly sensation from perception – what we feel from what we perceive' (*IP* II xvii, p. 265). The object of perception is a quality in the apple itself. However, the sensation is a mental act that has no object apart from itself. On some interpretations, Reid holds an adverbial theory of sensation.[19] To have a sensation of red is simply to sense 'redly'. An act of sensing bears no resemblance to any quality in a body.

Replacing ideas with sensations is not Reid's only departure from Locke. Reid claims that the foundation for the distinction is to be found in the *principles of our nature*. The basis of the distinction is not in the nature of the properties themselves.[20] The difference between primary and secondary qualities is a matter of a difference in human epistemic access to these qualities. We have substantial, direct knowledge of primary qualities. We only have limited, indirect knowledge of secondary qualities:

> ... our senses give us a direct and a distinct notion of the primary qualities, and inform us what they are in themselves; but of the secondary qualities, our senses give us only a relative and obscure notion. They inform us only, that they are qualities that affect us in a certain manner, that is, produce in us a certain sensation; but as to what they are in themselves, our senses leave us in the dark (*IP* II xvii, p. 252).

According to Reid, our senses give us only a relative and obscure notion of secondary qualities. Reid explains what he means by a relative notion: 'A relative notion of a thing, is, strictly speaking, no notion of the thing at all, but only of some relation which it bears to something else' (*IP* II xvii, p. 253).

[18] My interpretation of Reid here follows that of Vere Chappell, 'The Theory of Sensations', in M. Dalgarno and E. Matthews (eds), *The Philosophy of Thomas Reid* (Dordrecht: Kluwer, 1989), p. 51.

[19] This interpretation of Reid is proposed in E. Sosa and J. Van Cleve, 'Thomas Reid', in S.M. Emmanual (ed.), *The Blackwell Guide to Modern Philosophers: from Descartes to Nietzsche* (Oxford: Blackwell, 2001), p. 182. Reid seems non-committal: 'Sensation is the act, or the feeling, I dispute not which, of a sentient being' (*IP* II xvii, p. 255).

[20] Similarly, Keith Lehrer says that Reid's distinction is drawn 'on conceptual grounds, in terms of our ways of conceiving these qualities, rather than in terms of the nature of the qualities themselves': Lehrer, 'Reid on Primary and Secondary Qualities', *Monist*, 61 (1978), pp. 184–91, at p. 186.

If we have only a relative notion of a thing, we tend to pick it out by a relational specification. According to Reid, we pick out and refer to secondary qualities by the relation they bear to sensations. A secondary quality's paradigm specification is relational, because all that we know about the secondary quality is its relational properties – what it causes. (Strictly speaking, because of his views about causation, Reid does not think that the relation between qualities and sensations is genuinely causal. Rather, qualities 'suggest', 'occasion', or are conjoined by the laws of nature with, sensations. Nevertheless he is happy to use causal talk: see *Inq* V iii, p. 59.)

In sum, secondary qualities cause sensations, but we know little or nothing else about them. Reid explicates these ideas with the example of smelling a rose:

> The quality in the rose is something which occasions the sensation in me; but what that something is, I know not. My senses give me no information upon this point. The only notion therefore my senses give is this, that smell in the rose is an unknown quality or modification, which is the cause or occasion of a sensation which I know well (*IP* II xvii, p. 254).

I shall distinguish three properties here, using the terminology introduced earlier, to explicate Reid's view.

S is the fragrant sensation I am experiencing, the manifestation of the disposition

D is a property of the rose, a disposition to produce S in me

P is a property of the rose that causes S in me, the causal basis of D.

Which is the secondary quality for Reid, S, P or D? We can quickly eliminate S. I pointed out above that Reid rejects the view that secondary qualities are sensations. On his own account, a secondary quality is an 'unknown cause of a known effect' (*IP* II xviii, p. 274). The sensation is the known effect, not the unknown cause. Reid says, for example, that

> colour is not a sensation, but a secondary quality of bodies ... it is a certain power or virtue in bodies, that in fair daylight exhibits to the eye an appearance, which is very familiar to us, although it hath no name (*Inq* VI iv, p. 87).

Clearly Reid's secondary qualities are not sensations. His talk of a secondary quality being 'a certain power or virtue in bodies' seems to suggest that it is the disposition D. However, the secondary quality is unknown and obscure, which D is not. I know that the rose has the disposition to produce S in me. As Wolterstorff (p. 112) notes, 'If green were a disposition in things to cause certain sensations under certain conditions and not the physical basis of that disposition, we would know what it was'. We may not know the causal basis of the disposition, but that is not to say that the disposition itself is obscure.

Most of Reid's discussion supports the view that the secondary quality is *P*, the causal basis. *P* is the unknown cause of the known sensation. It fits the description of secondary qualities as qualities that 'affect us in a certain manner' and 'produce in us a certain sensation' (*IP* II xvii, p. 253). So it seems that a secondary quality is the causal basis of a disposition to produce a sensation. (Reid's view of colour is similar in broad outlines to that of Frank Jackson. However, perhaps ironically, Jackson calls his view 'the primary quality view of colour'. This goes to show how variable the uses of the terms 'primary quality' and 'secondary quality' are.)

How are we to interpret those passages in which Reid seems to be talking about secondary qualities as dispositions? Wolterstorff (p. 112) says that Reid 'doesn't speak consistently on the matter' of whether secondary qualities are dispositions to produce sensations, or causal bases of those dispositions. Perhaps. However, Wolterstorff assumes that Reid holds a certain view of dispositions according to which they are distinct from their causal bases. My suggestion is that Reid holds the identity view, according to which dispositions are identical with their causal bases. According to Reid, occult-quality expressions refer to unknown, underlying causal bases, rather than to powers over and above those intrinsic, physical properties. If he holds the identity view, then he is not being inconsistent when he speaks of secondary qualities sometimes as dispositions and at other times as causal bases.

So which is the secondary quality for Reid, the sensation, the disposition or the causal basis? Perhaps it is the disposition *and* the causal basis, since they are one and the same property, on the identity view. But how is it that this property is both known and unknown? Some things are known about it, others are not. We know that it typically has certain effects. That is to say, it is known *qua* disposition. However, we know nothing of its intrinsic nature. *Qua* causal basis, it is obscure.

V. IS REID CONSISTENT?

Reid is accused of a deeper, more troubling inconsistency.[21] He seems to hold

The semantic thesis. Sensations are semantic constituents of the meanings of secondary-quality terms.[22]

To conceive of a property as a secondary quality is to conceive of it as a cause of a sensation. Reid says 'We conceive it only as that which occasions

---

[21] This problem is discussed by Chappell, pp. 59–60.

[22] *IP* II xvii, p. 257; cf. Lehrer, *Thomas Reid* (London: Routledge, 1998), p. 47.

such a sensation, and therefore cannot reflect upon it without thinking of the sensation which it occasions' (*IP* II xvii, p. 257). For example, I shall call the type of sensation typically caused by redness 'R^*'. It is part of the meaning of 'redness' that it causes R^* (in normal humans in standard conditions). Reid seems committed to the view that, necessarily, redness causes R^*.

However, Reid also seems to hold

The contingency thesis. The connection between secondary qualities and the sensations they cause is contingent.

Secondary qualities might not have caused the sensations that they do cause. Reid says 'We might perhaps have had the perception of external objects, without ... sensations' (*Inq* VI xxi, p. 176). This suggests that redness might not have caused R^* sensations. So Reid also seems committed to the view that, possibly, redness does not cause R^*. So it appears as if he has an inconsistent view.

This problem can be resolved. The statement 'Redness causes R^*' is ambiguous. It admits of two readings, one of which is analytic or necessarily true, the other contingent. This kind of ambiguity is not uncommon, as in 'The President is the President'. This statement may be true in virtue of its meaning, but under some interpretations it expresses a contingent proposition. If it means 'For all x, if x is the President, then x is the President', then it does seem to be necessarily true. On the other hand 'the President' may be functioning as a name rather than a predicate. So the statement can be interpreted as 'George W. Bush is the President', which certainly could have been otherwise (in a very near possible world!). 'The cause of cancer causes cancer' is similar. Necessarily, whatever causes cancer causes cancer. But if we consider a particular carcinogen, say, dioxin, it seems possible that it might have been harmless.

To return to secondary qualities and 'Redness causes R^*', if we understand 'redness' as referring to whatsoever causes R^*, then the proposition expressed does seem necessary. However, if we think of 'redness' as rigidly designating the particular property that happens to cause R^* in this world, then we can allow that redness might not have caused R^*.

This ambiguity is likely to arise when one uses relational specifications. You can relationally specify something, and then say of that thing that it *stands in that very relation*. If that thing does not necessarily stand in that relation, then you have said something contingent. However, this statement may be confused with the necessary truth that whatsoever stands in that relation stands in that relation.

Dispelling this confusion allows us to see that Reid's view is coherent. Next, I consider whether Reid's view is stable.

VI. HAS REID ESTABLISHED A REAL DISTINCTION?

The similarities between primary qualities and secondary qualities, on Reid's view, are perhaps more striking than their differences. Like secondary qualities, 'The primary qualities are neither sensations, nor are they resemblances of sensations' (*IP* II xvii, p. 255). Both are causal bases of dispositions to cause sensations. Both produce sensations. Both fail to resemble those sensations. And yet Reid maintains that they differ. Prior to the statement of the distinction I have earlier quoted (p. 486 above), he says

> Every one knows that extension, divisibility, figure, motion, solidity, hardness, softness, and fluidity, were by Mr Locke called *primary qualities of body*; and that sound, colour, taste, smell, and heat or cold, were called *secondary qualities*. Is there a just foundation for this distinction? is there any thing common to the primary which belongs not to the secondary? And what is it?
>
>   I answer, that there appears to me to be a real foundation for the distinction (*IP* II xvii, p. 252).

Reid promises an account that classifies the sensible qualities as Locke does, but offers a better justification for classifying them in this way. In this section, I consider whether Reid delivers what he promises.

Reid's account of the foundation of the distinction is that the sensations caused by primary qualities suggest or signify something about the intrinsic nature of those qualities, while the sensations caused by secondary qualities signify only some unknown cause of that sensation. He gives an example:

> The sensation of heat, and the sensation we have by pressing a hard body, are equally feelings: nor can we by reasoning draw any conclusion from the one, but what may be drawn from the other: but, by our constitution, we conclude from the first an obscure or occult quality, of which we have only this relative conception, that it is something adapted to raise in us the sensation of heat; from the second, we conclude a quality of which we have a clear and distinct conception, to wit, the hardness of the body (*Inq* V v, p. 65).

Hardness is a primary quality. I shall call 'H_1*' the sensation hardness causes. H_1* does not resemble hardness. However, it conjures up the conception of hardness as firm cohesion of the parts of the body. How H_1* causes us to think of hardness we do not know. It is 'a natural kind of magic' (*Inq* V iii, p. 60). Heat is equally some real quality in the body, which nowadays we might think of as mean molecular kinetic energy. Heat causes sensation H_2*. But H_2* does not prompt us to think of heat as it is in itself, but only as something which causes H_2*. Hence heat is a secondary quality.

On this picture, the only difference between primary and secondary qualities is 'in the head', not in the properties. There is no metaphysical difference in the properties, only a difference in our epistemic access to them. $H_1{}^*$ and $H_2{}^*$ both lead us to believe that something is causing those sensations, but $H_2{}^*$ tells us nothing more. $H_1{}^*$ on the other hand gives us additional knowledge of the nature of hardness.

What accounts for this difference? Reid says it is a brute mysterious fact about our constitution. It could have been different. Pressing on a table might have caused a sensation of redness, and looking at a ripe apple might have produced $H_1{}^*$ (*Inq* VI xxi, p. 176; *IP* II xxi, p. 289). Or the sensation of redness might have conveyed to us information about the intrinsic nature of redness, and $H_1{}^*$ might have suggested only that some unknown cause is causing this sensation. Reid's view seems to imply that properties which are secondary qualities for us might be primary qualities for other creatures. We might have had a different constitution such that the primary qualities were secondary and the secondary qualities primary. We just happen to be constituted as we are.

These implications invite the following questions. Could this fact of our constitution change? Could our epistemic access to the secondary qualities change with experience? Could the human species evolve, learn or be trained to perceive the causes of our sensations which are currently unknown? Could $H_2{}^*$ ever give us knowledge of the intrinsic nature of heat?

Reid stresses again and again that secondary qualities are unknown and obscure, and that our senses give us no information about them, apart from their effect on us. We know they cause sensations, but 'as to what they are in themselves, our senses leave us in the dark' (*IP*, p. 252). But elsewhere he suggests that this could change. The nature of secondary qualities

> is a proper subject of philosophical disquisition; and in this, philosophy has made some progress. It has been discovered, that the sensation of smell is occasioned by the effluvia of bodies; that of sound by their vibration. The disposition of bodies to reflect a particular kind of light occasions the sensation of colour. Very curious discoveries have been made of the nature of heat, and an ample field of discovery in these subjects remains (*IP* II xvii, p. 256; see also xxi, pp. 305–8).

Apparently Reid did not think that secondary qualities must for ever remain shrouded in mystery. If our senses can give us knowledge of secondary qualities, then it looks as if the primary/secondary quality distinction turns on this contingent and variable epistemic difference. A quality's primary or secondary status seems to be entirely relative to individual humans, even in normal circumstances.[23]

---

[23] Cf. J.L. Ramsey, 'Realism, Essentialism, and Intrinsic Properties', in N. Bhushan and S. Rosenfeld (eds), *Of Minds and Molecules* (Oxford UP, 2000), pp. 117–28.

If the above claims are correct, Reid cannot say that smells are secondary *simpliciter*, but only in relation to those who glean nothing about their intrinsic natures through utilization of their senses. Reid does not propose some non-sensory way of learning about the intrinsic natures of latent qualities. He says that the man who has knowledge of sensible and latent qualities 'is informed *by his senses* of innumerable things' (*IP* II xxi, p. 307; my italics). Scientific investigation of latent qualities requires observation. When scientists investigate 'effluvia', they use their senses to learn about the intrinsic nature of smells. If they are successful, their senses tell them more about this property than that it is a cause of a certain sensation. By Reid's account, then, it seems that this property is no longer a secondary quality for those scientists. A property could cease to be secondary for someone if that person learns about its intrinsic nature through the senses.

This relativistic view is not what Reid advertised. I suppose there is nothing *wrong* with categorizing properties relative to individual perceivers' knowledge of their intrinsic natures; however, doing so will not reliably distinguish smells and colours on the one hand from size and shape on the other. In fact, this 'foundation' provides no reason for dividing the sensible qualities in any particular way. But this is precisely what Reid said that his account would do.

VII. SAVING THE DISTINCTION

This worry suggests that we have yet to understand Reid's view fully. We should note Reid's remarks that secondary qualities are such that 'we know no more *naturally*, than that they are adapted to raise certain sensations in us', and 'the latent qualities are such as are not *immediately* discovered by our senses' (*Inq* V iv, p. 61; *IP* II xxi, p. 307; my italics). This implies that perception of the intrinsic nature of a primary quality is immediate, but perception of the intrinsic nature of a secondary quality, if it occurs at all, is mediated.

To develop this idea further, we need to look to Reid's distinction between original and acquired perception:

> In original perception, the signs are the various sensations which are produced by the impressions made upon our organs. The things signified, are the objects perceived in consequence of those sensations, by the original constitution of our nature....
>
> In acquired perception, the sign may be either a sensation, or something originally perceived. The thing signified is something, which, by experience, has been found connected with that sign (*IP* II xxi, pp. 302–3).

For example, when I feel a ball in my hands, the sensation I get through touch signifies the spherical shape of the ball naturally, because of my constitution. However, it is said that someone who merely looked at a ball for the first time (or had recently acquired sight) would not be able to discern its spherical shape from its shading alone.[24] So the perception of three-dimensional shape through touch is an original perception, while the perception of three-dimensional shape through sight is an acquired perception. Other acquired perceptions can be more sophisticated and specialized, such as the perception that some hunk of metal is a carburettor.

What do original and acquired perceptions have to do with primary and secondary qualities? I understand Reid to be saying that one can have acquired perceptions of primary and secondary qualities, and one can have original perceptions of primary qualities, but one cannot have original perceptions of secondary qualities, except as unknown causes of sensations. Feeling a sphere's roundness is an original perception of a primary quality. *Seeing* its roundness is an acquired perception of a primary quality. We can also have *acquired* perceptions of secondary qualities. We can learn about the effluvia that produce olfactory sensations in us, and come to perceive that certain objects emit effluvia. But human beings do not *originally* perceive secondary qualities, except as unknown causes of sensations. It is not a part of our original constitution that sensations produced by secondary qualities give us perceptions of those qualities as they are in themselves.

This may sound odd. For example, it seems to imply that perception of colours, smells and tastes is acquired. However, according to Reid, these secondary qualities are properly conceived of as causal bases of dispositions to produce sensations. No one has original perceptions of the causal bases of colours, smells and tastes, other than those of unknown causes of sensations. The sensations caused by secondary qualities do not allow us to perceive the qualities as they are in themselves. However, we can have acquired perceptions of causal bases:

> No man can pretend to set limits to the discoveries that may be made by human genius and industry, of such connections between the latent and the sensible qualities of bodies. A wide field here opens to our view, whose boundaries no man can ascertain, of improvements that may hereafter be made in the information conveyed to us by our senses (*IP* II xxi, p. 308).

Perhaps, through investigation and training, we can come to perceive that some molecules are moving very fast, or that a surface has certain reflectance properties. This view has striking similarities to Paul Churchland's:

[24] For a discussion of this issue, see *IP* II xxi, p. 301; Locke, *Essay* II ix 8, p. 67; M. Morgan, *Molyneux's Question: Vision, Touch, and the Philosophy of Perception* (Cambridge UP, 1977).

... it is quite open to us to begin framing our spontaneous perceptual reports in the language of the more sophisticated reducing theory.... We can thus make more penetrating use of our native perceptual equipment.[25]

It is important for us to try to appreciate, if only dimly, the extent of the perceptual transformation here envisaged. These people do not sit on the beach and listen to the steady roar of the pounding surf. They sit on the beach and listen to the aperiodic atmospheric compression waves produced as the coherent energy of the ocean waves is audibly redistributed in the chaotic turbulence of the shallows.[26]

However, Reid is unlikely to go along with a wholesale revision of common sense conceptual frameworks. Because perception of secondary qualities is not original and natural, but mediated and acquired, the relational specification of secondary qualities is likely to remain the paradigm mode of reference.

This connection to original and acquired perceptions helps us to see why Reid's view does not reduce to the radical relativism discussed earlier. While the primary/secondary quality distinction may be relativized to the human race, it is not relativized to individual perceivers and times. Our epistemic situation may change, but we can still find a foundation for the distinction in the principles of our nature. Because of some natural principle of our constitution, we do not have original perceptions of the intrinsic natures of certain properties. When these properties cause sensations in us, we infer that the sensations have been caused by something or other, but we do not know by exactly what. If we want to refer to these properties, we have to pick them out in a relative way as whatever it is that causes these sensations. We have to use relational specifications of these properties, at least until we do some investigation and learn something about their intrinsic nature.

University of Alabama at Birmingham

---

[25] P. Churchland, 'Reduction, *Qualia*, and the Direct Introspection of Brain States', in *A Neurocomputational Perspective* (MIT Press, 1989), p. 53.

[26] Churchland, *Scientific Realism and the Plasticity of Mind* (Cambridge UP, 1979), p. 29.

6

REID, KANT AND THE PHILOSOPHY OF MIND

By Etienne Brun-Rovet

I suggest a possible rehabilitation of Reid's philosophy of mind by a constructive use of Kant's criticisms of the common sense tradition. Kant offers two criticisms, explicitly claiming that common sense philosophy is ill directed methodologically, and implicitly rejecting Reid's view that there is direct epistemological access by introspection to the ontology of mind. Putting the two views together reveals a tension between epistemology and ontology, but the problem which Kant finds in Reid also infects his own system, as his weaker ontological claims are undermined to such an extent by the necessary reintroduction of self-consciousness that the justification he seeks for reason fails to be reached epistemologically. Plausible solutions to these parallel tensions imply that both Reid and Kant have a pre-systematic concept of mind, and may lead to the conclusion that Reid's method is more economical in the elaboration of an ontology for the philosophy of mind.

Reid's metaphysics is primarily concerned with the philosophy of mind or 'pneumatology', 'the branch [of knowledge] which treats of the nature and operations of minds': 'The mind of man is the noblest work of God which reason discovers to us, and, therefore, on account of its dignity, deserves our study'.[1] It is in this field that his methodology, revelatory of his metaphysical assumptions, is of particular relevance to contemporary philosophy. For by asserting (*IP* I v, p. 238b) that 'the chief and proper source of this branch of knowledge is accurate reflection upon the operations of our own minds', and (p. 239b) that the 'power of the understanding to make its own perceptions its object, to attend to them, and examine them on all sides, is the power of reflection, by which alone we can have any distinct notion of the powers of our own or other minds', Reid defines a method in the philosophy of mind which assumes epistemological access to an ontological level, where epistemological access is understood as denoting a theory of knowledge according to which there is direct empirical access. Indeed, the first common sense principle 'taken for granted' in *Essays on the Intellectual Powers of Man* (I ii, pp. 230a–4a) is an identification of epistemological access with ontology: 'consciousness is the evidence, the only evidence, which we have

---

[1] Reid, *Essays on the Intellectual Powers of Man*, hereafter *IP*, in W. Hamilton (ed.), *The Works of Thomas Reid*, 6th edn (Edinburgh: MacLachlan & Stewart, 1863), preface, p. 217a.

or can have of [the] existence [of the operations of our minds]' (epistemo-logical access), and (p. 231b) what consciousness testifies is 'taken as a first principle', as that which defines these operations as mental (ontology). Keith Lehrer is correct in claiming that 'a state is mental only if we are conscious of it',[2] for Reid's distinction between consciousness and attentive reflection allows us to interpret his assertion (p. 239b) that 'although the mind is con-scious of its operations, it does not attend to them' as defining a criterion for the mental: 'conception of mental states is ... automatic, the product of consciousness, whether we attend to it or not' (Lehrer, p. 51). Reid's method, derived from the 'principles taken for granted', is therefore the practical manifestation of his metaphysics.

Reid's metaphysical legacy has, however, suffered from the explicit dis-missal of common sense philosophy by Kant. Reid's rehabilitation in this domain has depended either on arguments demonstrating the proximity of Reid and Kant in their anti-sceptical programme,[3] or on attempts to reduce Kant's programme to a metaphysical matter of choice.[4] Since both ap-proaches do violence to the specific differences of these philosophies, neither has been considered very convincing. As a consequence, Victor Cousin's 1857 appraisal (p. ix) is still pertinent: Reid's influence has tended to remain 'less ample and less widely propagated' than Kant's, but whereas Kant's 'name ... stands alone on the ruin of his doctrine' as 'his following has thrown itself in opposing directions', Reid's 'still lasts' with a school that 'follows his light'. Reid's metaphysics still suffers from the criticism of a philosopher whose following has been less loyal than his own.

Whatever Reid's importance in the history of philosophy, it is his direct relevance for contemporary philosophy of mind that makes it necessary to rehabilitate his metaphysics. Keith Lehrer's claim that 'Reid is a modern cognitive scientist as well as an eighteenth-century metaphysician', whose work is of 'paramount importance ... to the contemporary reader', may be an overstatement of the relevance of Reid for contemporary philosophy.[5] Nevertheless it is hard not to be struck by the close similarity of concerns between Reid and recent philosophers. His 'subservient' sources for know-ledge of our own minds – 'the structure of language' and 'the course of human actions and conduct' (pp. 238b–9a), his argument for the distinction

[2] K. Lehrer, 'Metamind: Belief, Consciousness, and Intentionality', in R.J. Bogdan (ed.), *Belief: Form, Content and Function* (Oxford UP, 1988), p. 50.
[3] V. Cousin, *Philosophie écossaise* (Paris: Librairie Nouvelle, 1857); T.J. Sutton, 'The Scottish Kant?', in M. Dalgarno and E. Matthews (eds), *The Philosophy of Thomas Reid* (Dordrecht: Kluwer, 1989), pp. 159–92.
[4] R.E. Beanblossom, 'Kant's Quarrel with Reid: the Role of Metaphysics', *History of Philosophy Quarterly*, 5 (1988), pp. 53–62.
[5] Lehrer, *Thomas Reid* (London: Routledge, 1989), p. 7; cf. John Haldane's review in *Philosophy*, 66 (1991), pp. 252–4.

between natural and artificial languages,[6] and his insistence on the importance of the 'social operations of the mind'[7] – all are, as Hennig Jensen and
Harré and Robinson underline, close to central Wittgensteinian themes,[8]
although Jensen's characterization (p. 367) of Reid's 'upgrading of language'
does not, on the evidence of §VIII of Hume's *Enquiry Concerning Human
Understanding*, or of §1 and Appendix IV of the *Enquiry Concerning the Principles of
Morals*, distinguish Reid's approach to language from Hume's. And, more
significantly, the debate on the consequences for the representational theory
of mind of Reid's attack on the theory of ideas demonstrates not only the
importance of a clear ontology in contemporary philosophy of mind, but
also the applicability of Reid's method to the field.[9]

I shall attempt to rehabilitate Reid's metaphysics by a constructive use of
Kant's criticisms. Kant's explicit dismissal rests on two points of disagreement: the absence of justification for, and the irrelevance of, common sense;
and Reid's claim for an epistemological access to the mind's ontology (§I).
Kant's attack on Reid's methodological choices points to a tension between
epistemology and ontology in Reid's philosophy of mind, but this tension
also exists in Kant (§II). Considerations as to its genesis help to find a
possible resolution (§III) which justifies common sense methodology, and
seem to validate the first two parts of Victor Cousin's claim (p. x) that Reid
'reached the truth first [before Kant] without so many deviations, deploying
less energy and more wisdom'.

I. THE KANTIAN ATTACK

Kant's criticism of Reid is twofold. The explicit condemnation comes in
Prolegomena, in which Kant deplores common sense philosophy's failure to
make anything of Hume's 'spark'.[10] Hume's inability to find an experiential
origin to the idea of necessary connection led him to the conclusion
'that there is no metaphysics at all, and cannot be any' (*Prolegomena*, p. 8).

---

[6] Reid, *An Inquiry into the Human Mind (Inq)*, in Hamilton (ed.), *The Works of Thomas Reid*,
IV ii, pp. 117b–18a.

[7] Reid, *Essays on the Active Powers of Man*, in Hamilton (ed.), *The Works of Thomas Reid*, V vi,
p. 664a.

[8] H. Jensen, 'Reid and Wittgenstein on Philosophy and Language', *Philosophical Studies*, 36
(1979), pp. 359–76; R. Harré and D.N. Robinson, 'What Makes Language Possible? Etho-
logical Foundationalism in Reid and Wittgenstein', *Review of Metaphysics*, 50 (1997), pp. 483–98.

[9] See Haldane, 'Whose Theory? Which Representations?', *Pacific Philosophical Quarterly*, 74
(1993), pp. 247–57, in response to R. Stecker, 'Does Reid Reject/Refute the Representational
Theory of Mind?', *Pacific Philosophical Quarterly*, 73 (1992), pp. 174–84, in response to Haldane,
'Reid, Scholasticism and Current Philosophy of Mind', in Dalgarno and Matthews (eds),
pp. 285–304; and Lehrer, *Thomas Reid*, pp. 290ff.

[10] Kant, *Prolegomena to Any Future Metaphysics*, ed. G. Hatfield (Cambridge UP, 1997), p. 7.

Although Kant finds this conclusion 'premature and erroneous', he accepts that it was 'founded on enquiry' of sufficient value for others to come to better conclusions. But he maintains that Reid and his followers did not understand Hume, that they 'missed the point of his problem', seeking, in the case of the concept of cause, to discuss the appropriateness of its use rather than its origin. The debate is therefore methodological: where the problem supposedly raised by Hume was (*Prolegomena*, p. 9) whether such a concept 'is thought through reason *a priori*, and in this way has an inner truth independent of all experience, and therefore also a much more widely extended use which is not merely limited to objects of experience', Reid's common sense tools for addressing such concepts are both too crude and too ill directed to provide a solution. By raising the question above the level of 'judgements that find their immediate application in experience', Kant breaks the limits of 'sound common sense' into those of 'speculative under-standing', applicable 'when judgements are to be made in a universal mode, out of mere concepts, as in metaphysics' (p. 10). So, according to Kant (pp. 9–10), not only does common sense not 'understand the justification for its own principles', and need to be kept 'in check' by 'a critical reason', 'for only so will it remain sound common sense', but even as a workable tool it is inapplicable to the metaphysical level on which Hume's conceptual questions ought to find their solution, the level of the critique of reason.

Kant's second criticism of Reid does not explicitly target common sense philosophy at all, but undermines the key premise of Reid's formulation of common sense in the philosophy of mind, according to which 'all we can know of the mind must be derived from a careful observation of its operation in ourselves' (*IP* II viii, p. 271b). According to Reid, 'the opera-tions of our minds are known, not by sense, but by consciousness, the authority of which is as certain and as irresistible as that of sense'; conscious-ness, coupled with careful reflection while they are exerted, allows us to form 'a distinct notion of any of the operations of our own minds' (II v, p. 258a). So Reid maintains that 'our consciousness and reflection inform us concerning the operations of our own minds' in a way symmetrical to that by which 'our senses inform us of external things', and that together they are the means by which the 'Supreme Being has given us some intelligence of his works' (II xv, p. 309b). This view is rejected by Kant, who states that if 'we admit that we know objects only in so far as we are externally affected, we must also recognize, as regards inner sense, that by means of it we intuit ourselves only as we are inwardly affected *by ourselves*; in other words, that, so far as inner intuition is concerned, we know our own subject only as appearance, not as it is in itself'.[11] Nor can consciousness be the means by

[11] Kant, *Critique of Pure Reason* (*CPR*), ed. N. Kemp Smith (London: Macmillan, 1929), B156.

which we obtain knowledge of our minds, because 'consciousness in itself is not a representation distinguishing a particular object, but a form of representation in general, that is, of representation in so far as it is to be entitled knowledge' (A346/B404). Reid's 'principles taken for granted' are therefore not only a means by which 'the dullest windbag can confidently take on the most profound thinker' (*Prolegomena*, p. 9), but also the source of a confusion between the actual operations of the mind and the representations we have of these operations.

This explicit condemnation has received a number of responses. Michel Malherbe, writing on the possibility of a philosophy of common sense, places the justification of common sense in 'reciprocal contamination' because of the dual status of its principles, both 'primary truths (with a meta-theoretical status) and final truths (objects of the theory)' whose duality is caused by the reflective method in Reid's philosophy of mind: 'the mind exercises its operations when it is the object of its scrutiny; and the evidence on which the meta-theory rests, the natural light which shines on all understanding and whose principles we can formulate, is precisely the object of the enquiry'.[12] This justification makes use of Reid's analysis of the ambiguity between mental operations and their object, in the term *idea*, which has a common and a philosophical use: commonly, and according to common sense, 'to have an idea of anything, is to conceive it' (*IP* I i, p. 224b), and conceiving is a simple operation of the mind which 'cannot be logically defined' (IV i, p. 360b); but 'according to the philosophical meaning of the word idea, it does not signify that act of the mind ... but some object of thought [or conception]' (I i, p. 225a). It is on this equivocation, 'built upon a philosophical opinion' (p. 226b), that the theory of ideas as immediate objects of thought is constructed.[13] Reid's sixth principle taken for granted stipulates instead that 'in most operations of the mind, there must be an [external] object distinct from the operation itself' (p. 233a). So when the mind operates on itself, it also posits itself as external, hence justifying both its existence (against Kant's implicit criticism) and the principles by which it reveals itself. However, Reid's account of intentionality, of 'creatures of the imagination' (IV i, p. 367b), blurs this picture. For although he claims that 'the powers of sensation, of perception, of memory, and of consciousness, are all employed solely about objects that do exist, or have existed', whereas 'conception is often employed about objects that neither do, nor did, nor will exist', the 'consciousness which we have of the operations of our own minds, implies a belief of the real existence of these

---

[12] M. Malherbe, 'Reid et la possibilité d'une philosophie du sens commun', *Revue de métaphysique et de morale*, 96 (1991), pp. 551–71, at p. 568.
[13] Cf. Lehrer, 'Metamind', pp. 39–41.

operations' (*IP* IV i, p. 368a), and not of any other external object, such as the mind itself. Reid might be content with the view that the mind is precisely the set of mental operations whose existence his method justifies, but cannot justify its embodiment in a distinct self except by the stipulation of another principle taken for granted, according to which 'I take it for granted that all the thoughts I am conscious of, or remember, are the thoughts of one and the same thinking principle, which I call MYSELF, or my MIND' (I ii, p. 232a). Malherbe's justification, therefore, although it seems somewhat coherentist,[14] since the plausibility of common sense is supported essentially by the compatibility of beliefs and operations of the mind, does not succeed without appeal to common sense principles that fall outside his 'reciprocal contamination' model, and resembles a rather more axiomatic scheme. This scheme remains open to Kant's implicit criticism, as the self-knowledge required to justify the principles Reid takes for granted is based on psychological reticences – the inability of the common sense thinker to deny their truth – which may well be due to our knowledge of our subject in its appearances rather than in itself, and which do not know their cause. So the response to the explicit argument is as exposed to the implicit criticism as that which it tries to justify.

The same is true of Sutton's interpretation (p. 159) of appeal to common sense 'as a form of transcendental argument'. The problem he finds (pp. 176–7) in Reid's justification of knowledge also concerns the status of the principles of common sense: is 'belief in the dictates of common sense a mere psychological impulse ... or is it necessary in a sense which provides a guarantee of the truth of what is believed?'. It is the same problem as he finds (p. 177) in Kant: does 'Kant's transcendental deduction guarantee that the categories we necessarily have to apply describe reality truly'? By this interpretation, the principles of common sense are taken to be preconditions for reason and knowledge, whose justification is an implicit transcendental argument. But, in so far as this explanation addresses Kant's explicit criticism of Reid, the 'difference' that Sutton (pp. 181–5) highlights between Reid and Kant leaves untouched the force of the implicit argument. For Kant's transcendental idealism renders an attack on the categories impossible, whereas Reid can only qualify such attacks as nonsensical. If 'pure concepts of understanding ... in relation to experience are indeed necessary, and this for the reason that our knowledge has to deal solely with appearances' (*CPR*, A130), questioning the applicability of the categories is trying to argue with words and concepts which, without the categories, are unavailable. Kant's distinction between the phenomenal and the noumenal,

---

[14] Cf. D. Schulthess, 'Did Reid Hold Coherentist Views?', in Dalgarno and Matthews (eds), pp. 193–203.

therefore, seems to defuse the implicit argument's force against himself, while preserving its force against Reid. It is Reid's claim to epistemological access to the ontology of mind, his refusal to draw Kant's distinction, that makes him vulnerable.

Ronald Beanblossom, in his 'Kant's Quarrel with Reid', also uses Kant's distinction between the phenomenal and the noumenal. He interprets Kant's transcendental idealism as a demonstration, against his explicit position, that metaphysical (ontological) assumptions are prior to epistemology. This approach blocks both criticisms by reducing Kant's quarrel with Reid to a speculative argument, but renders impossible the determination of the truth of either position (if not of any ontological position), and is therefore not satisfactory.

Kant's two criticisms of Reid, therefore, are reducible to the implicit argument that underpins the explicit condemnation. The principles of common sense require a justification beyond the merely psychological, if Reid's claim to epistemological access to ontology is to be supported. The position Strawson qualified as Kant's 'transcendental psychology' can only be held if a distinction is made between the ontological and that to which we have epistemological access. There is a tension in Reid between ontology and epistemology.

II. THE TENSION IN REID AND KANT

The issue between Reid and Kant is that of the foundation of reason and knowledge, against the sceptical threat posed by Hume. Reid makes a stronger claim for knowledge than Kant, believing knowledge of things in themselves to be accessible by the application of common sense principles. It is this belief that makes his position more vulnerable to a sceptical challenge, for Reid, unlike Kant, cannot refute his opponents' arguments by denying them the possibility of using words and concepts; their position must be simply incoherent or disingenuous. This problem manifests itself in two forms in Reid, within his system, and externally to it.

From within his system, Reid's problem is the product of two components of his position. On the one hand, consciousness is the only evidence we have for the existence of the operations of our minds; consciousness is 'employed solely about objects that do exist' (*IP* IV i, p. 368a). On the other hand, the intentionality of human thought allows the conception of things that do not exist, limited only by the 'ingredients' (p. 367a) of previous experience. Consciousness underpins conception, the only power of the mind 'that is not employed solely about things which have existence' (p. 368a). As Lehrer puts it, the 'conception of the operations of our minds ... is the result of a conceptual faculty that supplies those conceptions, the faculty of consciousness'.[15] Consciousness is a mental faculty that gives rise to the conception of mental operations. We can distinguish between operations of the mind and conceiving of these operations: the former (for instance, sensations) have no object, the latter do (for instance, conceiving of pain or pleasure has as object pain or pleasure). Consciousness and the principle of abstraction then permit us to have conceptions of individual qualities, while the principle of generalization allows us to form general conceptions which we use to conceive of things that do not exist. Consciousness and the principles of abstraction and generalization, which Lehrer calls 'metamental operations of the mind' ('Beyond Impressions', p. 393), are therefore the necessary conditions of intentionality. Since general conception is an operation of the mind irreducible to impressions and ideas, Reid's philosophy of mind is incompatible with a classical interpretation of Hume's theory of ideas – unless one accepts Galen Strawson's distinction between R-intelligibility and E-intelligibility, and the relativity of conceivability that follows[16] – and with representational theories of mind. But, more significantly, the formation of general conceptions is determined by utility, which allows for different means of giving general names to species of things (*IP* V iv, pp. 398a–403b). Furthermore, 'I can conceive a winged horse or a centaur, as easily and as distinctly as I can conceive a man whom I have seen' (IV i, p. 368a) without in any way inclining my judgement to belief in such things. Ontological dispute over the objects of combined general conceptions is therefore inevitable: whereas consciousness allows us to conceive of the individual qualities of all the operations of our minds, and thereby to determine mental ontology, general conception entails a certain plasticity in our higher-order ontology. This internal tension has the consequence of lending Reid his resemblance to Wittgenstein and other contemporary philosophers: the distinction between natural and artificial language, and the social aspect of his philosophy, are a direct consequence of what might be called not improperly his brand of ontological relativity, Reid's 'background language'[17] being that of primary qualities which arises from sensation 'by a natural kind of magic' (*Inq* V iii, p. 122a). It is this property of Reid's philosophy of mind and language that prevents him from denying sceptics the use of words and concepts in countering his position: to say that Reid's opponents are talking nonsense, in this context, is to say that they are speaking another

---

[15] Lehrer, 'Beyond Impressions and Ideas', *Monist*, 70 (1987), pp. 383–97, at p. 388.

[16] G. Strawson, *The Secret Connexion* (Oxford UP, 1989), pp. 127–8.

[17] See W.V.O. Quine, 'Ontological Relativity', in *Ontological Relativity and Other Essays* (Columbia UP, 1969), pp. 69–90, at p. 49.

language, possibly one that has formed different general conceptions. The ontological pretences of conceptualization are the cause of a new scepticism: scepticism over meaning and reference (higher-order ontology), rather than over minimal (first-order) ontology of mind.

Kant's position does not suffer from this internal tension, for by his transcendental idealism he abandons the ontological claims which oppose him to Reid. His implicit criticism of Reid, however, points to the more vital external tension between epistemology and ontology. For Reid's refusal to limit knowledge to phenomena also prevents him from denying sceptics the use of words and concepts in countering his position, because he cannot furnish an argument akin to the Transcendental Deduction which can guarantee 'the status as knowledge of what common sense prompts us to believe' and answer the question 'Does Reid's defence of first principles as acquired through our faculty of common sense' provide the guarantee that what common sense tells us is true?' (see Sutton, p. 177). As Sutton concedes (p. 181), a Reidian transcendental argument of the form

> First principles are the foundation of all reasoning
> We do engage in rational activity
> Therefore first principles can be taken for granted as true foundations for knowledge

does not 'guarantee ... that things are as we must believe they are'. But even if this were not considered a problem, the major difference between this transcendental argument and Kant's seems to disqualify a Kantian solution to Reid's problem. This difference can be presented as follows. Quassim Cassam argues that a possible analysis of transcendental arguments into a conceptual and a satisfaction component might help to reveal the structure of such arguments.[18] The conceptual component proposes a conceptual truth about experience or language, the satisfaction component shows that only a particular world can satisfy the conceptual component. By that analysis, Sutton's transcendental argument resolves into

C. We engage in rational activity and have knowledge
S. For rational activity and knowledge to be possible, there must be first principles of the mind.

But as Cassam points out (p. 361), a reformulation of the Transcendental Deduction in the form

C. For experience or knowledge to be possible, individual experiences must belong to a unified consciousness

---

[18] Q. Cassam, 'Transcendental Arguments, Transcendental Synthesis and Transcendental Idealism', *The Philosophical Quarterly*, 37 (1987), pp. 355–78.

S. For the unity of consciousness to be possible, appearances must display such unity and interconnectedness as is possible only if they are appearances of objects (that is, only experience of objects could provide a basis for the unity of consciousness)

suffers from the fact that it does not satisfy Kant's transcendental idealism, for the satisfaction component states how the world must be if the unity of consciousness is to be possible, whereas Kant's metaphysical concerns limit the Transcendental Deduction to a statement about how the world should *seem* to be for this condition to be satisfied. Understanding the arguments in this way, it is apparent that the satisfaction component in the Transcendental Deduction is of a nature different from that in the Reidian transcendental argument, and that therefore if the 'two components' proposal is valid (at the risk of 'reversing the order of [Kant's] priorities', Cassam, p. 363), a paradigmatic transcendental argument cannot answer Reid's ontological claim about epistemological access to the ontological.

This external tension in Reid, however, takes the form of two internal tensions in Kant. First, because as Cassam (p. 364) says, 'Transcendental idealism is itself a doctrine with numerous well documented defects, and there is no reason why these defects should be permitted to infect Kant's transcendental arguments'. If this line of argument were maintained, internal tensions within Kant would be deemed sufficient to subvert an important part of his metaphysics (pp. 368–70). There would then be no difference between the satisfaction components of Reid's transcendental argument and Kant's Transcendental Deduction. Their simultaneous validity would therefore vindicate Reid's claim to ontological access, while reinterpreting Kant as also enabling such access through transcendental arguments (so long as they are valid), to the detriment of his two criticisms.

But the second internal tension in Kant is more vital, as it strikes at the heart of his system, and deals with the problem of self-awareness central to Reid and to modern philosophy of mind. In the Refutation of Idealism, the demonstration of the thesis is followed by this note: 'The consciousness of myself is not an intuition, but a merely *intellectual* representation of the spontaneity of a thinking subject' (*CPR*, B278). The problem therein lies with the notion of an intellectual representation, sparsely used by Kant, and never defined. In this context, it seems to refer to a type of validity external to his system, for it is neither a figure (relation between a category and an intuition), nor the result of a search for possibility-conditions. Yet these being the only two criteria of validity available to Kant, the introduction of an altogether new notion to justify self-awareness implicitly leads him towards the same conclusion as Reid, whose fourth principle taken for granted is 'that all the thoughts I am conscious of, or remember, are the thoughts of one and the same thinking principle, which I call MYSELF, or my MIND' (*IP* I ii, p. 232a). This principle, which also seemed to elude Malherbe's reciprocal-contamination model, is therefore the common point of tension in both Kant and Reid: self-awareness, and the ability to fix at least in part the ontology of the mind by epistemological access, is presupposed in one way or another by both these philosophies of mind.

III. POSSIBLE RESOLUTION TO THE TENSION

Restated, the tension between ontology and epistemology is the following. On the one hand, Reid claims that consciousness reveals the existence of all the operations of the mind and defines a criterion for the mental. To this Kant opposes the claim that recourse to these operations is illegitimate because their mode of production is unknown or ill understood. Epistemological access to ontology is denied because self-knowledge is restricted to the way one *appears* to oneself, rather than to what one is as a thing in itself. On the other hand, Kant grants a special status to self-consciousness that eludes his stated modes of validity, since the restriction he imposes on the Transcendental Deduction is not only subject to criticism, but also fails to grant transcendental arguments a status sufficiently strong to enable anything to be said by them either about the world or about the self as they are in themselves. Kant's weaker ontological claims are therefore undermined to such an extent that the justification he seeks for reason fails to be epistemologically reached.

The simplest resolution of the tension therefore consists in a choice between either Reid's or Kant's methodology, followed by slight adjustments to the chosen path so as to iron out existing internal tensions. If one were to privilege Reid's account of a mind capable of revealing its own structure, one would have to live with the consequences of a system that provides an unequivocal ontology of primary qualities and operations of the mind, while allowing the ontology of higher-level general conceptions to be governed by pragmatic choices (sometimes naturally orientated) which imply ontological divergences or incompatibilities. Since such accounts are not foreign to modern analytic philosophy, either in mind or in language, this line might be tempting both as a philosophical explanation and as a solution to some of the problems of ontological 'grounding' that social models face. If, instead, one were to privilege Kant's account, one would have to opt either for the full story – excluding only the enigmatic status of self-awareness which opens the door to messy post-Kantian concerns – and accept that transcendental arguments must assume transcendental idealism and be limited to statements on how the world should seem, or opt for a drastic reinterpretation that would remove transcendental idealism from the account, and allow transcendental arguments to bridge the gap between epistemology and ontology. The first Kantian version justifies Kant's two criticisms of Reid; the second version renders a reduction of Kant to Reid likely, with common sense interpreted as a transcendental argument.

The three divergent paths suggested by the simple resolution are not satisfactory, however; they succeed in resolving the tension only by eluding it. In fact the significance of the tension between ontology and epistemology lies in the constitution of the concept of mind, and it is only in a re-conciliation between the two orders that the importance of the issue for the philosophy of mind can become apparent. The source of this reconciliation comes from Reid's method. As Cousin puts it (p. iii), the most important aspect of Reid's philosophy is 'that method of observation applied to human nature, which Reid called the reflective method'. Cousin traces this method to Descartes: it is this method that revealed to him 'the principle or rather the permanent and immortal fact upon which rests his whole system'. In Descartes, the permanent and immortal fact is the *cogito*, from which the existence of a 'thinking thing' is derived. In Reid, that fact is a 'thinking principle' that is both a mind and the self, constituted of those operations that are exhaustively derived by that very same method. But the significant point comes with the reason for adopting the method: in both Descartes and Reid, the method is determined by a search for certainty, for knowledge which can resist any sceptic's argument. The concept of knowledge or certainty implies the concepts of a thing that is known and of a thing that knows. According to Kant, in all judgements in which the relation of a subject to a predicate are at issue, there are two possibilities: either predicate F belongs to subject *a* and is implicitly contained by it (analytic judgement), or predicate F is linked to subject *a* without being contained by it (synthetic judgement) (*CPR* A6/B10–A10/B14). One can, therefore, using Kantian methodology, derive *a priori* the concept of a thing that knows from the concept of knowledge: the truth of this deduction is a simple analytic judge-ment. The concept of mind is only a step away, although it is complicated by the further requirement – in need of explanation – of self-awareness, which is close to that of consciousness: for how can something be known if there is no awareness of (access to) this knowledge? It is therefore inevitable that Descartes, Reid and Kant should come to face the problem of mind: their anti-sceptical programme is driven by the search for a concept that necessarily implies the existence of the mind. Taking a step further in this regressive line of reasoning, one finds that the concepts of knowledge and certainty are opposed to lack of knowledge and uncertainty: contained in the concept of certainty are therefore the concepts of that to which there is access, and of that to which there is not. It is the possibility of an inaccessible realm, together with considerations of intermediate forms of knowledge (akin to Hume's impressions of reflection), that founds the distinction between ontology and epistemology, between that which seems and that which is.

Such an account of the genesis of concepts is of course sufficiently open to leave room for a number of ambiguities, many of which are those which Reid tried to solve by an analysis of common language. The point is that a concept of mind or self is inherent to all philosophical procedures that stem from the insight that there is a set of things to be known. Claims to epistemological access and claims to ontology go hand in hand with these concepts: the access that the mind has is epistemological, and this access stands in an unknown relationship to the notional realm of all that really is, the ontological realm. The object of philosophy is the elucidation of this unknown relationship between epistemology and ontology. The object of modern science is to posit a set of ontological entities sufficiently rich to account for everything to which there is epistemological access. The naturalization of epistemology consists in abandonment of the notion of a fixed ontology, and in its scientific treatment by the positing of what might be described as a semantic ontology for the epistemology of all propositions believed to be true. But occasionally the scientific approach abandons the distinction between ontology and epistemology, and appeals to the as yet undefined relationship between the two, as in Wigner's 'mentalist solution' to the measurement problem in quantum mechanics that posits 'the existence of an influence of consciousness on the physical world', where consciousness is considered as a non-physical substance capable of operating the reduction of wave functions that determine the physical world.[19] In that case, an operation of which we are not conscious is defined as mental, contrary to Reid's definition.

These considerations prevent us from accepting all the consequences of Kant's transcendental idealism, whose ontological agnosticism falls short of our practice of ontological hypothesizing. But they do not force us to reduce Kant to Reid either. Instead, they present a justification of Reid's fourth principle in *Intellectual Powers of Man* and of the special status of self-consciousness as an intellectual representation in Kant. In both cases, the existence of a thinking principle is an irreducible fact. What is then at issue

[19] E. Wigner, 'Remarks on the Mind–Body Question', in *Symmetries and Reflections* (Indiana UP, 1967), pp. 171–84, at p. 181; cf. M. Bitbol, *Physique et philosophie de l'esprit* (Paris: Flammarion, 2000), pp. 39–45.

is the nature of the thinking principle. As Helen Steward puts it, since 'Few philosophers now believe in the existence of a substantial soul ... [as] a special kind of persisting object', philosophical considerations bearing on the mental make use of a 'fairly standard lexicon' that has given rise to 'a new ontology of mind, in which mental events, states and processes have replaced modifications of the soul', enabling philosophers 'to substitute for the view of the mind as a thing the alternative picture of the mind as a collection of things ... about whose connections with the physical world questions can then arise'.[20] The transition between these different pictures of the mind is apparent in the difference between Descartes' 'thinking thing', a substance located in the pineal gland, and Reid's 'thinking principle', constituted by a number of discrete operations. The irreducibility of Kant to Reid therefore holds in the specific ontological status each philosopher gives to the mind. In Reid, the mind is a collection of operations which cannot be denied, beyond which philosophical enquiry cannot regress. In Kant, the mind is in part the requirement, in the Transcendental Deduction, that there must be a connection between the possibility of experience and the unity of consciousness; transcendental idealism is then in fact a consequence of the subsequent dependency of the unity of consciousness on the unity and interconnectedness of appearances, which Kant requires to be more than a contingent matter of fact, and therefore associates to a natural realm defined as an aggregate of appearances, whose association is the product of a transcendental synthesis (cf. Cassam, pp. 368–9). But with knowledge thus vindicated, the mind is also constructed out of those elements that precede Kant's system, a concept generated in part by the analysis of knowledge (that which knows), and in part out of the natural prejudice according to which that which knows should be aware of at least some of its operations (at least of the fact that it knows), and should also be individuated. It is at this level that the intellectual representation of self-consciousness appears in Kant's system as an illegitimate element, completing our notion of mind by the juxtaposition of a unified consciousness with that of self-awareness.

The tension between epistemology (understood as an empirical theory of knowledge) and ontology is therefore not a destructive element within either Reid's or Kant's system of justification, but constitutes instead a matter of fact, arising out of pre-systematic conceptualization, for which these philosophies have to account. Evaluating how successful one system is relative to another in accounting for this fact amounts to evaluating methodologies, whose implicit metaphysical ambitions can result in failure to circumvent fully the naïve notion of mind.

[20] H. Steward, *The Ontology of Mind* (Oxford UP, 1997), pp. 1–3.

IV. MIND AND COMMON SENSE

The virtue of Reid's common sense philosophy of mind relative to these concerns is apparent. Kant's criticisms do not apply, since the principles of common sense explicitly attend to the fact of mind that results from the notion of knowledge: the principles are neither ill targeted philosophically (explicit criticism), nor used to obtain illegitimate access to ontology (implicit criticism), since the mind belongs to a realm akin to that of knowledge, being contained analytically by that concept. By refusing to distinguish between phenomena and noumena, Reid implicitly rejects the notion of an ontological realm parallel to epistemology and potentially inaccessible to it, thereby naturalizing his method of epistemological enquiry: epistemological access to ontology becomes the positing of an ontology sufficient to account for all that is known. The ontology Reid posits is that of the operations of the mind; these operations, operating on themselves and on individual conceptions by abstraction and generalization, allow the formation of a revisable, experimental, higher-order ontology of general conceptions. The mind therefore reveals the principles of its own operation, and these principles inform the mind of the existence of those things that are external to it: ontology of mind generates ontology in general. So the method by which the operations of the mind are discovered, the reflective method, functions symmetrically for external objects: common sense is sufficient to generate an ontology/epistemology of mind and world.

Reid's analysis of the origin of philosophical terms leads him to a pre-systematic origin in which mind is assumed to be an irreducible entity. The natural progression of his works then serves as an elucidation of that concept by the determination of an exhaustive set of operations. Philosophy of mind is therefore understood not so much as a foundationalist venture, but as a scientific programme. Kant's project is, on the contrary, a foundationalist enterprise whose explicit aim is the discovery of possibility-conditions of experience; as a continuation of Hume's, Kant's system seeks to show why such relations as causality are necessary for experience. The concept of mind therefore stands in need of justification, for Kant; in the absence of complete justification, the reintroduction of self-consciousness by the back door amounts to a reintroduction of the metaphysical concerns and occult qualities which his foundationalist method seeks to repel. But the paradox into which the abnormal status of self-consciousness leads Kant's system is symptomatic of his failure to realize that his application of the reflective method implies the existence of a concept of mind prior to the more precise, and more limited, notion of a unity of consciousness. As a result, his system rests somewhat uncomfortably between acceptance and rejection of a valid pre-systematic concept of mind.

Victor Cousin's comparative analysis of Reid and Kant therefore seems to be correct in so far as Reid makes a more direct and less problematic use of the reflective method. Reid's philosophy constitutes a philosophy of mind whose methodological thrust is the elaboration of a complete explicative ontology. Whether or not one agrees with Lehrer that Reid's philosophy of mind can be qualified as modern or as important to contemporary philosophy, his method of ontological elaboration is certainly still on the agenda of a discipline whose heterogeneity can only be compensated for by the choice of a common method and ontology.

7

REID AND PRIESTLEY ON METHOD AND THE MIND

By Alan Tapper

Reid said little in his published writings about his contemporary Joseph Priestley, but his unpublished work is largely devoted to the latter. Much of Priestley's philosophical thought – his materialism, his determinism, his Lockean scientific realism – was as antithetical to Reid's as was Hume's philosophy in a very different way. Neither Reid nor Priestley formulated a full response to the other. Priestley's response to Reid came very early in his career, and is marked by haste and immaturity. In his last decade Reid worried much about Priestley's materialism, but that concern never reached publication. I document Reid's unpublished response to Priestley, and also view Reid's response from Priestley's perspective, as deduced from his published works. Both thinkers attempted to base their arguments on Newtonian method. Reid's position is the more puzzling of the two, since he nowhere makes clear how Newtonian method favours mind–body dualism over materialism, which is the central debate between them.

I. INTRODUCTION

Readers of the *Critique of Pure Reason* must often experience some surprise when they find Kant discussing not just Hume and Reid but Joseph Priestley. Reid's philosophical reputation is now fairly secure, at least amongst philosophers with some respect for history; but as a philosopher Priestley's name is still little known. Yet Kant seems to have thought well of him. He portrays him as a Samson pulling down 'two such pillars of all religion as the freedom and immortality of the soul', but adds that he is motivated by 'concern for the interests of reason' and he 'knew how to combine his paradoxical teaching with the interests of religion' (A745–6; B773–4). He ranks Priestley even higher than Reid – but then it seems he knew Reid from Priestley's unflattering account in his 1774 *Examination* of the common sense philosophers, and this was very much a refracted image.

Reid too took Priestley seriously. Reid's main published works mention him, I think, only once, in *Active Powers* in connection with determinism, and even then Reid chooses not to use Priestley's name – he is 'a late zealous advocate for necessity'. But Reid also published anonymously a review of Priestley's 'Introduction' to his shortened edition of David Hartley's *Observations on Man*.[1] And in his unpublished writings dating from the 1780s or perhaps the early 1790s, now made readily accessible in Paul Wood's edition, Priestley's materialism is the dominant subject.[2] Why none of these thoughts on Priestley's materialism ever reached publication is far from clear. In his introduction to these papers (p. 52), Wood speaks of Reid's 'obsession with his opponent', and 'wonders if [he] ever succeeded in exorcizing the spectre of Priestley's materialism to his own satisfaction'. It is certainly a question worth pondering.

Reid was a philosopher all his adult life – it was the vocation from which he never strayed, except to carry out his clerical duties. Priestley, twenty-three years his junior, wrote as a philosopher for just a decade, from 1772 to 1782, in a burst of publishing which began with the *Examination*, his critique of the common sense Scots philosophers, and ended with a reply to Hume's *Dialogues Concerning Natural Religion*, and which coincided with the scientific work for which he is now best known. After 1782 his friends persuaded him that philosophy was not his *forte*, and he turned to history, politics and the defence of the phlogiston theory. Priestley and Reid were both deeply interested in the same metaphysical questions – the nature and powers of the mind, most importantly – yet the debate that might have taken place between them never happened. Some of the reasons for this are obvious. Priestley's treatment of Reid in his *Examination* had been offensive in both senses of the word, and Reid felt the slight. But there may also be reasons internal to the arguments which each employed. In reconstructing the dialectical situation of the 1780s I shall consider that possibility.

Debate between them would have been a clash of fundamentals. Their views on the nature of mind accord on almost nothing. The clash between them has an archetypal aspect, the confrontation of a sophisticated common sense realism with a robust scientific realism. Can there be debate between these positions? Or do they each simply deny the other's most basic assumptions? The case of Reid and Priestley is interesting just because, in his unpublished writings, Reid sought to meet Priestley on Priestley's chosen ground. That is, there was a common framework which each held as more basic than their respective philosophical creeds. The framework is that supplied by Newton in his 'Rules of Reasoning in Philosophy'. So those rules will be the central theme of this paper.

[1] Review of Priestley's *Hartley's Theory of the Human Mind* (1775), *Monthly Review*, 53 (1775), pp. 380–90, and 54 (1776), pp. 41–7.
[2] *Thomas Reid on the Animate Creation: Papers Relating to the Life Sciences* (hereafter *AC*), ed. Paul Wood (Edinburgh UP, 1995).

I shall be brief here about Reid and Priestley in the 1770s.[3] Priestley's 1774 *Examination* attacks Reid's *Inquiry* for three main reasons: its denial of the reality of 'ideas'; its supposed multitude of instincts and first principles; and its granting of epistemological authority to common sense.[4] Had the *Examination* been Priestley's only philosophical work, he would indeed be the minor figure in philosophy he is commonly thought to be. I shall move on to his later work, returning to the theory of ideas only at the end of this paper.

II. PRIESTLEY'S MATERIALISM

In 1777 Priestley published *Disquisitions Relating to Matter and Spirit* (hereafter *Disquisitions*). It is a substantial defence of materialism, of a kind rare in the history of British philosophy, perhaps the most substantial defence before the 1960s.[5] Priestley took it as given that as far as is known, all psychological phenomena have one-to-one physiological correlates. At least some dualists – David Hartley for instance, and perhaps Richard Price – conceded as much. He then argued for materialism on three philosophical grounds: from the nature of matter; from the problem of interaction that dualism entails; and from the principles of method articulated by Newton and generally taken as the canonical statement of the nature of modern science.

Priestley's first contention, opposing standard dualist doctrine, is that matter is far from powerless: on the contrary, the most advanced post-Newtonian physical theory shows it to be essentially powerful. Boscovich, he contended, had articulated a coherent and simple theory of matter, based on the idea of powerful point-particles. But if this is so, then one key defence of dualism, the assumption that matter has no powers, fails, and the possibility arises that, for all we can know *a priori*, matter's powers might extend to include the power of thought.

His second claim is that dualism requires interaction between substances with no common properties whatever (excepting temporality), so that

[3] James Somerville has explored this debate fully and perceptively in his *That Enigmatic Parting Shot: What was Hume's 'Compleat Answer to Dr Reid and to That Bigotted Silly Fellow Beattie'?* (Aldershot: Avebury, 1995), pp. 227–50. See also Alan Tapper, 'The Beginnings of Priestley's Materialism', *Enlightenment and Dissent*, 1 (1982), pp. 73–82.

[4] See *An Examination of Dr Reid's Inquiry into the Human Mind on the Principles of Common Sense, Dr Beattie's Essay on the Nature and Immutability of Truth, and Dr Oswald's Appeal to Common Sense on Behalf of Religion* (hereafter *Examination*), in *The Theological and Miscellaneous Works of Joseph Priestley, LL.D. F.R.S. &c.*, 25 vols, ed. J.T. Rutt (London: Smallfield, 1817–31; repr. New York: Kraus Reprint, 1972), Vol. III, pp. 25–67.

[5] John Yolton, in *Thinking Matter: Materialism in Eighteenth-Century Britain* (Oxford: Blackwell, 1984), his history of eighteenth-century British materialism, devotes ch. 6 (pp. 107–26) to Priestley's *Disquisitions*, though curiously he focuses mainly on Priestley's theory of matter, which formed the basis for only one of his three main arguments for materialism.

interaction between them is as good as inconceivable. Priestley recognizes that there are two forms of dualism, the Cartesian form in which mind is non-spatial, and a rival form which gives the soul spatial location and dimension. He argues that only the Cartesian position is fully coherent. But Cartesianism makes interaction unintelligible. Thus monism must be preferable to dualism, and materialism on those grounds must be preferable to Cartesianism.

Priestley's most important argument, and the one upon which he placed most weight, is that from Newton's rules. It is in fact his only direct argument in support of materialism. Newton's first rule, as phrased by Priestley, tells us that 'We are to admit no more causes of things than are sufficient to explain appearances'.[6] But, he asks, what appearances is the soul required to explain? If none, then it is redundant, and, by Newton's first rule, materialism is ontologically obligatory.

These are Priestley's central contentions, and he elaborates on them with various supporting considerations. Curiously, his second and third arguments point towards monism in general rather than materialism in particular, so they could be employed as a defence of immaterialism against dualism; and we know that as a young man Priestley was attracted to Berkeleian immaterialism: 'when I first entered upon metaphysical enquiries, I thought that either the *material* or *immaterial* part of the universal system was superfluous', he tells us (*Disquisitions*, p. 201). He came to reject Berkeley's scheme because it supposes a multitude of divine interpositions which, while not impossible, is not 'consonant to the course of nature in other respects' (*Examination*, p. 23). Thus immaterialism too fails on grounds of simplicity, though not ontological simplicity.

Priestley had been led from scientific realism to materialism. His scientific outlook wanted an account of the mind, one which preserves our knowledge of external realities, while acknowledging that this knowledge is mediated to us physiologically by 'ideas' or 'impressions'. His close acquaintance with the development of post-Newtonian matter theory had convinced him that the dualist assumption of matter's powerlessness is untenable. On methodological grounds, grounds he sees as Newtonian, he seeks a minimalist ontology. All this taken together drives him to materialism, which other arguments persuade him is at least consistent with Christianity, and possibly more suitable to the tenor of early Christianity than the Platonized metaphysical Christianity Priestley deplored. We should add that in 1774 Priestley had been in Paris with Lord Shelburne, where he had met D'Holbach and others, who were coming to take materialism for granted, and who simply

---

[6] *Disquisitions Relating to Matter and Spirit*, in *Works*, Vol. III, p. 221.

assumed that materialism excluded theism.[7] Part of his ambition was to turn the tide of the Enlightenment in the direction of a modernized minimalized Christianity. In all this Priestley's character shows through: intellectual boldness or audacity is his normal mode, with nothing held back, trusting that open debate will decide the outcome in the best interests of truth. Priestley's strange enterprise both deserved and needed criticism, and he was lucky to have on hand both a friendly critic, Richard Price, and an unfriendly one, Thomas Reid. Priestley's debate with Price is a lucid exchange of ideas on physics and the philosophy of mind, but Price nowhere touches on Priestley's use of Newton's rules.[8] Reid's deep commitment to those rules endows his response to Priestley's *Disquisitions* with a special interest, all the more so since the relevant papers have been for so long inaccessible.

III. NEWTON'S RULES AND THE NATURE OF MIND

Reid's response, in seven manuscripts, takes up no fewer than 77 pages (165–241) of Wood's edition. Four of these are simply notes; but documents IX, X and XI, as Wood classifies them, are carefully considered and polished statements of Reid's position. I shall start from the earliest and longest of these, IX, entitled 'Some Observations on the Modern System of Materialism', in which he sets out a close rebuttal of Priestley's argument.

Reid's 'Observations' has six sections or 'chapters'. The first sets Priestley in the context of modern, post-Cartesian philosophy. The second section tackles Priestley's interpretation of Newton's rules. Sections three, four and five are devoted entirely to contesting the theory of matter set forth by Priestley. The sixth wraps up Reid's case against his adversary. These proportions by themselves tell us much about Reid's position. Reid replies to Priestley on two and only two of the grounds staked out by Priestley. He tackles his methodological argument and his theory of matter. He says nothing about his argument from the problem of interaction and nothing about his empirical assumption that there is a universal correspondence

---

[7] D'Holbach's *Système de la nature* had been published in 1770. Priestley described it as 'the most plausible and seducing of any thing I have met with in support of atheism', *Works*, Vol. IV, p. 389.

[8] See *A Free Discussion of the Doctrines of Materialism and Philosophical Necessity, in a Correspondence between Dr Price and Dr Priestley*, of 1778. Price's main objection to materialism is that 'It is inconceivable to me how any person can think that many substances united can be one substance, or that all the parts of a system can perceive, and yet no single part be a percipient being'. Priestley's reply (*Works*, Vol. IV, p. 42) is that 'A system, though consisting of many beings or things, is nevertheless but one system. A brain, though consisting of many parts, is but one brain; and where can be the difficulty in conceiving that no single part of a brain should be a whole brain, or have the properties of a whole brain?'

between psychological and physiological facts. More than half of 'Observations' is devoted to refuting Priestley's account of matter. This is even more true of the other two long manuscripts, X and XI. Priestley's 'Modern System of Materialism' fails, in Reid's assessment, because it misconstrues Newton's rules, but even more because it misconceives the nature of matter.

First, then, Newton's rules, about the authority of which they are in complete agreement. Priestley had professed 'an uniform and rigorous adherence' to these rules, and had asked that his own reasoning 'be tried by this and no other test' (*Disquisitions*, p. 221). For Reid, the first rule 'is the true and proper test, by which what is sound and solid in philosophy may be distinguished from what is hollow and vain'.[9] 'So long as we follow these maxims, we may be confident that we walk on sure ground; but the moment we depart from them, we wander in regions of mere *fancy*, and are only entertaining ourselves and others with our own crude imaginations and conceits' (*Disquisitions*, p. 222). That is Priestley, but it might be Reid *verbatim*.

Priestley, Reid argues, has misstated the rules, and misstated them in just such a way as to make them favour the very thing that Newton sought to avoid, namely vain hypothesizing (*AC*, pp. 182–93). Reid translates the first rule thus: 'Of natural things no more causes ought to be admitted, than such as are both true and sufficient to explain their phaenomena'. Priestley's version of this rule, Reid correctly points out, omits the condition in Newton's original text requiring truth. The rule applies two tests, truth and sufficiency. By converting the rule into a one-test instrument, he represents it 'as if it gave a sanction to hypotheses, which have no evidence but that of explaining appearances', which is 'to contradict its main design'. The hypothesizing philosopher, seeking to explain some phenomenon, and applying his capacity for 'invention', 'hits upon an ingenious conjecture', one which is sufficient to provide an explanation, and he then concludes that 'by his sagacity he has discovered the Secret of Nature'. Hypotheses of this sort can be corrected by taking note of contradictory evidence, evidence that compels us to discard inadequate hypotheses and to form new and better ones. But even so, this method of argument is basically flawed, since all such hypotheses are 'grounded upon the same false notion, that human wit and invention is sufficient to discover the art of Nature' (*AC*, p. 187). Reid's heroes, Bacon, and following him, Newton, showed that explanations are valid only if both the truth condition and the sufficiency condition are met. The sufficiency condition standing on its own makes explanation a matter of ingenious invention. The truth condition crucially grounds explanation in the testimony of our senses.

---

[9] Reid, *Essays on the Intellectual Powers of Man* (hereafter *IP*), ed. W. Hamilton (Edinburgh: McLachlan & Stewart, 1846), I iv, p. 236a.

Reid similarly thinks Priestley has misconstrued Newton's second rule. Priestley's version is 'That to the same effects we must, as far as possible, assign the same causes'. Reid thinks that the phrase 'as far as possible' is 'purely an addition of the translator'. Wood has pointed out Reid's mistake here (*AC*, p. 72, fn. 153). In the third edition of Newton's *Principia* the rule is as Priestley has it. The earlier editions are as Reid contends: 'Of natural effects of the same kind, the causes are the same'. So both philosophers can find authority for their readings of the second rule. The philosophical point Reid wants to make is that Priestley's version leaves too much scope for those who are prone to see similitude of effects, 'when more accurate attention would discover [the effects] to be of a different kind'. 'The proper caution therefore with regard to this rule is, not That we assign Effects to the same Cause *as far as is possible*, but that we be sure the effects be of the same kind before we assign them to the same cause' (*AC*, p. 189).

Reid goes on to reproach Priestley for his failure to mention Newton's third rule. Since Reid uses this rule to debate the theory of matter and not the nature of mind, I shall pass over that point just now. Oddly, neither Priestley nor Reid makes mention of Newton's fourth rule.

Reid's interpretation of Newton's first rule is clear enough. What is quite unclear is how he thinks the rule applies to the theory of mind, and especially how it rebuts Priestley's claim that the rule warrants materialism. Neither in his 'Observations' nor in the other documents is there a single sentence on this point, which, however, seems to be the key point in this debate. At most he has shown that Priestley has misunderstood the first rule, and thus cannot claim Newton's authority for his position. To admit this is in no way to see how Reid thought he had refuted Priestley's materialism. But there is also a logical difficulty for Reid here, which, though never expressed, seems crucial to the dialectical situation. Priestley has open to him a reply that accepts all that Reid has so far claimed. He can accept the truth condition and turn it against the dualist. The materialist can claim his own 'true cause', the brain, an entity whose 'real existence' is not in doubt. What is the status of the soul? Is its existence not hypothetical? Since Reid's manuscripts were never published, Priestley never replied to them. But it is impossible to believe that, had they been published, Priestley would not have driven home this point with some force. His actual writings are never as explicit as Reid is about the distinction between truth and sufficiency in the first rule, but he clearly accepts that hypotheses are to be tried according to the truth test. Quite possibly, he trimmed the rule just because he thought the sufficiency issue, and not the truth criterion, is what the materialist must most explicitly satisfy, the truth condition being one which counts obviously in his own favour.

Reid's views on the application of the sufficiency criterion are also unclear. He might have tried to show the 'insufficiency' of the brain to account for mental phenomena. This could be done by nominating some mental state that lacks a physical correlate. He does not adopt this type of argument, and, for all we can tell, he may have thought that there is a complete correlation between the mental and the physical.

There are two interpretations that might make some sense of Reid's general strategy in his 'Observations'.

(1) Perhaps Reid is not arguing for dualism but simply against materialism, and his own position is one of ontological agnosticism about the nature of mind, an agnosticism backed by Newton's methodological principles. On this view both materialists *and* dualists are guilty of 'vain hypothesizing', and we must rest content in ignorance of mind's real nature. To take this interpretation seriously, we would have to imagine Reid as capable of attacking dualism with the same hostility as he evidently felt for Priestley's position, and there is nothing in Reid to suggest this possibility.

There is a suggestion in his discussion that the rules have their place in discovering the laws of nature, but not the essences of natural things. Pursuing this line of thought, we could think of science as discovering what laws govern the mind, but not telling us anything about its composition. Thus Newton's rules could be construed as ontologically agnostic. This reading requires that 'true causes' are simply antecedent events in a law-like statement. Reid, however, talks of 'true causes' as referring to 'real existences', and this phrase blocks the ontologically neutralist interpretation.

(2) A second interpretation is that he is not applying the rule to the nature of mind, but only to the nature of matter. Priestley had applied the rule to both; he held that it authorizes both materialism about the mind *and* Boscovichian matter-theory. Reid, it could be, is saying nothing about materialism itself, but he is trying to eliminate the support for it that Priestley derived from the theory that matter possesses real powers. The evidence in Reid's unpublished papers for this view is good. The main body and the concluding section of 'Observations' are about matter theory and not at all about materialism, showing that this was Reid's main concern. And Reid's later manuscript, XI in Wood's edition, is conclusive on this point: 'It was not the Intention of those Observations [on the Modern System of Materialism], to discuss the Question at large Whether the Soul be a material substance or not *but onely* to consider the Aid which that Author [Priestley] had endeavoured to give to Materialism, by giving a new Conception of the Nature of Body or Matter' (*AC*, p. 233).

This settles the matter of Reid's intentions, but of course it leaves open the question about Reid's own position on how the rules relate to the nature of mind, a question raised by the first interpretation, and the central issue between Priestley and Reid. Priestley's ontological challenge to the dualist is to defend dualism in some way that does not violate Newton's criteria.

Whether Reid thought this could be done remains puzzling. It is also unclear why he devotes so much space to the theory of matter, which was germane to only one of Priestley's three arguments for materialism. The best sense we can make of his thinking seems to be this. Priestley is to be answered by rebutting his theory of matter, with the help of Newton's 'rules of reasoning'. Rebutting the thesis that matter possesses powers will drive us to reject materialism, since if matter has no physical powers it can have no capacity to serve as the substrate of mind. That is, Reid will reinforce dualism's underpinnings in Newtonian physics. I turn now to that issue.

IV. THE THEORY OF MATTER

The very broad question of the nature of matter in the late eighteenth century is one about which there is already much scholarly literature. My focus here is on how Reid and Priestley employed Newton's 'rules of reasoning' in this controversy. Priestley's view is that the first rule requires us to ascribe powers to matter itself, for to ascribe them to something other than matter is to postulate a realm whose existence is hypothetical. That is, his argument rests mainly on the truth condition of the rule, the very condition Reid accused him of neglecting. To make out this case he adopts a hypothesis, Boscovich's theory of point-particles that exert their powers of attraction and repulsion at a distance. This theory, he contends, is sufficient to account for all the appearances of nature, and thus satisfies Newton's second desideratum. He has of course no direct proof of the real existence of point-particles.

In replying to this position, Reid might again have chosen ontological agnosticism, and attacked Priestley for going beyond the direct evidence of the senses. That is not his reply. Rather, Reid defends as strenuously as he can the theory of matter's powerlessness, which he equates with the Newtonian notion of inertia. Granted that matter itself has no power, and that nature exhibits power, it follows that nature contains non-material powers. Reid's insistence on matter's lack of power is designed to demonstrate the existence of immaterial but non-mental natural agents, which (like Newton) he refers to as *immaterial principles*. Thus Reid is committed to a dualistic natural science quite as much as he is committed to a dualism of mind and matter.

How exactly does Reid employ Newton's rules in defence of this position? How in particular does he show that his immaterial principles are not hypothetical entities? Part of the answer is that he turns to Newton's third rule, which, he observes, Priestley has ignored, but which Reid thinks governs exactly the point at issue in the theory of matter, namely, 'upon what evidence we are to hold a quality of bodies to be universal, or to belong to all Matter' (*AC*, p. 191).

The third rule permits us to treat as essential to matter only those qualities which 'admit neither of increase nor of diminution, and which are to be found to belong to all bodies on which we can make experiments' (Reid's translation: *AC*, p. 189). Reid thinks that inertia meets these requirements but Priestley's 'inherent powers of attraction and repulsion' do not, so that Priestley is unable to justify his account of matter by Newton's standards. Reid's physics requires both inertia and powers of attraction and repulsion, but he denies that both can be essential to matter (*AC*, pp. 203, 207). The onus is on Priestley to show how a mechanics without inertia might be at all plausible. On Reid's view, inertia is essential to mechanics, because without it 'the whole matter of the universe will require as little expense of force to move it, as an atom; and therefore the same impressed force may produce either a small or a great change of motion, which contradicts the second law of motion' (*AC*, p. 206).

Priestley's thesis is that a theory of powers of attraction and repulsion can replace talk of solidity, impenetrability and inertia, and that the first rule warrants this replacement. What we see in nature is the action of natural powers, and these powers are to be ascribed to matter, because to ascribe them to something else is to postulate something whose existence is not known to be true, and so is to breach the first rule. Reid's first reply is in terms of the third rule. But does he reply to Priestley's use of the first? He does: the first rule is the crux of his argument against Priestley. Priestley's assertion that powers such as gravitation are inherent in matter is mere conjecture, as Reid sees it. There are three equally eligible hypotheses available to us. Instead of A attracting B by an inherent power of attraction, A might move itself to B by an inherent power of self-motion; or some invisible matter between A and B may attract them to each other; or some invisible matter may propel A and B together (*AC*, p. 209). Priestley has not shown his hypothesis to be the true cause, nor has he shown it to explicate any phenomena, so he is violating the very rule he asked to be judged by. Reid's Newtonianism is thus the Newtonianism of *Hypotheses non fingo* and of Newton's Letter to Bentley.

Reid wonders, astringently, how Priestley can imagine that 'Sir Isaac Newton and the whole tribe of experimental philosophers for more than a century' could have reasoned fallaciously from the same evidence and by the same rules as Priestley accepts (*AC*, pp. 215–16). Is Priestley's position unintelligible, then? Not entirely. Two of the rival hypotheses Reid thinks he has not eliminated involve 'invisible matter'. Reid assumes we know true causes only when hypotheses of this sort are ruled out. Priestley, by contrast, takes the first rule as ruling out 'random hypotheses', and it seems likely that he would count talk of invisible matter as random. Reid's other hypothesis involves a power of motion inherent in matter, which makes it similar to Priestley's power of attraction in matter. Priestley cannot rule out that hypothesis on methodological grounds alone. But he can claim to defend 'true causes' if true causes are known real existents, since both parties to this debate think matter is a known real existent, and if, by the first rule, natural powers must be ascribed to known real existents and not to 'random hypotheses'. The clash between Reid and Priestley may be explicable, given these conflicting accounts of true causes and of the role of the first rule.

So far, so clear. But Reid does not leave it at that. His later documents are far from agnostic about natural powers. There is a startling statement in document X: 'the Philosophy of Matter naturally leads to the Philosophy of immaterial Being' (*AC*, p. 230). In that document he takes it as an assumption 'that Matter is that inert and passive substance which all natural philosophy teaches it to be' (p. 217). This assumption made, he then freely ascribes all natural powers to non-material agents. That is, he adopts a hypothesis – just the procedure for which he had earlier chastised Priestley. How might Newton's rules authorize Reid's move if they will not authorize Priestley's? Reid must show that his immaterial principles are true causes and sufficient to explain the phenomena. But plainly there can be no direct observation of these principles. Reid never attempts to square his account of natural powers with Newton's rules nor with his critique of Priestley, so documents X and XI look like lapses from his own methodological standards. Nor are they minor lapses. Many passages in Reid present an *immaterialist* natural science. Immaterial principles do all the work in nature, and the role of matter is merely to be that upon which those principles act. All this fits with Reid's account of causation and agency. But it does not fit with Newton's rules. As an interpreter of Reid I would like to remove this striking inconsistency, but I can see no way of doing so.

V. INTERACTIONISM

The theory of matter and issues of method inform attitudes to the problem of interaction. It is one of Priestley's three main arguments for materialism that dualism leaves mind–body interaction unintelligible. As I remarked above, in his youth he 'thought that either the *material* or *immaterial* part of the universal system was superfluous' (*Disquisitions*, p. 201). For him it is more certain that there are causal relations between matter and mind than that the mind is or is not material (p. 154). He rejected Berkeley's immaterialism because it supposes a multitude of divine interpositions that is not 'consonant to the course of nature in other respects' (*Examination*, p. 23) – that is, he rejected it on the ground of simplicity. In his *Examination* he argued that Reid's position approaches occasionalism, since Reid held that mind and body are so different that 'we can find no handle by which one may lay hold of the other' (p. 48). He quotes Reid from the *Inquiry*: 'I take it for granted, upon the testimony of common sense, that my mind is a substance ... and my reason convinces me that it is an unextended and indivisible substance; and hence I infer that there cannot be in it anything that resembles extension'.[10] By implication, no extended thing can act on an unextended one. Priestley's general objection to this position is to ask 'how can any thing act upon another but by means of some common property?' (p. 47).

In his unpublished papers Reid says little about this argument. If matter is passive, as these papers argue, then by definition it cannot act on mind. Given his theory of matter as passive, Reid might have replied that mind–body interaction must be interaction between two immaterial agencies. He does not say this, but it is his position.

VI. DUALISM AND THE COMMON SENSE PHILOSOPHY

I return now to the central topic, Reid's response to Priestley's materialism, as distinct from his theory of matter. Reid's unpublished papers show him attacking materialism by defending the doctrine of the passivity of matter, the doctrine that Priestley thought had been refuted by Boscovich and was contrary to Newton's rules. As already remarked, Reid nowhere debates Priestley's main argument, that Newton's rules authorize us to ascribe the powers of the mind to the brain. Why Reid passes over this is unclear. If he had an easy refutation he would have wanted to use it. Nor does he put forward any positive arguments for the mind's immateriality. In general, we can be sure that Reid was a dualist, and not an agnostic, about the mind. We therefore expect him to display something of his own positive position when he is replying to Priestley. In fact we get almost nothing. Why so little?

[10] *Examination*, p. 47. The source is Reid's *An Inquiry into the Human Mind*, ed. Hamilton, VII, p. 210b.

Reid is not agnostic about the nature of mind. It is true that he generally eschews speculation about the nature of mind. But one who ascribes immateriality to natural powers is hardly likely to be in doubt about the immateriality of the mind. As he puts the point in document X, 'if the meannest Animals and even Vegetables be endowed with an immaterial Principle there can remain no doubt of the existence of such a Principle in Man' (AC, p. 230). But animals and vegetables are endowed with an immaterial principle only in the sense in which non-living agents are, in Reid's opinion, so endowed. These agents are not themselves immaterial, but are animated by such a principle acting within them. (This line of argument may seem exactly opposite to that which we are accustomed to from Reid, who objected strenuously to all positive comparisons between material and immaterial entities. However, the comparison is really between various sorts of immaterial powers, and not between the mental and the physical.) The argument can work only against one who accepts such immaterial principles in nature; it can do nothing against a scientific realist like Priestley.

Is Reid perhaps an axiomatic dualist? Some interpreters have gone close to suggesting that he is. Selwyn Grave contends that for Reid 'common sense is implicitly dualist, root and branch. Bodies and minds are altogether different kinds of things, not things that might merge into identity below their manifested properties, though common sense has to wait on philosophy (on Descartes especially, Reid thinks) to know how to put the difference properly.'[11] Perhaps, as this suggests, Reid thought that both justification of dualism and refutation of materialism are equally impossible, since they would be argument framed in incommensurable terms. Against this, we can note that the refutation of immaterialism is also at issue here, and we have seen Reid using Newton's rules against that position.

More basically, this interpretation needs to account for the fact that Reid does not include the mind's immateriality amongst his twelve 'first principles', the principles definitive of common sense. Those principles include the claims that 'the thoughts of which I am conscious, are the thoughts of a being which I call MYSELF, my MIND, my PERSON'; that 'we have some degree of power over our actions, and the determinations of our will'; and that 'there is life and intelligence in our fellow-men with whom we converse' (IP VI v, pp. 443b–8b). They do not include anything about the substance of the mind or the substance of matter; nor do they include anything about the passivity of matter, though they do insist on the free activity of mind – the crucial terms informing his response to Priestley.

[11] S.A. Grave, The Scottish Philosophy of Common Sense (Oxford: Clarendon Press, 1960), p. 200. Grave observes (p. 199) that Reid's successor, Dugald Stewart, 'is less consistently sure than Reid that the difference between matter and mind goes beyond their phenomenal difference'.

Grave's interpretations can be defended if we emphasize 'implicitly' in the claim that 'common sense is *implicitly* dualist'. On this view, Reid's twelve 'first principles' are the *explicit* commitments of common sense, but there are other, implicit, commitments.

Reid does not regard his twelve principles as settled for all time ('I shall rejoice to see an enumeration more perfect', he says at *IP* VI v, p. 441b). They are a first attempt at discovering, inductively, the domain of common sense; with further thought, other principles may be added. But the idea of 'implicit common sense' runs into other difficulties. For Reid, first principles appear early in childhood, are indispensable in practical life, are felt to be undeniable, and are almost universally accepted as true (*IP* VI iv, pp. 438a–41b). Nowhere does he argue that either dualism or the passivity of matter meets these criteria.[12] And given these criteria, which seem to require that common sense must be explicit, it is far from clear what implicit common sense could be.

If the axiomatic interpretation is blocked, we seem forced back to the methodological approach to Reid's dualism. When Reid is not arguing from first principles, he commonly lets Newton's rules guide his thinking. Curiously, in these papers he is quite explicit that there is nothing in principle inappropriate in applying Newton's rules to the mind, as Priestley did, even though Newton may not have intended them for that purpose. ' ... the reason of them', Reid says, 'extends to these [natural phenomena of the mind], as well as to the phaenomena of the material system; and therefore they may be applied to both with equal propriety, and ought to be adhered to with equal strictness'. They should not be applied, however, to 'the voluntary actions of men', which are not natural phenomena.[13] Taking these two points together, it seems that Newton's rules extend only to the *phenomena* and not to the *substance* of the mind.

Elsewhere Reid does seem to use Newtonian method to reach ontological conclusions. In his *Inquiry* (V viii, p. 132a), Reid applied Newton's rules when objecting to Berkeley's immaterialism:

... this acute writer argues from a hypothesis against fact.... That we can have no conception of anything, unless there is some impression, sensation, or idea, in our

[12] Beattie, not surprisingly, does so argue. As Grave (p. 201) summarizes from Beattie's *Essay on the Nature and Immutability of Truth* (1772), 'it is the universal conviction of mankind, that we have souls which are completely different things from our bodies. No arguments are needed in support of this conviction; no arguments can shift it. It has intuitive evidence, "the evidence of internal sense".' Reid's writings are notable for the absence of any such claims.

[13] *AC*, p. 185. Reid's willingness to apply Newtonian method to the mind is present right at the beginning of *Intellectual Powers*: '[Newton's] *regulae philosophandi* are maxims of common sense ... and he who philosophizes by other rules, either concerning the material system or concerning the mind, mistakes his aim' (*IP* I i, p. 97b). There is no substance/phenomena distinction at this stage in Reid's thought.

minds which resembles it, is indeed an opinion which hath been very generally received among philosophers; but it is neither self-evident, nor hath it been clearly proved; and therefore it hath been more reasonable to call in question this doctrine of philosophers, than to discard the material world.

Here Berkeley's immaterialist 'hypothesis' – discarding the material world – is contrasted with Reid's dualistic direct realism, with the latter being preferred because it is not 'hypothetical'. In general too, Reid rejected the theory of ideas, because it supposed the existence of merely hypothetical entities, ideas.

Following this line of argument, he seems required to explain the methodological standing – its status as a 'true and sufficient cause' – of the immaterial mind. The place to find such an explanation, we might suppose, would be in his unpublished reply to Priestley's materialism, since for Priestley the brain is a 'true cause', but the soul cannot be. Reid's explanation is not there.

Edith Cowan University, Western Australia

8

COMMON SENSE AND THE THEORY OF HUMAN BEHAVIOUR

By Ferenc Huoranszki

I offer an analysis of Reid's notion of the will. Naturalism in the philosophy of action is defined as the attempt to eliminate the capacity of will and to reduce volition to some class of appetite or desire. Reid's arguments show, however, that volition plays a particular role in deliberation which cannot be reduced to some form of motivation present at the time of action. Deliberation is understood as an action over which the agent has control. Will is a higher-order mental capacity enabling us to control our own attitudes, decisions and actions. Reid investigates several distinct forms of this control. I conclude with some remarks about the relation between Reid's arguments about the function of the will and his moral rationalism.

One of the central problems in the philosophy of action concerns the structure of deliberation and its relation to the action in which it results. In this paper I shall attempt to reconstruct Reid's theory of action and to assess its historical and philosophical significance. I shall argue that Reid's answer is distinctively modern in the sense that his insights are not of only historical importance. In order to bring out his significance better it may be instructive to begin by setting Reid's arguments about voluntary action in the context of a more general problem. The more general problem concerns the relationship between naturalism and common sense understanding of human action. 'Philosophical naturalism', as I shall use the term here, signifies both a problem and a particular philosophical position. Naturalism, in a broader sense, was a problem for every philosopher who welcomed the 'new science of motion' and agreed that it carries important consequences with it as regards the problem of knowledge, morality and human action. In this broad sense, most of the philosophers of the seventeenth and eighteenth centuries can be classified as naturalists.

In the philosophy of action, however, there is also a narrower meaning of 'naturalism'. According to our common sense understanding, what is particular to human action is that at least some of our actions are *voluntary*. Not only humans act; animals act too. But their behaviour differs fundamentally from human actions in not being voluntarily controlled. They do what their instincts dictate to them. Humans, however, can consciously control their actions. The means of this control is what philosophers traditionally call the capacity of will. One way to characterize naturalism concerning the explanation of human action can therefore be based on what account philosophers give of this capacity. Naturalists in the narrower sense try to give an eliminativist account of volition, and a reductionist account of the will. They claim that the capacity of 'willing' either is senseless or should be reduced to some other mental state, generally to a certain class of motives or desires.[1]

It follows from the naturalistic conception of action that although beliefs and inferences are conscious states and operations of the mind, what we believe and how we infer are not under our conscious control. The same is true of our 'desires', 'passions' or 'appetites'. They set our purposes, direct our thoughts, and sometimes determine our actions. But they are not controlled by us. Beliefs and desires combine to give reasons for action. Reasons motivate: they move us to act. But there is no further control that we can exercise over our own motivation. Motives move us, as animals are moved by their natural drives. This is the general picture of human deliberation and action which is questioned by those who think humans can control their actions by means of the will.

This characterization of naturalism in the philosophy of action may help us to appreciate Reid's contribution to a philosophical theory of behaviour. Reid was an empiricist and a naturalist in the broad sense. He believed that Newtonian physics has a special role in our body of knowledge, and that we cannot dismiss its consequences with regard to the understanding of human action. But he did oppose naturalism in the narrower sense, to the extent that he denied that drawing the proper consequences requires the elimination of volition or reduction of the will. Animal behaviour is explainable in mechanistic terms.[2] But it is thus explainable only because animals are not capable of voluntarily controlling their actions, even if their actions are 'voluntary' in the very broad sense of being purposeful. Humans are

---

[1] The first philosopher in the modern age who explicitly formulated this claim was Hobbes: 'In *Deliberation*, the last Appetite, or Aversion, immediately adhaering to the action, or to the omission thereof, is that wee call the WILL': *Leviathan*, ed. C.B. MacPherson (Harmondsworth: Penguin, 1983), p. 127. Hume also arguably counts as a representative of the naturalist position, although his view on this issue, as on many others, is ambiguous. David Armstrong formulates it clearly: 'What we must reject is the idea that, over and above desires, there are further mental states or processes which are responsible for the translation of desires into action.... In an old-fashioned language, the Will is not a separate faculty from Desire', *A Materialist Theory of the Mind*, 2nd edn (London: Routledge, 1993), p. 152.

[2] In fact, for Reid, even the understanding of animal behaviour requires more than purely 'mechanical principles'. Only instincts and habits are 'mechanistic'; passions, appetites and desires are 'animal principles'. The ground of the distinction seems to be that the latter are intentional, whereas the former are not. This is, however, a highly questionable claim which I shall not consider further here.

animals, but of a very particular kind: they are, as the Aristotelian tradition has it, 'rational animals'. Rational behaviour, however, requires not only the capacity of reasoning but the capacity of a particular kind of conscious control over our actions and motives as well.

I. THE DEFINITION OF WILL AND VOLITION

Reid is known as the founder of the Scottish philosophy of common sense. He is also arguably a predecessor of what is now called 'ordinary-language philosophy'.[3] The problem of action provides a good example of the extent to which arguments from common sense can be used in philosophical reasoning. 'Volition' is a term of art. But our ideas concerning our capacity of will are fed by our common sense understanding of action. These notions are, however, sometimes in conflict. Some aspects of our common sense understanding of action, like the difference we find between human and animal behaviour, speak for our having a particular capacity, called 'the will'. But there is a rival view which makes the will seem to be somewhat mysterious. What is the will, and how can we identify a particular volition? Do we really need it in explaining human action? Why do desires and motives not suffice?

Undeniably, we do use the term 'will' in our common parlance. In some contexts, for instance, the use of the term refers to some kind of mental effort, or rather the lack of it. We say that people are 'weak-willed' if they are not able to act according to their best judgement. But this in itself is not sufficient evidence that there is such a thing as volition, since many think that the idea of acting against one's own best judgement is inconsistent.[4] What is more, it cannot be denied that one of the meanings of 'will' in normal usage is just to refer to wants or desires. Ordinary use of the term therefore can support both a reductive and a non-reductive analysis of volition. But Ockham's razor applied to mental capacities would dictate rejection of the 'special faculty' view. Therefore those who believe the will exists have to show that we cannot make good sense of other human capacities, nor of the notion of voluntary action, without assuming that will is a non-reducible mental capacity. This is exactly what Reid tries to do in his *Essays on the Active Powers of the Human Mind*. He gives the following definition of the will:

[3] Keith Lehrer provides a very concise and informative survey of Reid's influence on early twentieth-century philosophy in his *Thomas Reid* (London: Routledge, 1989), p. 6.

[4] Many twentieth-century philosophers of action have wrestled with this problem. For a survey of the debate, as well as a convincing argument supporting the possibility of acting against one's own best judgement, see A. Mele, *Irrationality* (Oxford UP, 1987), pp. 16–30.

> Every man is conscious of a power to determine, in things which he conceives to depend upon his determination. To this power we give the name of *Will*; and, as it is usual, in the operations of the mind, to give the same name to the power and to the act of the power, the term *will* is often put to signify the act of determining, which more properly is called *volition*.[5]

Alternatively, following and simplifying Locke's definition, he says that volition is 'The determination of the mind to do, or not to do, something which we conceive to be in our power' (*AP* II i, p. 58). He immediately remarks that this is of course not a 'strictly logical definition', since 'the determination of the mind is only another term for volition' (pp. 58, 59). This calls for some explanation. Reid thinks that there are many words referring to certain of our capacities which are not apt for what he calls 'logical definition'. A logical definition would be such that we understand the terms figuring in the *definiens* without understanding the *definiendum*. Many capacities cannot be defined in this way because there are no simpler and better understood concepts in terms of which we can explicate them. But why would this be the case with will, on the one hand, and determination of the mind to do what is in one's power, on the other? The two notions seem to be logically independent of each other.

Not for Reid, however. Reid has a very special account of power and determination. First, he believes that we can only call something a power if it is possible for it not to be exercised. One has the power to speak even if one is presently silent.[6] Reid's understanding of power therefore differs radically both from Hume's and from the one used in physics. For Hume, observation of the constant conjunction of logically distinct events gives rise to the idea of power.[7] On Reid's account, power is a logically primitive notion which we acquire *when* and *by acting*. The notion as it is used in physics refers to certain dispositions. Since there is a logical connection between physical dispositions and their manifestations, physical power requires that, given the circumstances in which it *can* be exercised, it is *impossible* for it not to be exercised. If one body is in such a situation that it has the power to exercise gravitational attraction on another, it is obviously not possible for the former not to exercise that power.

For Reid, however, power is 'active', and activity precludes the possibility of not having control over the exertion. Therefore neither constant conjunctions nor physical forces are 'powers' in the proper sense of the word. Hume

---

[5] Reid, *Essays on the Active Powers of the Human Mind*, ed. Baruch A. Brody (MIT Press, 1969, hereafter *AP*), II i, p. 57.

[6] Reid, 'Of Power' (hereafter OP), this volume, pp. 14–23, at pp. 18–19.

[7] Hume, *A Treatise of Human Nature*, ed. P.H. Nidditch (Oxford: Clarendon Press, 1998), pp. 165–6.

was right in claiming that Newtonian laws are nothing but mathematical descriptions of certain regularities. But he was wrong in assuming that these laws really refer to powers or involve causation, and do not only state 'general facts', or regularities:

> But those of juster discernment see, that laws of nature are not agents. They are not endowed with active power, and therefore cannot be causes in the proper sense. They are only rules according to which the unknown cause acts (*AP* IV iii, p. 280).

According to Reid, therefore, there is a close link between the notions of will and volition, and that of 'the power to determine':

> ... will is necessarily implied in the notion of power. Volition and what follows upon our volitions is all that we conceive to be in our power (OP, p. 19).

This explains his contention that the definition he has given is not a 'strictly logical definition'. It also explains in what sense he meant that we can only call something a power if it is possible both to have it and, at the same time, not to exercise it. Power to determine is will, and we can have the power to will something without exercising it.

> When I will to rise and walk immediately, the exertion seems inseparably conjoined with the volition, and both appear as one and the same act of mind: but I resolve to rise and walk an hour hence. This is a deliberate act of will, as well as the will to do it immediately; but no exertion follows for an hour. Here the will is disjoined from exertion therefore they are different (OP, p. 14).

This feature of the will as the power of delayed exertion is essential to the understanding of its function in the structure of deliberation and action. But before I turn to Reid's argument concerning the function of volition in human deliberation and action, I need to face another difficulty with his definition of the will.

The difficulty concerns the phrase 'Every man is conscious of a power to determine'. In the first chapter of *Essays on the Active Powers* Reid gives a general characterization of what he calls 'power'. The very first remark he makes about power (*AP* I i, pp. 5–6) is that

> Power is not an object of any of our external senses, nor even an object of consciousness.... That we are not conscious of it, in the proper sense of that word, will be no less evident, if we reflect, that consciousness is that power of the mind by which it has an immediate knowledge of its own operations. Power is not an operation of the mind, and therefore no object of consciousness.

How is this to be reconciled with his definition of the will? I think there is an explanation, which brings us closer to an important point concerning the nature of will as a mental capacity. As I have noted above, there is a common sense view which speaks against the existence of 'acts of will', on the ground that they are somewhat 'mysterious': although they are the acts of our own minds, they require the existence of a mental capacity to the workings of which we have no direct access whatsoever.

If we combine Reid's characterization of power and his definition of the will, however, we can explain away the mystery. Reid argues that there are certain things of which we have only a 'relative conception'. We are not conscious of them immediately but only via some of their essential or accidental qualities or attributes (*AP* I i, pp. 7–8). Such is the concept of a body, for instance. We know that bodies have certain properties: they are extended, solid, divisible. These properties do not provide a definition of what a body is. Yet only in relation to these or some other properties can we understand the notion of a body. The case is similar with the mind and some of its powers. Whenever the will is exercised, we know that there is a power in the mind which is responsible for the exertion. But the power itself is a derived notion (*AP* I v, p. 36):

> From the consciousness of our own activity, seems to be derived, not only the clearest, but the only conception we can form of activity, or the exertion of active power.

This, I think, clarifies the otherwise very obscure second part of the definition, which claims that everyone is conscious of a power to determine 'in things which he conceives to depend upon his determination'. What we conceive as depending on our determination is 'our own activity'; and 'activity', as I shall show later, in the case of humans always means 'action'.[8]

To put all this in somewhat more interpretative terms, Reid responds to the objection that there is something mysterious about the faculty of will by saying that the identification of acts of volition cannot be achieved directly. We are not directly aware of the actions of our wills. This explains the feeling of 'mysteriousness'. But if we recognize that the will, being a power, is only a relative notion, the mystery dissipates. Will (like body and mind) is a relative notion, because we can only identify it in relation to some of its attributes. The will has the attribute of being the ultimate determinant of action; and since we are conscious of at least some features of our own actions, we do have attributes relative to which we can identify the will.

II. THE FUNCTION OF THE WILL

But things are more complicated, because, as we have already been told, there could be, and in fact there is, a sense in which there must be power

---

[8] Reid uses 'activity' in a broader sense too, in which it covers all events and processes expressed by active words. But in the genuine sense of the word only humans and God can be active, since only they can *act*.

without exercise. How can we know, then, that there is a volition involved in the action? To this question, not explicitly addressed by Reid, we can offer the following answer. We have already seen that for Reid will is a causal notion. Even more than that: determining the will is the only way to acquire the notion of causation. We have also seen that will and volition are theoretical notions, in that we are not immediately conscious of them. What I suggest is that Reid's 'will' refers to what we would call today a functional property.

I am using the notion *functional property* in a very broad sense. Functional concepts refer to powers or capacities which are identified by their role in the processes which result in an action. Some such roles can be identified by reference to others with which they conjoin to produce certain types of behaviour. On this broadly functional account, we are justified in believing in the existence of a mental capacity only if, given a background of other already identified functions, it fulfils an identifiable role by which we can explain behaviour better. This explanation of human behaviour is closely connected with making sense of it (in that the roles identified also provide reasons for actions), and so the functions bring certain normative consequences with them.

I shall argue that some of Reid's arguments support the idea that 'will' is a term of which a functional analysis can be given. What we have to explain is the consistency of the following two claims: (a) will can only be identified with reference to its exertion; but (b) it can only exist if it is possible for it not to be exercised. The two claims patently apply to most of the dispositional–functional capacities. There are many actual functional powers or capacities which are never 'exercised'. A magnet will never exercise its power to attract iron if it is never sufficiently close to any piece of iron. But if there is a piece of iron near enough, the magnetic power must be exercised. What is particular about the will is that there are no circumstances which would compel the exertion of a particular volition. There are no such circumstances, because agents *can control* their own wills. The capacity of the will therefore has a very peculiar but also identifiable function. Will is the means of control. Consequently, if for our common sense explanation of human behaviour the notion of such control is necessary, we have good reason to accept the capacity of will as a functional power by which the control is exercised.

It has still to be shown, however, why we need the non-reducible capacity of will when making sense of certain types of action; and we also have to give an account of how the will combines with, and is to be distinguished from, other mental capacities which also have a role in the determination of action. I shall turn first to the latter issue.

Reid gives us a very detailed characterization concerning what is special to the faculty of will and its exertion. Will is similar to other mental states in that every volition must have content:

> Every act of will must have an object. He that wills must will something; and that which he wills is called the object of his volition. As a man cannot think without thinking of something, nor remember without remembering something, so neither can he will without willing something (*AP* II i, p. 59).

This may give the impression that will is only a general term which covers many other 'pro-attitudes', like desires, appetites, preferences, etc. This, however, is not so, because will has an intentional object of a very specific kind: 'the immediate object of the will must be some action of our own' (p. 60). As stated, this criterion is surely not sufficient to distinguish the will from desire. We can and do sometimes desire our own actions. One can desire to have fun, to present a paper or to make love; and all these are one's own actions. It is true that one can only desire a *future* action of one's own, whereas one wills an action when one does it. But this does not distinguish will from desire either, because we can will our future actions too. In fact this is one of the fundamental functions of willing, as Reid himself admits. Consequently, for an attitude to be an instance of will, it is *necessary* for it to have the subject's own action as its 'immediate object'. But this cannot be sufficient.

What is characteristic of the will, and distinguishes it from desire, is that 'when we will to do a thing immediately, *the volition is accompanied with an effort to execute* that which we willed' (*AP* II ii, p. 63; my italics). Desires and other pro-attitudes are not accompanied by effort. One can desire to have or to do something without ever making any effort to satisfy one's desire. But one cannot will to do something without trying to execute the action.

This criterion indeed applies as long as we talk about the 'will to do a thing immediately', but what about the actions which we will to do in the future? What if 'I resolve to rise and walk an hour hence'?

> A fixed purpose to do, some time hence, something which we believe shall then be in our power, is strictly and properly a determination of will, no less than a determination to do it instantly. Every definition of volition agrees to it.... A purpose, or a resolution, therefore, is truly and properly an act of will (*AP* II iii, p. 84).

When the object of volition lies in the future, the will is characterized by a particular kind of *act of commitment* concerning our own future actions. This act of commitment determines what one has resolved to do when the time of the performance of the action arrives. This resolution is just as uncharacteristic of desires as the effort to execute an action. I can desire to have something or to do something without any resolution that when the time comes to get it or do it, I shall act so as to satisfy the desire. Perhaps I do not like my own desire; or perhaps it is not strong enough to elicit any effort on my part.

Consequently volition is characterized by Reid as a mental event, the object of which is our own action, and which is either accompanied by some effort to execute the action, or requires resolution to act. But Reid says more of the capacity of will. He does not only tell us what is specific to this faculty. He also indicates how it is connected with other mental attitudes like desires and beliefs. It seems to be obvious that something that lacks the capacity of having beliefs and desires cannot have the capacity of will either. Will, for Reid, as we have seen, is the power to determine what to do. But will itself can never provide the purpose of the action. Rather, 'in all determinations of the mind that are of any importance, there must be something in the preceding state of the mind that disposes or inclines us to that determination' (*AP* II i, p. 63). This something may be a passion, a desire, a motive, or any other purposeful mental state. Without these 'dispositions' or 'inclinations', volition would be goalless and empty. Furthermore, it follows from the definition of the will that volition has a particular connection with what one believes: 'the object of our volition must be something which we believe to be in our power, and to depend upon our will' (p. 62). This is again a characteristic of the will which does not apply to desires. Desires are not connected with beliefs in this particular way. We can, and sometimes do, desire actions or states of affairs which we believe are not in our power to determine.

To summarize, Reid provides an interesting and, to my mind, highly plausible account of the capacity of will. In modern terminology, the will is a functional capacity of the mind. Volition in turn plays a particular causal role in the production of action. This role is to be distinguished from that of desires by being accompanied by a conscious effort to perform some action or by requiring an act of resolution concerning our future actions. The will, however, is not independent of beliefs and desires. Only those beings (for Reid, normal adults and God) can have the capacity of will who have beliefs and desires.

III. MOTIVES AND THE WILL

Reid provides a characterization of the will which makes it perfectly clear how it differs from, and how it is connected with, other mental attitudes and capacities. But it is still not sufficient to convince those who deny that the invocation of volition is indispensable in the common understanding of at least certain types of action.[9] A reductionist would say, with Hume, that will is but 'the internal impression we feel and are conscious of, when we knowingly give rise to any new motion of our body, or new perception of our mind' (*Treatise*, p. 399). It may be true that the desires, passions or motives which in fact cause the action are accompanied by a feeling, the 'impression' of effort. But this may only be a mental epiphenomenon. We feel the presence of effort, but it has no causal role in the determination of action. In Reid's words, it is always 'the strongest motive' which determines action.

Reid argues that this is not the case. There is a wide range of actions, of many different types, for the explanation of which it is insufficient to cite the motives only. By 'motive' we mean the desire or 'passion' which gives the purpose of the action, or sometimes the desire and the conjoined beliefs about the best means to attain the desired goal. What Reid endeavours to show is that this 'Humean' account concerning the explanation of human action is highly oversimplified. The structure of reasons which we use in our common sense explanation of behaviour is a lot more complicated than this. I turn next to his arguments which consider the essential role of volition in the explanation of certain types of action.

Reid has defined will as the 'power to determine'. It follows from this definition that the types of action for which volition seems to be necessary are those of which it is sensible to ask whether the agent who performed the action could control it. Reid's main argument against those who believe that motives are sufficient to explain all kinds of action rests on his attempt to prove that the control of action by agents would not be possible without their possessing the capacity of will. Either motives are not under agents' control or, if they are, then their being controlled by the agents themselves requires volition. To show why, I have to say more about the structure of deliberation and decision which eventually results in an action.

On the reductionist account, deliberation explains, and may cause, the action, but deliberation itself is not an action. To simplify, whatever goes on in our minds which eventually causes us to act in a certain way rather then another is not under our control. According to the Hobbesian tradition, actions are controlled by agents themselves if they can do what they decide to do. But we cannot control our own decisions, because decision is not an action; it is a necessary outcome of the desires and beliefs we have. Reid thinks otherwise. For him, decision consists in the determination of the will which is 'the first part of the action' (*AP* IV i, p. 264). It is not true, therefore, that agents cannot have control over their deliberations.

---

[9] Reid's claim is stronger. In modern terms, he is a 'volitionist': he claims that what makes an event an action is that it is caused by a volition. Therefore there could be no action without volition. I shall not consider the plausibility of this stronger claim here.

Reid's arguments come from three directions. First, he argues negatively that no one has convincingly shown that it is always the strongest motive which determines the action. Secondly, he mentions that there are situations in which there is no reason to mention motives at all. Thirdly, he argues that there are situations in which, albeit the weighing of the motives is essential, comparison of them can only make sense if we regard deliberation and decision as actions controlled by agents themselves.

There are two kinds of case in which it makes no sense to talk about the strongest motive determining the action. In one, there are motives both for doing and for not doing an action. Reid (*AP* IV iv, p. 287) observes of this

> When it is said, that of contrary motives the strongest always prevails, this can neither be affirmed nor denied with understanding, until we know distinctly what is meant by the strongest motive.
>
> I do not find, that those who have advanced this as a self-evident axiom, have ever attempted to explain what they mean by the strongest motive, or have given any rule by which we may judge which of two motives is the strongest.
>
> ... There must be some test by which their strength is to be tried, some balance in which they may be weighed, otherwise, to say that the strongest motive always prevails, is to speak without any meaning.... I grant, that when the contrary motives are of the same kind, and differ only in quantity, it may be easy to say which is the strongest. Thus a bribe of a thousand pounds is a stronger motive than a bribe of a hundred pounds. But when the motives are of different kinds – as money and fame, duty and worldly interest, health and strength, riches and honour – by what rule shall we judge which is the strongest motive?

This argument, as it stands, is not convincing. First, it was Reid himself who claimed that powers can only be known by their effects. Powers also may come in degrees. Some powers are stronger than others, since although 'volition ... does not admit degrees', its exertion does (OP, p. 14). Therefore it is perfectly reasonable to claim that the strongest motive is the exertion of power to which we infer from its effect, i.e., from the action done. In fact this is how modern utility theory is often interpreted. Utility, in the technical sense, is whatever agents maximize by their actions. It is indeed true that, in this model of rational action, what maximal utility *is* cannot be identified independently of how one actually acts. Further, there is no question about how one can prove that it is so. The assumption that agents always perform those actions which bring maximal utility to them is a postulate without which the formal representations of decisions cannot get off the ground.

But even if Reid's argument is not persuasive, it is not indefensible either. Utility as it is used by formal decision theory is a technical notion. Utility theory is a way to measure the strength of preferences. But the proper use of the concept of utility as a unit of weighing preferences does not in itself imply that there is anything psychologically real to which utilities cor-respond. With reference to utilities as measures, we may explain or 'make sense of' actions without claiming that, by the same token, we have identified their psychological or mental causes. Reid's argument can be used at least to indicate why we find the explanation of human actions in terms of the 'strongest motive' so meagre. 'Strongest motive', unlike the modern notion of utility, is a psychological notion. By reference to it, philosophers aim to give a mental–causal explanation of action. Reid's examples suggest, even if they do not prove, that the invocation of the strongest motive is in many cases not sufficient to explain the structure of deliberation which leads to a certain action.[10]

But Reid also cites another kind of case in which the assumption that the strongest motive prevails makes no sense. It is possible that there is only a motive on the one side, and yet that it does not determine the action.

> It can never been proved, that when there is a motive on one side only, that motive must determine the action.
>
> ... Is there no such thing as wilfulness, caprice, or obstinacy, among mankind? If there be not, it is wonderful, that they should have names in all languages. If there be such things, a single motive, or even many motives, may be resisted (*AP* IV iv, pp. 286–7).

For this argument to make sense, 'motives' must mean desires (or pro-attitudes) *conjoined with* beliefs. If 'motive' means a sudden desire or a pure 'passion', it is just too easy to respond that this is exactly what is required by 'the strongest motive determining action'. But motives, as Reid takes them here, imply beliefs concerning what ought to be done either on moral or on prudential grounds. Briefly, motives are reasons. Reid wants to call our attention to the possibility of *irrational action*, and shows how this possibility speaks against the view that the strongest motive must always determine action.

Of course there is a simple response to this argument: motives *do* include passions, which sometimes determine actions even against the agent's own reason. But taken together the two arguments are somewhat stronger. Someone who claims that the strongest motive always determines action owes us an account of what exactly 'the strongest motive' means. Sometimes it seems to mean 'reason'. But if it does, then the strongest motive does not always determine action, as the examples just cited show. Therefore the strongest motives must include irrational forms of motivation too. But if they do, we cannot infer from the action to what the strongest motive was, as is required by the first case, since this inference presupposes that the motive

---

[10] For further arguments against the idea that the strongest motive always determines action (with extensive reference to Reid), see C. Ginet, *On Action* (Cambridge UP, 1990), pp. 131–6.

makes sense of the action. Consequently we cannot say whether the action was determined by reason or by some irrational motivation; and if we assume that there is no such difference, then we cannot distinguish between rational and irrational action either. Since in our common sense explanation of action we do make such a distinction, however, a theory which renders doing so impossible cannot be endorsed.

All this is of course not yet conclusive. But it does prepare the ground for some stronger arguments. The second kind of argument invokes situations in which the performance of a particular action does not require the presence of a particular motive (*AP* IV iv, pp. 285–6):

> Cases frequently occur, in which an end, that is of some importance, may be answered equally well by any one of several different means. In such cases, a man who intends the end finds not the least difficulty in taking one of these means, though he be firmly persuaded, that it has no title to be preferred to any of the others....
>
> How insignificant soever, in moral estimation, the actions may be which are done without any motive, they are of moment in the question concerning moral liberty.

This argument is central to the issue about the existence of the capacity of the will, and has, as Reid himself remarks, a long history. There are cases, sometimes called 'Buridan cases' (though the famous example has not been found in Buridan's writings) in which the agent has no reason to do one thing rather than another.

The usual retort is to deny the significance of such cases. It can be argued that such actions are based on arbitrary decisions, and no action the ground of which is arbitrary can be morally or prudentially approved or disapproved. People cannot be blamed or criticized for performing a particular action if they had no reason to do one thing rather than another. But Reid correctly points out that this, even if true, is irrelevant to the question whether only motives can determine action. For even if an arbitrary action cannot be morally or prudentially estimated, *it can be done*. Consequently the normal human response to such situations, which occur very frequently indeed, proves that we have the power to act even in the absence of determining motives.

But Reid of course does not want to argue that volition is important *only* in the cases of action which are morally or prudentially insignificant. Just the contrary. What he endeavours to show, on the final account, is exactly that volition is necessary for the moral estimation of action. This leads us to the third kind of case where the will is shown to be necessary for *evaluation* of the conflicting motives. This is indeed at the heart of Reid's arguments. He argues that the *estimations of the motives are themselves actions*, and that this kind of action requires the capacity of will.

> I grant that all rational beings are influenced, and ought to be influenced, by motives. But the influence of motives is of a very different nature from that of efficient causes.... We cannot, without absurdity, suppose a motive either to act, or to be acted upon; it is equally incapable of action and of passion; ... [Motives] may *influence* to action, but they do not act. They may be compared to advice, or exhortation, which leaves a man still at liberty (*AP* IV iv, p. 283).

Reid's main argument for volition is, therefore, based on the assumption that there are cases when we can and do control our own motives. We cannot, of course, control whether we have them or not, but we can control whether we act upon them or not. Motives, no matter whether they are desires, passions or reasons, can be 'heard' or 'neglected', just as advice can be. Without this control over motives as determiners, rational action would be impossible in many cases; and (p. 284) it is only by their volition that agents can exercise control:

> Rational beings, in proportion as they are wise and good, will act according to the best motives; and every rational being who does otherwise, abuses his liberty.

People can reflect on their motives, judge them, and decide if they want to act upon them or not. But this is only possible if they have the higher-order capacity of will. The essence of the argument is the following: rational action requires judgement over the motives, not merely the existence of motives; and this judgement is possible only if we have the capacity of will.[11] Reid distinguishes the following functions ('operations') of the will: 'attention, deliberation, and fixed purpose, or resolution' (*AP* II iii, p. 76).

I shall start with deliberation. Rational action, in many cases, is based on prior deliberation about how to act. But not every situation requires deliberation. 'No man deliberates whether he ought to choose happiness or misery' (p. 80). Some actions require long and careful deliberation, others a quick decision. We have to start to deliberate and finish deliberation in due time. All this means that deliberation is itself an action, which agents have to control. Obviously they need a faculty with which they can exercise the control. This higher-order capacity (a capacity which directs the working of other capacities) is the will, by means of which agents control their own deliberations.

Next, deliberation itself, as well as many other actions, is impossible without conscious attention. The mind has to focus on a problem or on the performance of a particular action (like writing a novel, playing the piano, hitting a good service). Concentration of attention, however, is a kind of

---

[11] For contemporary 'hierarchical theories' of the will, cf. H.G. Frankfurt, 'Freedom of the Will and the Concept of a Person', *Journal of Philosophy*, 72 (1975), pp. 205–20. There is a difference: for Frankfurt, we desire our desires, whereas for Reid, we judge them.

conscious effort which requires control over our own mental states. It is only the faculty of will which can make this control possible.

Last, but not least, we not only deliberate about what to do immediately, but also what to do in the long run. We form intentions about what to do in the future, execute plans, and stick to our former decisions to a greater or lesser extent. All this requires the faculty of will. It is obvious that the resolution to carry out a long-term plan, like following a profession, requires control over what alternatives we should take into account when we deliberate. It is not that we are not conscious of the existence of other alternatives. But we have to select for deliberation those alternatives which are in line with our previously fixed purpose. If one wishes to give a lecture on the philosophy of the end of the eighteenth century, one can deliberate whether it is better to speak about, and therefore immerse oneself in, the writings of Reid or of Kant. But it is not reasonable to consider whether it would be the right thing to read a novel by Agatha Christie, even if one had the inclination to do so. A conscious effort is required to concentrate on the *relevant decision*, the focus of which is determined by the prior resolution. So the three kinds of operation which are exercised by the will and are necessary for many kinds of rational action are closely connected with one another.

To summarize, Reid argues that rational action, in many cases, requires will and volition. Motives, of course, do *influence* actions. By attributing motives we can form expectations concerning what other people will do. But this does not imply that motives would *determine* actions. Since we possess the faculty of will, we can control the influence of our motives on our actions.

> It is true that we reason from men's motives to their actions, and, in many cases, with great probability, but never with absolute certainty. And to infer from this, that men are necessarily determined by motives, is very weak reasoning (*AP* IV iv, p. 291).

IV. THE MORAL SIGNIFICANCE OF VOLITION

Reid's aim was to reconcile our common sense understanding of human actions with the explanation of purely physical events. This reconciliation, even if based on concepts and experiences derived from our common sense, required a theory of human action. This theory attempted to prove that there is no way to explain a large class of characteristically human actions without admitting that humans have a special faculty not possessed by 'other animals': the faculty of will. Reid does not deny that human actions are sometimes influenced by 'mechanical principles' (like instinct or habit) or by 'animal principles' (like appetites, passions or desires). Unlike animals, however, humans have the capacity to control their instincts, habits, appetites, passions and desires. But is there any purpose for the sake of which this control is necessary?

In the twentieth century, most philosophers of action emphasized that their interest in the problem of action and volition is to be separated from moral considerations.[12] Answers to the problem concerning the capacity of will or the possibility and meaning of freedom have no direct consequences for the issue of moral responsibility. In this respect Reid was a philosopher of his own age. His primary interest in the philosophy of action, like that of all his contemporaries, was ethical, but 'ethical' in the broad sense of the word, which includes not only other-regarding but also self-regarding prudential actions.

Reid was a moral rationalist. He believed that, in addition to the 'mechanical' and 'animal' principles, there also exist innate rational principles of action. These principles are both prudential and moral. They tell us how we should behave towards our future selves as well as towards others. But these principles, although known for each of us by reflection, do not compel. Rather they are like advice: they provide us with information about the right conduct. It is up to us whether we comply with the advice or not. Compliance is possible, however, only if we can control our behaviour; and control would be impossible without the faculty of will.

In this context there is a further argument put forward by those who think that the will is to be reduced to some appetites, passions or desires. The charge is that if will is an independent means of control, then moral estimation of action becomes impossible: 'if men are not necessarily determined by motives, all their actions must be capricious' and 'rewards and punishments would have no effect' (*AP* IV iv, pp. 292, 293). Reid believes this to be bad reasoning. Just the opposite is true. Without the will, humans could not act according to rational principles of action; they could only be motivated by 'animal principles', and this, if anything, would make behaviour 'capricious' and render moral estimation of action impossible.[13]

Consequently there is an intimate connection between his ethical rationalism and his arguments concerning the nature of will. Reid did accept the Hutchesonian–Humean doctrine of the moral sense: the postulation of an innate capacity that elicits moral response immediately in certain situations. But he did not take moral sense to be a purely uncontrolled and uncontrollable emotive response. For him it is a partly rational capacity, since it

---

[12] For instance, Frankfurt; cf. T. Pink, *The Psychology of Freedom* (Cambridge UP, 1996), p. 12.

[13] Reid also argues for a stronger claim, that actions can only be praised or blamed if they are free. He is probably not right in that, but I shall not discuss here the complicated relation between responsibility and freedom. For an instructive discussion of Reid's argument, see Lehrer, pp. 273–6.

always involves judgement.[14] Moral sense presupposes the *recognition* of what is right and what is wrong. Without this recognition, no action can conform to our duties and obligations. Moral sense, if it is to play any role in moral estimation, must be a cognitive capacity. But cognition and volition

> are easily distinguished in thought, but very rarely, if ever, disjoined in operation.
>
> In most, perhaps in all the operations of mind for which we have names in language, both faculties are employed, and we are both intellective and active.
>
> Whether it be possible that intelligence may exist without some degree of activity, or impossible, is, perhaps, beyond the reach of our faculties to determine; but, I apprehend, that, in fact, they are always conjoined in the operations of our minds (*AP* II iii, p. 76).

I have already shown that volition plays an important role in deliberation. In fact, deliberation itself is in many cases voluntary. We have control over what to deliberate about and what not to deliberate about. We can also voluntarily concentrate our attention on solving a particular problem or making a decision. Our active powers are controlled and executed by our will, and active powers are woven into all mental operations.

Whether this extremely inclusive role attributed to the will is a plausible doctrine or not is difficult to assess. It depends to a large extent what 'mental operations' can include. For Reid, as for all eighteenth-century philosophers, the idea of unconscious mental states and processes was inconceivable. If we admit that the mental can extend to what is unconscious, Reid's claim that all actual mental processes are 'active' and in principle controllable by agents themselves is obviously untenable. But if we restrict our considerations to conscious processes, the idea may not seem so indefensible. In fact it may be interpreted as analytic. We may define conscious states as the states over which the agent has *some* control. But defence of this claim would require a more detailed analysis of what control by agents over their own attitudes means, and that is beyond the scope of this paper.

What I have tried to show is that some of Reid's arguments concerning the existence of will as a separate mental capacity are distinctively modern and worth considering. Of course the philosophical position Reid intends to defend is not new at all. It was the widely accepted view before the rise of the new science of motion. Reid's was a response to the challenge of those philosophers who thought the new science had consequences for our understanding of human action. He endeavoured to show that this new response, the elimination of volition, was, as an attempt to 'naturalize' the human

---

[14] 'When Mr Hume derives moral distinctions from a moral sense, I agree with him in words, but we differ about the meaning of the word *sense*. Every power to which the name of a sense has been given, is a power of judging of the objects of that sense, and has been accounted' such in all ages; the moral sense therefore is the power of judging in morals' (*AP* V vii, p. 468).

mind and action, a difficult position to accept. But he did not, and could not, *prove* that it was impossible. His arguments rest on the assumption that our common sense explanation of human behaviour, and some of our first-person reflective beliefs about how deliberations determine actions, provide us with reliable evidence about the nature of human action. His criticism of naturalism is, I believe, strong and effective. But it is strong and effective only so far as naturalists share his view about what counts as reliable evidence. The naturalists with whom he argued would probably not have denied the relevance of our common sense and our first-person reflective convictions. But for a naturalist who claims that all these seeming evidences are in fact the result of a giant cognitive illusion, and are not to be relied upon, Reid's arguments against the reductionist and eliminativist view of will and volition are obviously idle.

There is a last problem, however, which cannot pass unmentioned. Reid not only aims to save the faculty of the will from reductionist attempts, but also argues for a special model of causation. For him, as for Aristotle, 'efficient causes' are not events but substances. Humans are free *because* they are agents. Causation means control, and requires that agents themselves, and not things which happen to them, cause and thereby control their actions. To many ears this is a strange doctrine. Most, if not all, contemporary philosophers would be reluctant to endorse it. Although I count myself among the minority who do not find the idea of agent causation so obviously incomprehensible, I need not discuss the problem here. In reconstructing Reid's argument for the capacity of will and volition, I have tried to avoid making any reference to the doctrine of agent causation. If my reconstruction of his arguments is near to being correct, it shows that endorsement of this highly questionable doctrine is not a precondition for proper appreciation of the force of his arguments concerning the will and volition. Volition is a means to control; and a means requires a user, as control requires a controller. The only assumption which has to be accepted for Reid's argument to work, therefore, is that we are *agents*, in some sense. But his arguments about the unreducibility of will and volition apply without his view of the agent as a peculiar form of cause.[15]

Central European University, Budapest

---

[15] For an attempt to understand agency without agent causation, see D. Velleman, 'What Happens When Someone Acts?', *Mind*, 101 (1992), pp. 461–81.

I thank Howard P. Robinson, Thomas Pink, Tim Crane, Katalin Farkas and Loránd Ambrus-Lakatos for discussion and comments.

9

HOW TO REID MOORE

By John Greco

Moore's 'Proof of an External World' has evoked a variety of responses from philosophers, including bafflement, indignation and sympathetic reconstruction. I argue that Moore should be understood as following Thomas Reid on a variety of points, both epistemological and methodological. Moreover, Moore and Reid are exactly right on all of these points. Hence what I present is a defence of Moore's 'Proof', as well as an interpretation. Finally, I argue that the Reid–Moore position is useful for resolving an issue that has recently received attention in epistemology, namely, how is it that one knows that one is not a brain in a vat?

Some years ago, G.E. Moore held up one hand and then another, and claimed to have thereby proved that external things exist. Moore's subsequent paper, 'Proof of an External World', has since evoked a variety of responses from philosophers, including bafflement, indignation and sympathetic reconstruction.[1]

Philosophers have disagreed not only about the success of Moore's alleged proof, but also over what he was trying to do in the first place. For example, some have interpreted Moore as an ordinary-language philosopher. According to Norman Malcolm, 'The essence of Moore's technique of refuting philosophical statements consists in pointing out that these statements *go against ordinary language*'.[2] Alice Ambrose took a similar view:

> It is clear that Moore is in effect insisting on retaining conventions already established in the language about the usage of the words 'know' and 'believe', and that the consequence of what he says is the preservation of the linguistic *status quo*.[3]

As Barry Stroud points out, however, Moore effectively repudiates any such interpretation. In Moore's reply to Ambrose, he says flatly 'I could not have

[1] G.E. Moore, 'Proof of an External World', presented on 22 November 1939, and published in *Proceedings of the British Academy*, 25 (1939), pp. 273–300, repr. in Moore, *Philosophical Papers* (New York: Collier, 1962), pp. 126–48, to which page numbers below refer.
[2] N. Malcolm, 'Moore and Ordinary Language', in P.A. Schilpp (ed.), *The Philosophy of G.E. Moore* (La Salle: Open Court, 1942), pp. 343–68, at p. 349.
[3] A. Ambrose, 'Moore's "Proof of an External World"', in Schilpp, pp. 395–417, at p. 415.

supposed that the fact that I have a hand proved anything as to how the expression "external objects" *ought* to be used'.[4]

Stroud's interpretation of Moore's proof seems no more plausible, however. According to him, the question whether we know anything about the external world can be taken in an internal or an external sense. In the internal sense, the question can be answered from 'within' one's current knowledge; hence one can answer it by pointing out some things that one knows, such as that here is a hand. In the external sense, however, the question is put in a 'detached' and 'philosophical' way:

> If we have the feeling that Moore nevertheless fails to answer the philosophical question about our knowledge of external things, as we do, it is because we understand that question as requiring a certain withdrawal or detachment from the whole body of our knowledge of the world. We recognize that when I ask in that detached philosophical way whether I know that there are external things, I am not supposed to be allowed to appeal to other things I think I know about external things in order to help me settle the question.[5]

According to Stroud, Moore's proof is a perfectly good one in response to the internal question, but fails miserably in response to the external or 'philosophical' question. In fact, Stroud argues, Moore's failure to respond to the philosophical question is so obvious that it cries out for an explanation – hence Malcolm's and Ambrose's ordinary-language interpretations. Stroud (p. 119) offers a different explanation for Moore's failure to address the philosophical question: '[Moore] resists, or more probably does not even feel, the pressure towards the philosophical project as it is understood by the philosophers he discusses'. Or again (p. 125), 'we are left with the conclusion that Moore really did not understand the philosopher's assertions in any way other than the everyday "internal" way he seems to have understood them'. The problem with this interpretation, of course, is that it makes Moore out to be an idiot. Is it really possible that Moore, the great Cambridge philosopher, did not understand that other philosophers were raising a philosophical question?

I shall opt for a more straightforward and more generous interpretation of what Moore is doing in his 'Proof of an External World', one on which it does not matter that Moore fails to answer the sceptic's external question, or that he otherwise fails to answer the sceptic in a non-question-begging way. I shall argue that Moore is following Thomas Reid on a variety of points, both epistemological and methodological. Moreover, I shall argue that Moore and Reid are exactly right on all of these points. Hence I shall be

---

[4] Moore, 'A Reply to My Critics', in Schilpp, pp. 533–677, at p. 674.
[5] B. Stroud, *The Significance of Philosophical Scepticism* (Oxford: Clarendon Press, 1984), pp. 117–18.

offering not only an interpretation of Moore's paper, but a defence of it as well.

My evidence for the proposed interpretation is, first, that we know that Moore was familiar with and admired Reid.[6] Secondly, interpreting Moore as following Reid makes otherwise puzzling and dubious aspects of 'Proof of an External World' both clearly intelligible and eminently plausible. Finally, the proposed interpretation shows how Moore's 'Proof of an External World' is related to other works of Moore's, by showing how all of these fit into the context of a broader philosophical project. I shall argue for my substantive thesis, that the Reid–Moore position is correct, largely by letting Reid speak for himself. But I shall also add my own two cents' worth where appropriate, and at the end of the paper I shall show how the position neatly addresses an issue in epistemology that has received recent attention.

Here is the interpretation in a nutshell: in giving his proof, Moore knows full well that the sceptics will not be satisfied with it. Moore is not trying to give the sceptics something that they will be satisfied with. Moore's point, rather, is that we do not know that external things exist by proving this. On the contrary, we know that external things exist by perceiving them, and therefore sceptics are misguided in wanting a proof in the first place. When Moore gives his proof, therefore, his tongue is in his cheek. (There is a common sort of joke among analytic philosophers, and it is very British as well: that is, to give someone what they literally asked for, even though you know that it is not what they want.) It is not that Moore does not understand the sceptics' question, or that he does not understand what sceptics want when they request a proof that external things exist: he understands perfectly well what the sceptics are requesting, and he is challenging a variety of assumptions behind that request.

In the remainder of the paper I shall proceed as follows. In §I, I shall go over some salient aspects of Moore's 'Proof of an External World', including some remarks about what he intends to be proving, the proofs themselves, and some remarks which Moore makes in response to anticipated objections. In §II, I shall discuss some epistemological principles from Reid, and in §III, I shall discuss some methodological principles. In §IV, I shall look at some objections to what I have said so far. In §V, I shall apply the

6 See K. Lehrer, 'Reid's Influence on Contemporary American and British Philosophy', in S.F. Barker and T.L. Beauchamp (eds), *Thomas Reid: Critical Interpretations* (Temple UP, 1976), pp. 1–8; and J. Haldane, 'Thomas Reid: Life and Work', in *American Catholic Philosophical Quarterly*, 74 (2000), pp. 317–25. As Lehrer notes, one of Moore's early papers contains frequent references to Reid, 'The Nature and Reality of Objects of Perception', *Proceedings of the Aristotelian Society*, 6 (1905–6), pp. 68–127, repr. in Moore, *Philosophical Studies* (London: Routledge & Kegan Paul, 1922), pp. 31–96.

Reid–Moore position to the question, much discussed in recent epistemology, of how it is that one knows that one is not a brain in a vat.[7]

I. MOORE'S 'PROOF OF AN EXTERNAL WORLD'

Moore tells us that he is able to prove that external things exist, and that, in
fact, he can give us many such proofs. But what is meant by 'external
things'? By way of explanation, Moore tells us (p. 128) that 'external things'
means 'things external to our minds', as opposed to 'external to our bodies'.
Thus external things are 'things which are to be met with in space', our
bodies included (p. 129). Examples of such things would be 'the bodies of
men and of animals, plants, stars, houses, chairs, and shadows' (p. 136). If
you can prove that any two such things exist, Moore says, you will *ipso facto*
have proved that there are external things in the relevant sense.

Well, Moore thinks (p. 144), *that* is easy!

> I can prove now, for instance, that two human hands exist. How? By holding up my
> two hands, and saying, as I make a certain gesture with the right hand, 'Here is one
> hand', and adding, as I make a certain gesture with the left, 'and here is another'. And
> if, by doing this, I have proved *ipso facto* the existence of external things, you will all
> see that I can also do it now in numbers of other ways: there is no need to multiply
> examples.

Moore (p. 146) thinks he can also prove that external things have existed in
the past:

> Here is one proof. I can say: 'I held up two hands above this desk not very long ago;
> therefore two hands existed not very long ago; therefore at least two external objects
> have existed some time in the past, Q.E.D.'

I shall now look at some remarks that Moore makes by way of elaboration,
and by way of answering some anticipated objections to his proofs. All of
these remarks, I shall argue, tie into points that we can find in Reid.

First, Moore insists that the first proof he gave is a 'perfectly rigorous
one'. And indeed (p. 144), 'that it is perhaps impossible to give a better or
more rigorous proof of anything whatever'. One thing that a proof requires
is that one knows its premises. But he certainly did know that here is one
hand and here is another, Moore (p. 145) insists: 'How absurd it would be to
suggest that I did not know it.' He says similar things (p. 146) regarding his
second proof: 'This is a perfectly good proof, provided I *know* what is

---

[7] For example, see K. DeRose, 'How Can We Know that We're Not Brains in Vats?',
Southern Journal of Philosophy, 88 (2000), Supp. Vol., pp. 121–48; and S. Cohen, 'Basic
Knowledge and the Problem of Easy Knowledge', forthcoming in *Philosophy and Pheno-
menological Research*.

asserted in the premise. But I *do* know that I held up my two hands above this desk not very long ago. As a matter of fact, in this case you all know it too. There's no doubt whatever that I did.'

Next, Moore responds to philosophers who he 'is perfectly well aware' will not be satisfied with his proofs. One reason why some will not be satisfied, he says, is because they want Moore to prove his premises, i.e., they want a proof that 'Here's one hand and here's another'. Moore's reply to this sort of dissatisfaction is important for the proposed interpretation. First, he admits that he has not given any such proof. Secondly, he says that he does not think that any such proof can be given. Here (p. 148) are his reasons why such a proof is not possible:

> How am I to prove now that 'Here's one hand, and here's another'? I do not believe I can do it. In order to do it, I should need to prove for one thing, as Descartes pointed out, that I am not now dreaming. But how can I prove that I am not?

Moore's next comments are especially interesting:

> I have, no doubt, conclusive reasons for asserting that I am not now dreaming; I have conclusive evidence that I am awake: but that is a very different thing from being able to prove it. I could not tell you what all my evidence is; and I should require to do this at least, in order to give you a proof.

Finally, Moore considers one more source of dissatisfaction with his proofs: some will think that if he has not proved his premises, then he does not know them at all. This is a common view among philosophers, Moore thinks (p. 148), but one that is clearly wrong: 'I can know things, which I cannot prove; and among things which I certainly did know, even if (as I think) I could not prove them, were the premises of my two proofs'.

It seems to me that everything Moore says in these passages is exactly right. Moreover, we can see better that he is right by turning to various observations and arguments advanced by Thomas Reid.

II. EPISTEMOLOGICAL PRINCIPLES IN REID

I have elsewhere described Reid as defending a moderate and broad foundationalism.[8] His foundationalism is 'moderate', in the sense that he does not require infallibility for knowledge. Neither does he require in-defeasibility or unrevisability, or some other high-powered epistemic status. It is 'broad', in the sense that he allows a wide variety of sources of both foundational and non-foundational knowledge. For Reid, introspective

---

[8] See my 'Reid's Critique of Berkeley and Hume: What's the Big Idea?', *Philosophy and Phenomenological Research*, 55 (1995), pp. 279–96.

consciousness, perception, memory, testimony, deductive reasoning and inductive reasoning are all possible sources of knowledge. For present purposes, I can emphasize Reid's point that demonstrative reasoning (or proving) is only one source of knowledge among many. Here, then, is the first principle on which Moore follows Reid:

E1.   Not everything we know is known by proof.

Reasoning in general is defined by Reid as follows.[9]

> Reasoning is the process by which we pass from one judgement to another, which is the consequence of it.... In all reasoning, therefore, there must be a proposition inferred, and one or more from which it is inferred. And this power of inferring, or drawing a conclusion, is only another name for reasoning; the proposition inferred being called the *conclusion*, and the proposition or propositions from which it is inferred, the *premises* (*IP* VII i, p. 475a).

There are many kinds of reasoning, but the most important distinction, Reid thinks (p. 476b), is that between demonstrative and probable. A proof, then, would require demonstrative reasoning. But not everything that we know is known by proof, Reid insists. In fact, not everything we know is known by reasoning in general, nor could it be. Rather, reasoning in general 'is like a telescope, which may help a man to see farther, who hath eyes; but, without eyes, a telescope shews nothing at all'. In other words, reasoning in general, and demonstration in particular, need premises. Hence reasoning can extend knowledge, but we must admit other sources of knowledge as well.

The second epistemological principle on which Moore follows Reid is

E2.   External objects are known by perception, not by proof.

First, perception gives us knowledge of *external* objects, or objects that exist even when no one is perceiving them.

> Ideas are said to be things internal and present, which have no existence but during the moment they are in the mind. The objects of sense are things external, which have a continued existence (*IP* III vii, p. 358a).

Secondly, perception does not involve proving, nor any kind of reasoning at all.

> If, therefore, we attend to that act of our mind which we call the perception of an external object of sense, we shall find in it these three things: – *First*, Some conception or notion of the object perceived; *Secondly*, A strong and irresistible conviction and

---

[9] All references to Reid are to *An Inquiry into the Human Mind on the Principles of Common Sense* (*Inq*) and *Essays on the Intellectual Powers of Man* (*IP*), both in Reid, *Philosophical Works*, ed. H.M. Bracken (Hildesheim: Olms, 1983).

belief of its present existence; and, *Thirdly*, That this conviction and belief are immediate, and not the effect of reasoning (*IP* II v, p. 258a).

> ... it is not by a train of reasoning and argumentation that we come to be convinced of the existence of what we perceive; we ask no argument for the existence of the object, but that we perceive it; perception commands our belief upon its own authority, and disdains to rest its authority upon any reasoning whatsoever (p. 259b).

This is not to say that the perception of objects is never learnt or acquired. Most perception, Reid thinks, is acquired perception (*Inq* VI xx, p. 185a). But even acquired perception is devoid of reasoning.

> This power which we acquire of perceiving things by our senses, which originally we should not have perceived, is not the effect of any reasoning on our part: it is the result of our constitution, and of the situations in which we happen to be placed (*IP* II xxi, p. 332b).

Perception does not involve reasoning, because reasoning is grounded on prior beliefs acting as premises. But perception is grounded in sensory experience, which produces a belief in the external object either by nature or by acquired habit.

> When I grasp an ivory ball in my hand, I feel a certain sensation of touch. In the sensation there is nothing external, nothing corporeal. The sensation is neither round nor hard; it is an act of feeling of the mind, from which I cannot, by reasoning, infer the existence of any body. But, by the constitution of my nature, the sensation carries along with it the conception and belief of a round hard body really existing in my hand (*IP* VI v, p. 450a).

> In acquired perception, the sign may be either a sensation, or something originally perceived. The thing signified, is something which, by experience, has been found connected with that sign (*IP* II xxi, p. 332a).

Perceptual signs, Reid observes, become the grounds for belief without becoming objects of beliefs themselves. For example, sensations are able to act as signs for external objects, even though the sensations themselves are not noticed at all.

> There is, no doubt, a sensation by which we perceive a body to be hard or soft.... We are so accustomed to use the sensation as a sign, and to pass immediately to the hardness signified, that, as far as appears, it was never made an object of thought, either by the vulgar or by philosophers; nor has it a name in any language. There is no sensation more distinct, or more frequent; yet it is never attended to, but passes through the mind instantaneously, and serves only to introduce that quality in bodies, which, by a law of our constitution, it suggests (*Inq* V ii, p. 120a).

But if we do not even think about sensations in the typical case, then we do not typically have beliefs about them, and they do not act as premises in our reasoning. In other words, perception is not a kind of reasoning.

The third epistemological principle on which Moore follows Reid (see *IP* II xx, p. 328a) is

E3.   The evidence of sense is no less reasonable than that of demonstration.

In other words, the evidence of reasoning (or demonstration, or proof) should not be privileged over the evidence of perception.[10] Here (*Inq* VI xx, p. 183b) Reid finds the sceptic about perception to be inconsistent:

> Reason, says the sceptic, is the only judge of truth, and you ought to throw off every opinion and every belief that is not grounded on reason. Why, sir, should I believe the faculty of reason more than that of perception? – they came both out of the same shop, and were made by the same artist; and if he puts one piece of false ware into my hands, what should hinder him from putting another?

In fact, Reid observes, reason and perception are in the same boat with respect to their trustworthiness:

> The imagination, the memory, the judging and reasoning powers, are all liable to be hurt, or even destroyed, by disorders of the body, as well as our powers of perception; but we do not on this account call them fallacious (*IP* II xxii, p. 335a).

> They are all limited and imperfect.... We are liable to error and wrong judgement in the use of them all; but as little in the informations of sense as in the deductions of reasoning (*IP* II xxii, p. 339a).

Moore insists that he knows the premises of his proof, i.e., that here is one hand and here is another. He also (p. 145) claims to know this as well as anything: 'I certainly did at the moment *know* that which I expressed by the combination of certain gestures with saying the words "Here is one hand and here is another".... How absurd it would be to suggest that I did not know it, but only believed it, and that perhaps it was not the case!' Here Moore is simply following Reid's (E3) above: the evidence of perception is perfectly good evidence, and not less good than the evidence of, for example, mathematical demonstration. Hence Moore's reasoning from his perceptual knowledge is 'perfectly rigorous', and 'it is perhaps impossible to give a better or more rigorous proof of anything whatsoever' (p. 144).

The present interpretation also helps us to understand Moore's comments (p. 148) regarding dreaming:

> I have, no doubt, conclusive reasons for asserting that I am not now dreaming; I have conclusive evidence that I am awake: but that is a very different thing from being able to prove it. I could not tell you what all my evidence is; and I should require to do this at least, in order to give you a proof.

---

[10] Reid is not entirely consistent on this point. See *IP* II xx, p. 330a, where he says 'the evidence of reasoning, and that of some necessary and self-evident truths, seems to be the least mysterious, and the most perfectly comprehended'.

The passage may be read like this: 'I certainly know that I am not dreaming, because I can *see* that I am awake. My conclusive evidence for my belief that I am awake and not dreaming is my sensory experience. But I cannot give *you* that evidence – it is not propositional evidence, and so I cannot cite it as premises from which I can demonstrate that I am not dreaming, as I would have to do in order to prove it.'

Reid does not say exactly the same thing. In one place Reid claims to know that he is not dreaming, but confesses that he does not know how he knows (*Inq* II v, p. 107b). But the present position on how one knows that one is not dreaming, or how one knows that one is awake, is perfectly consistent with everything Reid does say.

In sum, Moore's remarks in 'Proof of an External World' are both intelligible and plausible in the light of Reid's three epistemological principles above. All of those principles are perfectly correct, in my view, and Moore's remarks follow from them straightforwardly. But Moore does not follow Reid only on epistemological points. He also follows him on some important methodological points as well.

III. METHODOLOGICAL PRINCIPLES IN REID

Reid's methodological principles concern how one should proceed in doing epistemology, and in particular, how one should proceed in addressing the sceptic. The first methodological principle I want to discuss is

M1. One should not try to prove what is not known by proof.

Reid gives us several reasons for adopting this principle. First, reason is most open to error when in this sort of employment: 'One is never in greater danger of transgressing against the rules of logic than in attempting to prove what needs no proof' (*IP* VII iv, p. 486a). In particular, he thinks, attempts by philosophers to prove the existence of external things have gone terribly wrong. 'Des Cartes, Malebranche, and Locke, have all employed their genius and skill to prove the existence of a material world; and with very bad success' (*Inq* I iii, p. 100b).

Secondly, when one sees the fallacy of such arguments, one is apt to doubt that which was to be proved (*IP* I ii, p. 231a):

> When men attempt to deduce such self-evident principles from others more evident, they always fall into inconclusive reasoning: and the consequence of this has been, that others, such as Berkeley and Hume, finding the arguments brought to prove such first principles to be weak and inconclusive, have been tempted first to doubt of them, and afterwards to deny them.

The last reason why we should not try to prove what is not known by proof is that people who deny first principles are not fit to be reasoned with, and therefore reasoning is no remedy for the problem. For example (*IP* I ii, p. 232b),

> ... by my senses, I perceive figure, colour, hardness, softness, motion, resistance, and such like things.... If any man should think fit to deny that these things are qualities, or that they require any subject, I leave him to enjoy his opinion as a man who denies first principles, and is not fit to be reasoned with.

One should not try to prove that which is not known by proof. But there are other strategies for responding to philosophers who deny first principles. First, such principles can be 'illustrated', or can 'be placed in a proper point of view' (*IP* I ii, p. 231b). Secondly, the denial of first principles is not only false, but absurd. And this allows another strategy for responding to their denial (*IP* VI iv, p. 438b):

> ... to discountenance absurdity, Nature hath given us a particular emotion – to wit, that of ridicule – which seems intended for this very purpose of putting out of countenance what is absurd, either in opinion or practice.
>
> This weapon, when properly applied, cuts with as keen an edge as argument. Nature hath furnished us with the first to expose absurdity; as with the last to refute error. Both are well fitted for their several offices, and are equally friendly to truth when properly used.

Moore employs both strategies. Hence he holds up his hands for all to see, placing two external objects 'in a proper point of view'. And he insists 'How absurd it would be to suggest that I did not know [that here is a hand], but only believed it, and that perhaps it was not the case!'. Moore goes on 'You might as well suggest that I do not know that I am now standing up and talking – that perhaps after all I'm not, and that it's not quite certain that I am!'. Of course the sceptic *would* insist on just that, and Moore very well knows it. He is ridiculing his sceptical opponents, as he was when he gave his proofs in the first place.

A second methodological principle that Moore adopts from Reid is this:

M2. Rather than trying to prove that external things exist, or that we know that external things exist, we should take a close look at the sceptic's reasons for saying that we do not know this.

Reid and Moore have each been understood as simply insisting that we know what the sceptic denies that we know. But neither do this. Rather, each is a brilliant critic of sceptical arguments. Thus Reid takes a careful look at numerous arguments from Berkeley, Hume and other sceptical philosophers, and offers sharp analyses of where they go wrong. Moore does a little of this at the end of 'Proof of an External World', but much more so in 'Four Forms of Scepticism'. In the latter paper he offers devastating criticisms of several sceptical arguments from Bertrand Russell, by first dis-ambiguating Russell's claims, and then showing how each of Russell's arguments rests on either (a) an assumption that is implausible, (b) an assumption that is clearly false, or (c) a fallacy in reasoning.[11]

Of course there is no guarantee that we shall always be able to identify a mistake in the sceptic's reasoning. We must analyse sceptical arguments one at a time, and there is no guarantee that the next one will not be better than the last. However, adopting Reid's methodology turns the tables on the sceptic in a way that is absolutely essential in mounting a successful response to scepticism. For the consequence of (M1) is that one gives up the imposs-ible task of proving what is not known by proof. The consequence of (M2) is that one replaces that task with something more promising. There is still no guarantee that one wins this game, but at least there is no guarantee that one loses it.

Finally, Reid thinks that success at this new game is more than just promising. For once the tables have been turned in this way, the sceptic incurs a heavy burden of proof. This is directly related to the third methodological principle on which Moore follows Reid:

M3. Common sense has defeasible authority over philosophical theory.

Common sense, according to Reid, is a gift of nature. It concerns that which we know immediately, by the natural operation of our cognitive powers, as opposed to that which is known only by special training or by reasoning. Hence the knowledge of common sense is found universally among healthy human beings, and occurs at an early age. In fact, Reid thinks, it is reflected in the structure of all human languages (*IP* VI v, p. 440b). For present pur-poses, it is important to note that Reid closely associates common sense with the knowledge of first principles.

> We ascribe to reason two offices, or two degrees. The first is to judge of things self-evident; the second to draw conclusions that are not self-evident from those that are. The first of these is the province, and the sole province, of common sense (*IP* VI ii, p. 425b).

> Such original and natural judgements are ... a part of our constitution; and all the discoveries of our reason are grounded upon them. They make up what is called *the common sense of mankind*; and, what is manifestly contrary to any of those first principles, is what we call *absurd* (*Inq* VII, p. 209b).

The first principles of common sense have a great authority. Specifically,

---

[11] Moore, 'Four Forms of Scepticism', in *Philosophical Papers*, pp. 193–222.

they have authority over speculation and theory, both in general and in philosophy in particular. This is partly because speculation and theory are unreliable, as is demonstrated by the history of science. '[Scientific] discoveries have always tended to refute, but not to confirm, the theories and hypotheses which ingenious men have invented' (*IP* I iii, p. 235b).

In philosophy too, however, we should be wary of conjectures that contradict common sense. For example, Reid finds that Berkeley's arguments against a material world rest on the dubious assumption that we can have no conception of anything unless there is some sensation in our minds that resembles it. Reid observes that this hypothesis has wide currency among philosophers, 'but it is neither self-evident, nor hath it been clearly proved; and therefore it hath been more reasonable to call in question this doctrine of philosophers, than to discard the material world' (*Inq* V viii, p. 132b). For this reason, he thinks, it is legitimate to argue against a philosophical theory by invoking common sense. In fact, in one place (*IP* II xiv, pp. 302b–3a), Reid uses arguments against Hume which are reminiscent of Moore's proofs. Here the target is Hume's thesis that the immediate object of thought is never an external object, but always some image or perception in the mind:

> ... I beg leave to dissent from philosophy till she gives me reason for what she teaches. For, though common sense and external senses demand my assent to their dictates upon their own authority, yet philosophy is not entitled to this privilege. But, that I may not dissent from so grave a personage [i.e., Hume] without giving a reason of my dissent: – I see the sun when he shines; I remember the battle of Culloden; and neither of these objects is an image or perception.

Reid does not think that common sense is infallible or that its first principles are indefeasible. On the contrary, it is possible to be mistaken regarding first principles.[12] The point is rather that one needs a *good reason* for rejecting common sense in favour of a philosophical position. Hence it is 'more reasonable' to question Berkeley's unsupported principle than to accept scepticism about the material world. Moore makes a similar point at the end of 'Four Forms of Scepticism' (p. 222):

> What I want, however, finally to emphasize is this: Russell's view that I do not know for certain that this is a pencil or that you are conscious rests, if I am right, on no less than four distinct assumptions.... And what I can't help asking myself is this: is it, in fact, as certain that all these four assumptions are true, as that I *do* know that this is a pencil and that you are conscious? I cannot help answering: it seems to me *more*

---

[12] Perhaps we should say more precisely that it is possible to be mistaken regarding what counts as a first principle. This is because, by definition, first principles are true. Nevertheless, Reid thinks we can err with regard to what really is a first principle and what is not. For example, see *IP* I ii, p. 231a.

certain that I *do* know that this is a pencil and that you are conscious, than that any single one of these four assumptions is true, let alone all four.

Common sense has defeasible authority over philosophical theory. To think the contrary is only philosophical arrogance, which is both misplaced and ill advised.

I return now to Stroud's interpretation of 'Proof of an External World'. According to Stroud, the question whether external things exist can be raised in an ordinary and 'internal' sense, or in a philosophical and 'external' sense. However, Stroud thinks, Moore 'resists, or probably does not even feel' the external sense that philosophers intend.

My interpretation allows the following reply on behalf of Moore. His paper is a response to Kant's and other philosophers' request for a proof that external things exist. If we take that request in an internal sense, in which we are allowed to proceed from things that we know, then Moore agrees with Stroud (a) that such a proof is easy, and (b) that it is of no consequence, i.e., of no importance philosophically. The reason why it is of no consequence, Moore thinks, is that we do not know external things by proving their existence, but by perceiving them. If we take the request for a proof in the external sense, in which we are required to prove the thing in question without relying on any knowledge of the external world, then again Moore agrees with Stroud (a) that such a proof is impossible. However, he insists (b) that this is still of no consequence. And the reason why is the same as before: we do not know external things by proving their existence, but by perceiving them. Failure to answer Stroud's external question amounts to this: that we cannot prove the existence of external things from a set of premises restricted in a certain way. But this is of no more consequence than that we cannot prove Euclid's theorems from a set of axioms restricted in a certain way. Nor can we know mathematical truths by perception, nor truths about the present by memory. Nothing follows from this except that these are not the ways in which we know such things.

IV. SOME OBJECTIONS

In this section I shall consider two objections to what I have said so far. The first is an objection to my claim that Moore is following Reid, the second to the position which I have attributed to both Reid and Moore.

One might object to my interpretation of Moore as follows: 'You claim that in his response to scepticism, Moore is following Reid. However, central to Reid's rejection of scepticism is his rejection of the theory of ideas. Reid thought, in fact, that the theory of ideas was sufficient to ground all of

Berkeley's and Hume's sceptical conclusions. But Moore accepts a sense-datum theory about the perception of external things, and the sense-datum theory is a version of the theory of ideas. Therefore Moore's response to scepticism cannot follow Reid.'

The problem with this objection is that it associates Moore's sense-datum theory of perception too closely with the theory of ideas which Reid rejects. When Reid talks about the theory of ideas, what he has in mind is a particularly strong version of representationalism. According to that theory, external objects are not perceived directly, but only indirectly by means of ideas in the mind that resemble them. This account of perception, Reid thinks, is sufficient to entail scepticism about external things.[13] It is not clear, however, that Moore's commitment to sense-data commits him to this kind of representationalism about external things. On the contrary, what Moore means by sense-data is 'whatever are the direct objects of perception', and he leaves it open whether such things are ideas or images in the mind, or the surfaces of external objects.[14] So even though Moore thinks that we do not perceive hands directly, he thinks we might perceive the surfaces of hands directly, and the surfaces of hands are external objects, on Moore's view.

But even if Moore's sense-datum theory did commit him to representationalism about external things, it would still not commit him to the theory of ideas in the sense which Reid thinks is sufficient for scepticism. For the theory of ideas constitutes a particularly strong version of representationalism – one where the representatives of external things must be resemblances, or images, or pictures of them. And it is this stronger commitment, Reid thinks, that is essential to Berkeley's and Hume's sceptical arguments.

> [Berkeley] concludes, that we can have no conception of an inanimate substance, such as matter is conceived to be, or of any of its qualities; and that there is the strongest ground to believe that there is no existence in nature but minds, sensations, and ideas.... But how does this follow? Why, thus: we can have no conception of anything but what resembles some sensation or idea in our minds; but the sensations and ideas in our minds can resemble nothing but the sensations and ideas in other minds; therefore, the conclusion is evident (*Inq* V viii, pp. 132a).

[13] I discuss relationships among the theory of ideas, representationalism and scepticism in 'Reid's Critique of Berkeley and Hume', and in *Putting Skeptics in their Place: the Nature of Skeptical Arguments and their Role in Philosophical Inquiry* (Cambridge UP, 2000), esp. ch. 4.

[14] See for example, Moore, 'A Defence of Common Sense', repr. in *Philosophical Papers*, pp. 32–59, esp. pp. 53–6; see also 'A Reply to my Critics', in Schilpp, esp. p. 643. As Lehrer notes, Moore's earlier work is unambiguous regarding the possibility of perceiving material objects directly. In a paper first published in 1903 Moore writes 'I am as directly aware of the existence of material things in space as of my own sensations, and what I am aware of with regard to each is exactly the same – namely, that in one case the material thing, and in the other case my sensation does really exist': 'The Refutation of Idealism', *Mind*, 12 (1903), pp. 433–53, repr. in his *Philosophical Studies*, quoted by Lehrer, 'Reid's Influence', p. 4.

This argument can be reconstructed as follows.

1. The only immediate objects of thought are ideas and sensations
2. All thought of other (mediate) objects must be by means of ideas or sensations which represent them
3. In the case of external objects, the ideas or sensations which mediate our thought must be images or resemblances of those objects
4. No idea or sensation resembles any external object
5. Therefore there is no thought or perception of external objects.

Since Moore is not committed to either premise (3) or premise (4) of the above argument, he can reject the argument as well as Reid can.

Reid thinks there is another route by which the theory of ideas leads to scepticism, however, and we should see how Moore can respond to this one.

> When it is maintained that all we immediately perceive is only ideas or phantasms, how can we, from the existence of those phantasms, conclude the existence of an external world corresponding to them?
>
> This difficult question seemed not to have occurred to the Peripatetics. Des Cartes saw the difficulty, and endeavoured to find out arguments by which, from the existence of our phantasms or ideas, we might infer the existence of external objects. The same course was followed by Malebranche, Arnauld, and Locke; but Berkeley and Hume easily refuted all their arguments, and demonstrated that there is no strength in them (*IP* III vii, p. 358a).

This second argument can be reconstructed as follows.

1. All knowledge is either non-inferential, or reached by means of an adequate inference from knowledge that is non-inferential
2. All non-inferential knowledge is about our ideas or sensations
3. Therefore if we are to have knowledge of external objects, it must be by means of an adequate inference from knowledge of our sensations
4. But there is no adequate inference from knowledge of our sensations to our beliefs about external objects
5. Therefore we can have no knowledge of external objects.

Again, if sense-data can be the external surfaces of external objects, then Moore need not be committed to premise (2). But even if sense-data are mental objects, Moore still does not have to accept premise (2). For the thesis that external objects must be represented by mental objects does not commit one to the thesis that external objects must be inferred from mental objects. In other words, representationalism does not commit one to an inferential theory of perception.[15]

---

[15] Moore is aware of the point. See Moore, *Some Main Problems of Philosophy* (London: George Allen & Unwin, 1953), p. 125.

It is true that Moore sometimes talks as if he thinks there is an inference from sense-data to the existence of external things. For example, in 'Four Forms of Scepticism' (p. 221), he says 'But I cannot help agreeing with Russell that I never know immediately such a thing as "That person is conscious" or "This is a pencil"'. But Moore speaks very carefully about this issue, and it is important to pay attention to his hedges and qualifications. For example, he agrees (p. 222) that *if* he does not know external things immediately, then his knowledge of them must be 'in some sense' based on an inductive argument. And he says of that conditional proposition that 'this must be true in some sense or other, though it seems to me terribly difficult to say exactly what that sense is'. Nothing here commits him to the position that perception involves 'reasoning' in the sense in which Reid understands this term. In other words, nothing here commits Moore to the thesis that perception involves a 'process by which we pass from one judgement to another, which is the consequence of it', or that it involves 'a proposition inferred, and one or more from which it is inferred'. On the contrary, it seems to me that what Moore says here and elsewhere is perfectly compatible with what Reid says in the following passage (*Inq* V v, p. 125a):

> Let a man press his hand against the table – *he feels it hard*. But what is the meaning of this? – The meaning undoubtedly is, that he hath a certain feeling of touch, from which he concludes, without any reasoning, or comparing ideas, that there is something external really existing, whose parts stick so firmly together, that they cannot be displaced without considerable force.
>
> There is here a feeling, and a conclusion drawn from it, or some way suggested by it.

In short, perception involves a movement in thought from sensation to object. But we need not conceive all movements in thought as involving an inference from one proposition to another, as in reasoning proper. Hence Reid says that the sensation 'suggests' an external object: 'I beg leave to make use of the word *suggestion*, because I know not one more proper, to express a power of the mind, which seems entirely to have escaped the notice of philosophers' (*Inq* II vii, p. 111a).

The next objection I shall consider regards the adequacy of the position which I am attributing to both Reid and Moore. Specifically, Reid and Moore agree that we know external things through perception rather than reasoning. In Reid's terminology, our knowledge that external things exist is a first principle, and therefore does not admit of proof.[16] The objection, in short, is that this position is dogmatic.

---

[16] More exactly, such things do not admit of direct proof. Reid thinks that first principles can sometimes be proved indirectly, by *reductio ad absurdum* (*IP* VI iv, p. 439b).

But what does it mean to say that a position is 'dogmatic', or that it is 'held dogmatically'? One thing this might mean is that the person who holds the position is not willing to consider arguments against it. However, we have seen that both Reid and Moore do consider sceptical arguments against their position: they consider sceptical arguments very carefully, and find them wanting. Another thing the charge could mean is that the position is held to be indefeasible: thus although one is willing to consider arguments against the position, one insists that no such argument could overturn it. However, we have seen that Reid thinks that his position is not indefeasible. Specifically, what one takes to be a first principle might turn out not to be, and philosophers must be open to this possibility.

> Upon the whole, I acknowledge that we ought to be cautious that we do not adopt opinions as first principles which are not entitled to that character.... We do not pretend that those things that are laid down as first principles may not be examined, and that we ought not to have our ears open to what may be pleaded against their being admitted as such (*IP* I ii, p. 234a).

I see nothing in Moore that contradicts this attitude in Reid.

Finally, the charge of dogmatism might mean that one is not willing to give reasons for one's view. But if this charge is directed against Moore's belief that here is a hand, then it begs the question against the Reid–Moore position, which is that some things can be known without being based on reasons. If the charge is directed against the Reid–Moore position itself, i.e., that some things can be known without reasons, then the charge is false. Reid gives many reasons for thinking that some things can be known without reasons, as does Moore.

V. THE PROBLEM OF EASY KNOWLEDGE

Suppose, with Reid and Moore, that I can know that here is a hand without first having to prove it. For example, to know that here is a hand, it is not necessary first to prove that my perceptual faculties are reliable. Any such position is potentially open to the following problem: it now seems too easy to know all sorts of things. For example, from my knowledge that here is a hand, I can easily infer that I am not a brain in a vat, and am not merely deceived into thinking that here is a hand. Likewise, I may easily infer that I am not a disembodied spirit, deceived by a Cartesian demon. The problem in such cases is that it seems wrong that I can come to know such things by such inferences. And this suggests either (a) that I did not know my premise in the first place, or (b) that I did know it, but that I also knew other things, such as that my perceptual faculties are reliable, and this additional knowledge is part of my grounds for the inferences I actually make.[17]

A somewhat similar problem arises for a variety of contextualist theories. As Keith DeRose notes, many contextualist positions entail the result that, at least by normal standards, one knows that one is not a brain in a vat without any evidence at all.[18] On DeRose's own view (p. 136), for example, we know because 'We're naturally disposed to reject such hypotheses as that we're brains in vats, and to thereby come to believe *and to know (with a high degree of warrant)* that these hypotheses are false, upon coming to consider them'. Some might think that this is a problematic position, and for a similar reason to that offered above. That is, just as it seems that I cannot know that I am not a brain in a vat by inferring it from 'Here is a hand', it seems that I cannot know such a thing on no evidence at all.

How does the Reid–Moore position defended above fare on this issue? Here I shall defend two claims.

First, it is consistent with that position that I know that I am not a brain in a vat, and that I know this neither by an easy inference nor by no evidence at all. How *does* one know that one is not a brain in a vat, or that one is not deceived by an evil demon? Moore and Reid are for the most part silent on this issue. But a natural extension of their view is that one knows it by perceiving it. In other words, I know that I am not a brain in a vat because I can see that I am not. Of course this position is a non-starter if one thinks that, on the basis of one's sensory experience, one must reason to the conclusion that one is not a brain in a vat in order to know it. But once we have given up the idea that perception is a kind of reasoning from experience, it becomes much more plausible that one could perceive such a thing. Just as I can perceive that some animal is not a dog, one might think, I can perceive that I am not a brain in a vat. Thus the Reid–Moore position can give a plausible account of our knowledge in some problematic cases. In particular, it allows us to say that certain cases of knowledge are neither known without evidence nor got by easy inference from other things that we know.

My second claim is that, once we give up the theoretical background which the Reid–Moore position effectively refutes, it is no longer a philosophically interesting question how we know such things; that is, it is no longer philosophically interesting whether we know them without evidence,

[17] The problem is framed in this way by Stewart Cohen, 'Basic Knowledge and the Problem of Easy Knowledge'.

[18] DeRose, 'How Can We Know that We're Not Brains in Vats?', p. 135. DeRose notes that the same result is defended in Gail Stine, 'Skepticism, Relevant Alternatives and Deductive Closure', *Philosophical Studies*, 29 (1976), p. 258; S. Cohen, 'How to be a Fallibilist', *Philosophical Perspectives*, 2 (1988), pp. 112–15; and D. Lewis, 'Elusive Knowledge', *Australasian Journal of Philosophy*, 74 (1996), pp. 561–2.

or by an easy inference, or by perception. Rather this becomes an empirical question about how our cognition actually works.

The theoretical background which the sceptic employs, and which Reid and Moore refute, is broadly rationalist. In particular, it involves the idea that all evidential relations must be logical or *quasi*-logical, in other words, that our evidence must have some necessary relation (either logical or probabilistic) to the beliefs that it makes evident. This background makes it plausible that our knowledge of external things, which has sensory experience as its evidence, must proceed by some sort of inference or reasoning from experience. The alternative to this broadly rationalist view must be broadly reliabilist. That is, if our evidence does not indicate the truth of our beliefs by virtue of some necessary relation, then it must do so by virtue of some contingent relation. And this, of course, is exactly what reliabilism says. In short, the rejection of rationalism about evidence leads naturally to reliabilism about evidence.

And now the point is this: once we are reliabilists about evidence, inference or reasoning is not so special any more. In fact, once we are reliabilists about evidence, *evidence* is not so special any more. What matters is that however we form our beliefs, they are formed in ways that are reliable. Some of these ways might involve reasoning from evidence, some might involve evidence without reasoning, and some might involve no evidence at all.[19]

We can see that this is exactly what happens in Reid's epistemology. According to Reid, some knowledge results from our reasoning faculties, and some from the faculties that give us first principles. Among knowledge of first principles, some is grounded in experience, and some is not grounded in experience. For example, Reid thinks that it is a first principle that like causes will have like effects, and that this is known neither by reasoning nor by experience (*IP* VI v, p. 451b). Similarly, he thinks that it is a first principle that our natural faculties are not fallacious, and that this too is known neither by reasoning nor by experience (pp. 447a–8a). Moreover, all such knowledge is equally good, being equally the product of our natural constitution: 'The first principles of every kind of reasoning are given us by Nature, and are of equal authority with the faculty of reason itself, which is also the gift of Nature' (*Inq* VI xx, p. 185b).

Sometimes it is difficult to distinguish first principles from products of reasoning:

> ... there are some propositions which lie so near to axioms, that it is difficult to say whether they ought to be held as axioms, or demonstrated as propositions. The same thing holds with regard to perception, and the conclusions drawn from it. Some of

---

[19] I defend the present line of argument in greater detail in my 'Agent Reliabilism', *Philosophical Perspectives*, 13 (1999), pp. 273–96, and in *Putting Skeptics in their Place*, esp. ch. 7.

these conclusions follow our perceptions so easily, and are so immediately connected with them, that it is difficult to fix the limit which divides the one from the other (*IP* VI xx, p. 185b).

Moreover, whether a given belief is the result of perception or easy inference becomes unimportant. This is because, whatever you call it, the thing is the result of our natural and non-fallacious cognitive faculties. And as such, it has positive epistemic status.

Similar things can be said regarding my belief that I am not a brain in a vat. Is such a belief 'hard-wired', so to speak, like the principle that like causes have like effects, or the principle that my natural faculties are not fallacious? Or do I perceive that I am not a brain in a vat, or do I infer it from what I perceive? I have suggested that I perceive it. It is certainly possible, however, that we do not perceive such things, but infer them from other things we do perceive. It is also possible that the belief, or something very much like it, is hard-wired. The point is that it really does not matter much from the present perspective. For if my belief arises in any of these ways, then it is the result of my natural, non-fallacious constitution, and therefore has its status as knowledge. The questions that remain are empirical questions, regarding how human beings are in fact built, and how our cognitive faculties in fact operate.[20]

Fordham University

[20] I would like to thank Ernest Sosa and an anonymous referee for their comments on an earlier version of this paper.

10

A DEFENCE OF SCOTTISH COMMON SENSE

By Michael Pakaluk

I provide a reading of Reid as an 'encyclopaedist', in Alasdair MacIntyre's sense, that is, as a scientist who conceives of himself as part of a broader scientific community, and who aims to make a contribution through work in a particular field. Reid's field is pneumatology. On this conception, Reid's recourse to 'common sense' is of a piece with the postulation, by any scientist, of a natural endowment for members of the same ostensible kind. Reid should therefore be understood as rejecting the classical tradition of epistemology and any conception of epistemology as first philosophy. His view resembles, rather, the modern position of 'natural epistemology', though admittedly, on account of his doctrine of active power, he is not committed to 'naturalism' in the contemporary sense.

Nicholas Wolterstorff holds that the notion of common sense (hereafter CS) is the deepest but also the most confusing element of Reid's philosophy. He maintains that Reid had no clear idea of what he meant by 'common sense', and in particular, that he put forward two different and apparently non-identical stipulations of it: (1) CS as consisting of self-evident principles that everyone believes; and (2) CS as consisting of basic presumptions that we must 'take for granted' in everyday life. Wolterstorff speculates that Reid probably intended (2), but that he was led to accept (1), on the false assumption that we could not take something for granted without believing it: but once these things are thought to be *believed*, then we must be concerned about their evidence, and, since this evidence is clearly not inferential in character, it must amount to 'self-evidence'.[1]

I maintain, on the contrary, that Reid had a very clear notion of what CS was. It was not a private notion; he shared this notion with other members of the 'common sense school', principally James Oswald and James Beattie. Together with the great majority of scientific thinkers in Enlightenment Scotland, these philosophers regarded the existence of CS as something almost pedestrian and undeniable. The common sense school understood itself not as discovering or articulating anything particularly new, but rather as simply restating the obvious – lost sight of for only a brief while, they

[1] N. Wolterstorff, *Thomas Reid and the Story of Epistemology* (Cambridge UP, 2001), p. 240.

thought, because of a momentary and eccentric eruption of scepticism, consequent upon some bad science served up by Descartes and Hume.[2] Furthermore, the notion of CS which they shared is captured well by neither of Wolterstorff's two characterizations, since it was, we may say, a 'scientific' rather than a 'philosophical' notion.

I suspect that this shared conception of CS avoids, or can respond to, all of the objections typically raised against it. However, it must do so in a 'deflationary' way. The cost of adherence to this conception of CS – a justifiable adherence, perhaps – would be abandonment, as misguided and pointless, of large parts of what is regarded as 'philosophy' today.[3] It is a consequence of the doctrine of CS that the scope of philosophy must be seriously restricted, if indeed there is anything at all left to philosophy after its development, or ramification, into particular fields of science. Indeed, we miss much of the force of Reid's claims about CS because the heirs of Reid's project today are to be found not in academic philosophy, but in the fields of anthropology, behavioural economics and human ecology.

To structure my discussion, I have collated the principal objections that may be brought against the notion of CS. I can identify six:

1. Talk of CS is too easy; it is a grand *petitio principii*, or perhaps we should say, a *petitio principii primi*. To assert that a claim should be believed because it belongs to CS has 'all the advantages of theft over honest toil', as Russell famously quipped.

2. To classify a principle as belonging to CS seems unreflective and uncritical in spirit, since when something is assigned to the 'human constitution', it apparently becomes removed from the realm of dispute and critical examination – as indeed happens to a principle of government when it is moved from a legislative to a constitutional basis. The commonsensical is therefore that which is uncritically accepted.

3. Talk of CS appears indeterminate, since there are no criteria for distinguishing it from what is simply acquired and deeply entrenched opinion.

---

[2] 'The old system [i.e., of Plato and Aristotle] admitted all the principles of common sense as first principles, without requiring any proof of them; and, therefore, though its reasoning was commonly vague, analogical, and dark, yet it was built upon a broad foundation, and had no tendency to scepticism': Reid, *An Inquiry into the Human Mind on the Principles of Common Sense* (hereafter *Inq*), ed. D.R. Brookes (Edinburgh UP, 1997), VII iii, p. 210.

[3] James Beattie is not being a religious polemicist when he remarks 'I know not but it may be urged as an objection to this doctrine, that, if we grant common sense to be the ultimate judge in all disputes, a great part of ancient and modern philosophy becomes useless. I admit the objection with all my heart, in all its force, and with all its consequences', *Essay on the Nature and Immutability of Truth* (Edinburgh: Kincaid & Bell, 1770), I ii 9, p. 143. His reasons for disregarding so large a portion of philosophy are, however, scientific, not religious or anti-intellectual: as I shall show, they do not differ significantly from Quine's. Beattie, in effect, wants to promote philosophy in the sense of 'science' and dismiss philosophy in any other sense.

4. An appeal to CS has no more weight than an appeal to an authority; and, in the end, it is an appeal to mob opinion.

5. Any appeal to CS, by the nature of the case, is redundant: either one's interlocutor shares CS, or not; if so, a mere statement of the relevant point should be sufficient, apart from any identification of that point as belonging to CS; if not, then no force can accrue to the point under dispute by the mere assertion that it belongs to CS.

6. The very idea of CS confusedly blends together the descriptive and the normative, the compulsory and the justified. In doing so, it raises 'the problem of the truth-value gap', as Keith Lehrer has called it: even if our nature *compels* us to believe in various things, what reason do we have for regarding what we thus believe as *true*?

I. REID'S PROJECT

I shall say here a few general things about the character of Reid's philosophical project, with the intention of evoking a kind of *gestalt* change, whereby we might perhaps come to see what Reid is up to in a new and slightly different light. I should say that I regard Reid's project as fundamentally the same as Beattie's and Oswald's, although this may be obscured by the fact that the latter two appeal to CS principally to defend what they regard as attacks upon morality and religion. This explains the unpleasant, polemical character of their writing, absent in Reid. Reid's immediate interests lie elsewhere; but the differences are merely superficial.

Reid is above all an 'encyclopaedist', in Alasdair MacIntyre's sense.[4] This is in fact typical of an educated Scotsman in his day. He regards scientific knowledge as a coherent body of truths about the world, continually being added to and improved upon; the arts are similarly constantly being improved. Reid regards himself as playing a role within this project, as a member of a community of scientific enquirers. Within this outlook and approach, Reid's particular contribution is to the discipline of 'pneumatology', the study of spiritual or thinking creation, as opposed to material creation. The division is of course Cartesian in its immediate origin, but Reid would have regarded its ultimate provenance as ancient:

> As, therefore, all our knowledge is confined to body and mind, or things belonging to them, there are two great branches of philosophy, one relating to body, the other to mind. The properties of body, and the laws that obtain in the material system, are the objects of natural philosophy, as that word is now used. The branch which treats

[4] A. MacIntyre, *Three Rival Versions of Moral Enquiry*, Gifford Lectures 1988 (Univ. of Notre Dame Press, 1990), pp. 14–24.

of the nature and operations of minds has, by some, been called Pneumatology. And to the one or the other of these branches, the principles of all sciences belong.[5]

However, although Reid accepts Newtonian principles of induction for pneumatology (*Inq* I i, p. 12), he does not make the crude mistake of thinking that the characteristics of spiritual beings must be understood on the model of material beings (as La Mettrie may be understood as holding in *L'homme machine*, and as Hume maintains frequently, e.g., in his dissertation 'Of the Passions'), because Reid regards only minds as having active power.

Two important consequences of Reid's 'encyclopaedism' are that, first, he regards himself as free to use, in his enquiries, the results of other particular sciences, as in fact any scientist does; and, secondly, he views it as a constraint on his theorizing that what he says, in articulating a theory, must be consistent with other scientific results, and in particular, that it cannot undermine any received results, or imply the impossibility or misguidedness of these results:

> ... it was taken to be the outcome of the successful application of methods to facts that there is a continuous progress in supplying ever more adequate unifying conceptions which specify ever more fundamental laws. So it is characteristic of genuine science, as contrasted with the thought of the prescientific and the non-scientific, that it has a particular kind of history, one of relatively continuous progress (MacIntyre, p. 20).

All that I have said so far may be expressed by saying that Reid regards 'pneumatology' as something to be carried out from a suitably informed 'third-person point of view', not from a 'first-person point of view'. Reid, like a practitioner of 'natural epistemology' of today, regards the enquiry into how human beings acquire knowledge, and thus how they practice science, as itself a branch of science – though on account of his views on active power, he is a natural epistemologist without the naturalism. We might also put the point in this way: Reid's conversion away from Berkeleianism involved not merely a change in doctrine ('There are material things now, in addition to ideas'), but also a change in method and goals. His break from Berkeley did not involve merely admitting the existence of a greater number or variety of objects, but also adopting new standards for correct results: the results of (what we would call) epistemology must cohere in the right sort of way with the results and reliability of other branches of science. It is correct, then, to construe Reid's conversion away from Berkeleianism as a rejection of First Philosophy.

---

[5] Reid, *Essays on the Intellectual Powers of Man* (henceforth *IP*), ed. Baruch A. Brody (MIT Press, 1969), Preface, pp. xxxiv–xxxv. Although he uses the term 'pneumatology' sparingly in his published writings, it is clear from the manuscripts in the Reid Archives that he viewed his work as a contribution to this discipline.

II. NATURAL SCIENCE AS IDENTIFYING THE
NATURES OF THINGS

We know that Reid regarded scientific explanation as well captured by Newton's nomological approach, according to which a phenomenon is explained by subsuming it under a law; and a law is explained by subsuming it under a higher law; and so on, until one reaches what is apparently a highest law in some domain. Reid many times insists that a law of this sort is to be accounted for simply by 'resolving it into the will of the Maker'. That is to say: we do not know what the reason is for this law, but there is indeed a reason, in God's mind.

This strategy of explanation is not unlike what Richard Swinburne has called 'personal' as opposed to 'physical' explanation.[6] Swinburne insists that 'personal' explanations differ in kind from 'scientific' explanations, because the former appeal to intentions and beliefs, the latter to 'liabilities and powers', yet statements regarding intentions and beliefs cannot be analysed in terms of those regarding liabilities and powers. But here is a significant difference from Reid, who thinks that, ultimately, non-persons have only liabilities, or 'passive powers', not active powers; yet scientific explanation, in so far as it must appeal to laws, relies upon notions of agency that are properly applied only to persons. Thus whereas Swinburne takes 'personal' and 'scientific' explanations to be distinct but co-ordinate, Reid regards scientific explanations, if properly understood, as parasitic upon personal explanations. The appeal to God's will here is not feckless or a superstitious genuflection to religion; rather it is the claim that some explanation belonging to a general type is true, even if it remains unknown *which* particular explanation of that type is true.

This, so far, is standard Newtonianism, which Reid shares with Hume, apart from the appeal to God. Reid appeals to God where Hume does not, not because Reid is a specifically 'religious' thinker, but rather because he regards the existence of God as a reasonable postulate given the evidence, not unlike Cleanthes in Hume's *Dialogues*. Reid uses this appeal in a specific way. It seems clear that one kind of lawfulness he allows is the recurrence of exactly similar sets of powers or properties in things that are initially identified by phenomenal characteristics: that is, things have 'natures' which they share with other things of the same kind. We may therefore say that a 'nature' is akin to a highest law of explanation; and to say that a power or property belongs to the nature of a thing is simply to say that explanation,

---

[6] R. Swinburne, *The Existence of God* (Oxford UP, 1979), pp. 25–50.

for scientific purposes, must stop here, with the mere identification of something as belonging to a thing's nature. That is, the postulation of a nature and the identification of a highest law in a domain are exactly on a par. We may thus construe Reid's talk of 'natures' as a transposition into Aristotelian language of his Newtonianism.

Reid regards things' having natures as typically falling into patterns which evince 'intelligence or design' and which therefore license speculation about what the 'intention of nature' was in introducing them. This means, of course, giving an account of a nature that exhibits design, by showing how its having such a nature works out for the good of the things that have that nature, or of systems to which things of that nature belong. (This view of a 'nature' underwrites Reid's talk of the 'constitution' of things, since the term 'constitution' connotes both that of which something essentially consists, and also the harmonious structure and mutual adaptation of the fundamental parts of a thing.) That is, Reid makes use of 'final causes'. He is aware of this, aware that he departs in this respect from the strictures of Bacon's *Novum Organum*; yet he is insistent that good science requires it. And in this respect Reid took himself simply to be following what he reasonably regarded as good and well established scientific practice: form does follow function; and living things do behave in a goal-directed manner.

The nature of a thing may be viewed as its *endowment*: it constrains how that thing may be acted upon or changed, and, for things with active power, how such things are able and disposed to act. The basic properties of chemical substances, for instance, would be their nature or endowment; the use of such things in chemical reactions would be something superadded by nature or human invention. On this way of looking at things, it is trivial that human beings have a natural endowment: how could they be a distinct kind of thing, as they are, without their having a definite nature, the 'human constitution'? In fact, the scientific (or 'philosophical') study of human beings, as indeed with any science, must begin with the assumption that there is a definite sort of thing, the properties of which (its 'powers' or 'faculties') must be discovered. But there must be some natural endowment relative to every natural activity of a thing. If, therefore, one of the things which human beings do is discover the truth – and the success of science ('philosophy') in accordance with the encyclopaedist project shows clearly that science is something we engage in and succeed at – then some part at least of that with which human beings are endowed by nature must move or direct them towards the discovery of the truth, and these are the first principles of the human mind.

It is in this light that we should understand the ferocity of the Scottish common sense school's attack on Locke's image of a *tabula rasa*. A human being could not be originally indefinite, any more than anything else in nature. Beattie scolds Locke on this point:

> It is a favourite maxim with Mr LOCKE, as it was with some ancient philosophers, that the human soul, previous to education, is like a piece of white paper, or *tabula rasa*; and this simile, harmless as it may appear, betrays our great modern into several important mistakes. It is indeed one of the most unlucky allusions that could have been chosen. The human soul, when it begins to think, is not extended, nor inert, nor of a white colour, nor incapable of energy, nor wholly unfurnished with ideas, (for if it think at all, it must have some ideas, according to Mr LOCKE's definition[7] of the word) nor as susceptible of any one impression or character as of any other. In what respect then does the human soul resemble a piece of white paper? To this philosophical conundrum I confess I can give no serious answer.[8]

Beattie (pp. 140–2) has a neat argument that there must be shared principles constituting the nature of the human mind and inclining it towards truth. There is a determinate way in which the world is arranged (to admit this is simply to admit the 'distinction between truth and falsehood'); human beings succeed in coming to know how the world is; all reasoning, by the nature of the case, is from first principles; if these were not true, we could not succeed in coming to know how the world is; therefore the first principles of human reasoning are true.

Beattie (p. 140) initiates this argument dialectically with the consideration 'If there be any creatures in human shape, who deny the distinction between truth and falsehood, or who are unconscious of that distinction, they are far beyond the reach of philosophy, and therefore have no concern in this inquiry'. 'Philosophy' here again means science: such persons as deny the distinction remove themselves from the project of science. Only a creature that was human in shape alone could adopt this position, or so Beattie thinks, consistently with his view that the pursuit of scientific truth in accordance with the encyclopaedist conception is simply an expression of human nature. Hence that human nature is such that it enables human beings to arrive at science must itself be a conclusion of science.[9]

I have claimed that a 'nature' may be seen as a 'highest law' that governs the uniform behaviour of things falling in a kind. As such, a nature functions as a kind of first cause in a series of causes: we trace the activity of a thing

---

[7] Here Beattie is quoting Locke: 'The word *idea* serves best to stand for whatsoever is the object of the understanding when a man thinks. – I have used it to express whatever it is which the mind can be employed about in thinking' (*Essay*, Introduction, §8).

[8] Beattie, *Essay on the Nature and Immutability of Truth*, I ii 9, pp. 152–3.

[9] This is Beattie's analogue to what Quine would call the containment of epistemology within psychology: 'Epistemology in its new setting ... is contained in natural science, as a chapter of psychology': W.V.O. Quine, 'Epistemology Naturalized', in *Ontological Relativity and Other Essays* (Columbia UP, 1969), pp. 69–90, at p. 83. See also fn. 17 below.

back to elements of its nature, at which point, except for teleological elucidations of its function, we can say little more than that God has constituted that thing in that way. An element or part of the nature of a thing, and even the nature itself, is referred to by Reid as a 'principle' of a thing of that kind. So, for instance, if being attracted to other matter in accordance with Newton's law of general gravitation is part of the nature of matter, then it is a 'principle' of matter that it must be so attracted. Here Reid is simply following traditional usage: the Latin *principium* is the equivalent of the Greek *arche*, which was in fact the original word used in the early development of science among the pre-Socratics for denoting a basic cause of a thing.

But this usage of 'principle' makes possible an ambiguity when Reid talks about human nature, and Reid regarded himself as justified in exploiting both senses of the term. Along with Beattie, he regards human nature as consisting of basic determinations of thought and action, which enable human beings to arrive successfully at scientific truth. These basic determinations may be arrived at from observing how human beings act, and by attending to the reasons they give in theorizing. We presume the existence of such causes, and hypothesize about what should be included within that class, as we do with respect to the endowment of any kind of thing whatsoever. Therefore these basic determinations may appropriately be called 'principles', in the sense of basic causes. Yet additionally, these determinations, given that they admit of explicit formulation, may be grasped and deliberately accepted by us – 'deliberately', not in the sense that we deduce them or reason to them, but rather in the sense that we can become convinced, for our own part, by reflecting on the requirements of science, and applying marks of something's belonging to the human constitution, that they are part of the nature of a human being that enables us to arrive at truth successfully. Thus the principles may serve as 'principles' in the sense of axioms for the (immanent) activity of thought and the (transitive) activity of human action.

There are many passages in which Reid employs both senses of the word 'principle' – 'principle' as *cause* and 'principle' as *reason* – and moves freely back and forth between them. For instance, in his discussion of 'First Principles of Contingent Truths' in *IP* VI v, p. 632, Reid remarks

> We may here take notice of a property of the principle under consideration, that seems to be common to it with many other first principles, and which can hardly be found in any principle that is built solely upon reasoning; and that is, that in most men it produces its effect without ever being attended to, or made an object of thought. No man ever thinks of this principle, unless when he considers the grounds of scepticism; yet it invariably governs his opinions.

The principle Reid is talking about is 'that the natural faculties, by which we distinguish truth from error, are not fallacious'. Yet he speaks of it as a cause: 'it produces its effect without ever being attended to', and as a reason, 'No man ever thinks of this principle, unless when he considers the grounds of scepticism'. This way of speaking is intelligible on the broadly behaviouristic assumptions that to every action that displays intelligence there may be assigned a belief, which is a partial cause of that action; that every belief as regards action of a certain sort will in fact have effects discernible in action of that sort; that we may have beliefs of which we are unaware; and that reliance upon, or trust in, one's 'natural faculties' displays intelligence.

In holding that 'the natural faculties, by which we distinguish truth from error, are not fallacious', Reid rejects the high tradition of epistemology beginning with Descartes, which aims to determine, all at once instead of piecemeal, the reliability and proper limits of operation of the 'human understanding'.[10] Reid (*IP* VI v, p. 631) recognizes this implication: 'Des Cartes certainly made a false step in this matter', he observes, and after summarizing the difficulty of the Cartesian circle, notes that 'the reason why Des Cartes satisfied himself with so weak an argument for the truth of his faculties, most probably was, that he never seriously doubted of it'. Since Reid holds that the principle of trust in one's natural faculties is a part of the human constitution, he must believe that everyone always in fact believes it, and that no serious investigation into how people actually reason can begin by calling this into question.

In the Introduction to his *Treatise*, Hume avows that 'the science of man is the only solid foundation for the other sciences', and that ' ... all the sciences have a relation, greater or less, to human nature'. He wonders 'what changes and improvements we might make in these sciences were we thoroughly acquainted with the extent and force of human understanding, and cou'd explain the nature of the ideas we employ, and of the operations we perform in our reasonings'.[11] From the point of view of the CS school, this sort of speculation is deeply confused. The only dependence one sees among sciences is causal dependence, and the objects studied in the various sciences do not depend causally on human nature; furthermore, precisely because the human endowment is fixed and everywhere operative, we should expect no general changes or improvements in scientific theorizing generally, from a better specification of this endowment.

---

[10] Hume expresses in his first *Enquiry* his belief that 'The only method of freeing learning, at once, from these abstruse questions, is to enquire seriously into the nature of human understanding, and show, from an exact analysis of its powers and capacity, that it is by no means fitted for such remote and abstruse subjects. We must submit to this fatigue, in order to live at ease ever after', §1 para 12.

[11] Hume, *A Treatise of Human Nature* (Oxford: Clarendon Press, 1978), Intro., pp. xv–xvi.

III. WHAT IS THE 'IDEAL SYSTEM'?

We can understand a philosopher's position better by understanding better what view he takes it to work against. Of course Reid is the great critic of Hume, but perhaps Hume is too close to Reid to provide us with the best contrast with Reid. It is more useful to look first to Descartes, whom Reid regarded, famously, as initiating a misguided tradition that finds its culmination in Hume. For my present purposes, I wish simply to call attention to an oddity in Reid's interpretation of Descartes, which tells us something significant about him.

We tend to read Descartes as a 'foundationalist', and indeed as the first modern philosopher to engage seriously in philosophical epistemology. As I have remarked, Reid's understanding of CS is such that he must reject this kind of investigation as feckless. Thus if Reid is to give Descartes any weight at all, he must understand him to be engaged in some other kind of project. Thus it happens that through an application of the principle of charity in interpretation, Reid interprets, or rather misinterprets, Descartes as a natural scientist, engaged in roughly the same project as himself, and in particular as a psychologist, who aims to uncover the laws and principles governing the operation of the human mind.[12] Descartes aimed to contribute to 'our philosophy concerning the mind and its faculties', that is, he aimed to 'consider the phaenomena of human thoughts, opinions, and perceptions, and ... trace them to the general laws and the first principles of our constitution'; but because he found 'nothing established in this part of philosophy', his enquiry almost immediately went astray (*Inq* I iii, p. 16).

In order to explain how it is that Reid understands Descartes, I shall introduce the notion of 'rehearsing an argument'. To rehearse an argument is not to think it through for oneself so much as to see whether it describes a possible path of reasoning for someone who is described as having abilities of a certain sort. To think about an argument in this way is therefore to adopt, in a limited respect at least, a third-person as opposed to a first-person point of view as regards that argument.

Suppose we understand reason simply to be one among many elements or parts of human nature. Reason has its own powers, abilities and characteristic operations, which we may stipulate with greater or lesser precision. Yet we hold that there are other elements of human nature,

---

[12] We might say that Wolterstorff's misunderstanding (p. 183) of CS derives from his taking Reid's target to be a variety of foundationalism. But Reid rather regards Cartesian doubt as simply an exaggerated response to the disarray in the scientific study of the human mind.

which may similarly be specified. We take for granted, as was said, that human beings arrive at truths about the world, and we are concerned with a matter of causation and fact: how precisely do they arrive at truth? We do not presume in advance that one element in human nature alone is responsible for human beings arriving at truth. Suppose for instance that human beings typically succeed in coming to know p. Suppose we wish to investigate whether belief in p can be attributed to that element of human nature which we have identified as 'reason' – whether reason alone can suffice to explain it. If there is some specification of the faculty of reason, and some valid argument relative to that specification, according to which it follows that p, then we may rightly attribute belief in p to reason. (Presumably the axioms and rules of inference we allow to reason must be ones that are plausible upon reflection.) If such an argument is or appears impossible, then either we must expand the powers we ascribe to reason – by adding premises and principles of inference, say – or we are constrained to attribute the belief that p to some power of human nature other than reason, or to some power working in conjunction with reason.

This testing of arguments to see whether, on a certain model of reasoning, one may arrive at p, may be called 'rehearsing' those arguments. For instance, Reid reasons in *Inquiry* that sensations of touch are so far different from tangible magnitude that no line of reasoning, on any plausible model of reason, suffices to take us from one to the other; therefore judgements regarding tangible magnitude must be explained in terms of some other power (sense-perception, Reid says). In general, we may understand Reid's theory of *perception* to be simply the view that the sense faculties are elements of the human constitution which are responsible for our arriving at some classes of truths. His theory of perception is important not so much because it aims to show that reason plays a vital role even in supposedly brute sensation (somewhat as in Kant's maxim 'intuition is blind without understanding'), but rather because it is an important first admission that some faculty other than reason can be the direct means by which human beings attain to truth.

We may now characterize Reid's misinterpretation of Descartes as follows: Reid thinks that Descartes' *cogito* should be understood as Descartes' rehearsal of arguments that begin from the following meagre materials: (i) the observation that one is thinking; (ii) the principle that 'whatever is given to consciousness is true'. Descartes, however, applied his model poorly, and in particular he committed the fallacy of circular reasoning, which is not, on any account, a proper functioning of reason. As a consequence, he failed to see that his initial model was impoverished, and that it needed to be supplemented with a richer natural endowment: he needed to supply it with more first principles. Thus, according to Reid, Descartes is twice guilty: guilty of circular reasoning, and guilty of bad science – bad pneumatology – since Descartes' mistakes in reasoning hindered him from seeing how he had misconstrued the way in which the mind operates. It is this second censure that makes Reid's interpretation of Descartes so odd.

Descartes 'resolved not to believe his own existence', yet it is clear, from how he acted and what he said, that he never succeeded in doubting this. So there is a question of fact: what caused him, after his resolve, to believe his own existence? If we rehearse his arguments, we see that those arguments could not have been the cause, as Descartes misguidedly thought. Now we might presume that some *other* argument, more rigorous but not yet discovered, was in fact the cause; but Malebranche, Locke and others have shown that this kind of explanation is fruitless: ' ... however lame and imperfect the system may be, they have opened the way to future discoveries, and are justly entitled to a great share in the merit of them' (*Inq* I iv, p. 18). They have shown that kind of explanation to be fruitless, not as a logician shows a result to be impossible, but in the way in which it may become clear that scientists working on a particular theory have played out all of the resources of that theory: through their efforts, that line of enquiry or research now appears pointless.

Reid interprets Hume similarly, and with better reason, since Hume of course regarded himself as a pioneer in the scientific study of the mind. This interpretation is evident in one of Reid's most basic criticisms of Hume. Hume notoriously wished to argue that our inability to derive some idea from impressions could serve to indicate that there was no such idea: 'When we entertain, therefore, any suspicion, that a philosophical term is employed without any meaning or idea (as is too frequent), we need but enquire, from what impression is that supposed idea derived? And if it be impossible to assign any, this will serve to confirm our suspicion' (First *Enquiry*, §I para. 9). But Reid regarded this as bad science: we have such ideas, as we can see, not simply from introspection but also from 'the structure of all languages' (which is the force or role of this appeal), and from the fact that our assertions involving that idea are predictable and have structure.[13] A good pneumatologist ought to conclude, therefore, from rehearsing Hume's arguments, that Hume's model of the natural endowment of the human mind is false.

---

[13] The criterion is ultimately behavioural in a broad sense: 'If power were a thing of which we have no idea, as some philosophers have taken much pains to prove – that is, if power were a word without any meaning – we could neither affirm nor deny anything concerning it with understanding. We should have equal reason to say that it is a substance, as that it is a quality; that it does not admit of degrees as that it does': Reid, *Essays on the Active Powers* (*AP*), I i.

What I have called a 'model', Reid calls a 'system'. It is essential to the understanding of Reid to see that by a 'system' he means not a philosophical or epistemological *account*, which is supposed to be convincing because of its conceptual plausibility, but rather a proposed *theory* of the operation of the human mind, of the sort that should be devised within pneumatology. The term is introduced early on in *Inquiry* (I ii), where Reid distinguishes between an *analysis* and a *system* of the human mind:

> It must therefore require great caution, and great application of mind, for a man that is grown up in all the prejudices of education, fashion, and philosophy, to unravel his notions and opinions, till he find out the simple and original principles of his constitution, of which no account can be given but the will of our Maker. This may be truly called an *analysis* of the human faculties; and, till this is performed, it is in vain we expect any just *system* of the mind – that is, an enumeration of the original powers and laws of our constitution, and an explication from them of the various phaenomena of human nature.

Analysis must always precede and govern the construction of a system: analysis is the tracing back of all of the phenomena of the mind, dispassionately and accurately, until one arrives at 'simple and original' principles sufficient to explain them. A system is a model of the human mind, used to predict the nature and limits of the mind's activity. Reid's criticism of Hume, in brief, is that Hume constructs a system without having first carried out an adequate analysis. Hume therefore relies on his model to dismiss evidence, rather than finding in recalcitrant data the need to revise his model.

The 'ideal system' is simply a model of the human mind (or, rather, a family of such models), which postulates a certain sort of theoretical entity playing a certain role – ideas – in order to account for the mind and its operations. A system of the human mind will be conducive to scepticism if it predicts or implies results about human thought or action so different from what is evidently the case that, to the extent that one accepts that system, one feels put upon by one's original observations.[14] The 'ideal system' is of this sort, hence Reid calls it also the 'sceptical system'.[15] It is a consequence of Reid's understanding of Hume, then, that he interprets Hume's scepticism in a very different way from Hume himself. Hume regarded his scepticism as a philosophical attitude, and compared himself to philosophers

[14] ' ... I find I have been only in an enchanted castle, imposed upon by spectres and apparitions. I blush inwardly to think how I have been deluded', Reid remarks, characterizing what he takes to be a natural reaction to Hume's views, at *Inq* I vi, p. 22.

[15] 'These facts, which are undeniable, do, indeed, give reason to apprehend, that Des Cartes' system of the human understanding, which I shall beg leave to call *the ideal system*, and which, with some improvements made by later writers, is now generally received, hath some original defect; that this scepticism is inlaid in it, and reared along with it' (*Inq* I vii, p. 23).

in the Academic and Pyrrhonian movements. Reid understands it in a deflationary way, as fundamentally a condition in which we have been led to reject the proper starting points of scientific investigation, on account of bad science. It is not a scientific theory, but an overturning of science, or rather, what amounts to the same thing, a separation of oneself from the project of science. In this respect Reid's criticism of Hume is like Aristotle's of Parmenides. The thesis 'Nothing is in motion' is not a claim within physics, but a position implying the abolition of physics. It is 'philosophical' in a feckless and irresponsible sense.

But perhaps Reid's sharpest complaint against Hume is not, *pace* Kemp Smith, that Hume's philosophy leads to a general suspension of judgement, and thus to either 'idealism' or 'universal scepticism', but rather that Hume's conclusions are so much at odds with what people otherwise, and responsibly, accept, that they are likely to discredit the proper study of human nature. Reid's indignation is of the sort that is characteristic of a professional and working scientist. It is not unlike that which might be adopted by an astronomer towards a proposed theory, putatively an astronomical theory, which implied that we are all deceived and mistaken in believing that the stars appear to rotate around the Pole Star: if this theory were widely accepted, or even if people simply came to believe that astronomers seriously entertained theories of this sort, it would bring derision upon astronomy.

> The mind of man is the noblest work of God which reason discovers to us, and, therefore, on account of its dignity, deserves our study. It must, indeed, be acknowledged, that, although it is of all objects the nearest to us, and seems the most within our reach, it is very difficult to attend to its operations so as to form a distinct notion of them; and on that account there is no branch of knowledge in which the ingenious and speculative have fallen into so great errors, and even absurdities. These errors and absurdities have given rise to a general prejudice against all inquiries of this nature.[16]

Even though the 'ideal system' thus threatened to call pneumatology into disrepute, Reid genuinely admired Hume's contribution, as we have seen, because he regarded it as closing off a fruitless area of investigation and making the alternative seem unavoidable. Not all of the common sense school had so sanguine an outlook. Perhaps again because he was more concerned with accounting for human ethical action and religious belief, Beattie, in contrast, disdained Hume's contribution. Referring to the 'useless and mischievous' controversies stirred up by followers of the way of ideas,

[16] *IP* Preface, pp. xxxv–xxxvi. Of course anyone who shared this view might quite reasonably oppose Hume's appointment to a chair in pneumatology.

Beattie writes 'But it is said, that they improve their understanding, and render it more capable of discovering truth, and detecting error. – Be it so: – but though bars and locks render our houses secure, and though acuteness of hearing and feeling be a valuable endowment, it will not follow, that thieves are a public blessing; or that a man is entitled to my gratitude, who quickens my touch and hearing, by putting out my eyes' (*Truth* II 9, p. 146).

I have called Reid a 'scientist', and of course he called himself a 'philosopher'. Yet he uses the term 'philosophy' to mean not merely 'science', but also in another sense; and to get clear on this is to get clear on how Reid regarded his project as different from what we would today regard as 'philosophy' in its usual sense. Einstein remarked that all of science is nothing but the careful elaboration of common sense. Reid's view is similarly that 'philosophy' in the sense of 'science' is appropriately based upon, and therefore indebted to, common sense: 'Philosophy ... has no other root but the principles of Common Sense; it grows out of them, and draws its nourishment from them. Severed from this root, its honours wither, its sap is dried up, it dies and rots.'[17] There should be, and in the past there has been, he remarks, a 'cordial friendship' between CS and philosophy.

I have shown that Reid's assessment of the 'ideal system' is that it postulates too sparse a model of the human mind, and that proponents of this system, rather than sensibly amplifying that model to accommodate the facts, prefer to deny the evidence that comes in conflict with it – and this is why Reid calls it a 'sceptical system'. But it is important to appreciate how perverse this 'philosophy' seemed to Reid. Because of the dependence of science on common sense, a philosopher of the human mind who persists in not according the proper role to common sense persists in ignoring what his very activity as an investigator presupposes. His misguided theories, which fail to acknowledge the role of a natural endowment, need therefore to be explained not only as bad science, but also as the manifestation of some kind of pride or *hubris*.

That is, on Reid's view, the 'votaries of the ideal system' display *hubris* not simply because they do not patiently observe nature and impute no laws to it beyond what the phenomena require, but also because they prefer *their own* imaginings and thoughts, as Reid saw it, to nature's laws:

> Conjectures and theories are the creatures of men, and will always be found very much unlike the creatures of God. If we would know the works of God, we must consult themselves with attention and humility, without daring to add any thing of ours to what they declare (*Inq* I i, p. 12).

[17] *Inq* I iv, p. 19. This is Reid's analogue to what Quine would call the converse containment of science within 'epistemology': 'Epistemology Naturalized', p. 83. See also fn. 9 above.

In that respect, to be sure, they show the same sort of *hubris* as does any bad scientist, in whatever field he works. But additionally they show *hubris* in so far as they exhibit a misguided tendency, one which particularly afflicts educated persons, of identifying themselves with only a part of what they really are, their faculty of reason.

Reasoning, as Reid sees it, is an activity that develops over time, only with careful cultivation, and only with the thoroughgoing assistance of parts of our nature other than reason. This is a view that runs throughout Reid's discussions in *Essays on the Active Powers*. For example, in his discussion of instinct (*AP* IIIa ii) he insists, rightly, that we need instincts to keep us safe before the development of reason, and to help us carry out complicated or quick movements, aimed at our own good, after the development of reason. It is a fallacy of 'philosophers' in the bad sense to regard their power of reasoning as self-sufficient, free-standing and autonomous, when in fact it is everywhere indebted to natural endowments, for which we can claim no responsibility, but with respect to which we are in debt. Philosophical *hubris*, so considered, is a kind of natural impiety, a negligence of the debt we owe to nature in being able to reason now at all. 'Philosophy', then, in so far as it is distinct from science, involves a curious reflexive mistake: someone who engages in that sort of investigation misconstrues what he is actually like, yet that misconstruction itself provides perhaps the best evidence of his error.

IV. THE OBVIOUSNESS OF COMMON SENSE

At this point it should be clear, at least, why the common sense school was satisfied that it had responded adequately to Hume. It regarded Hume's work as an unfortunate digression in the progress of the scientific study of human nature, which was liable to cause people, temporarily, to lose sight of some obvious truths about human nature and enquiry. This view of Hume has perhaps since been vindicated, in the sense that Hume's work is not today typically regarded as the foundation of or even ancestor to received theories of human thought and behaviour. Despite what is regarded as a naturalistic temperament in Hume, we do not place his *Treatise* in the tradition of experimental psychology, ethology, behavioural ecology or sociobiology, but rather in the tradition which runs through Kant to the *Aufbau* and beyond.

But what of the objections to common sense formulated earlier? How might they be answered, if we understand common sense and the appeal to common sense in the manner explained here? In fact they can be disposed of fairly easily.

1. The appeal to common sense is clearly not a *petitio principii*, at least, not in its intention or spirit, since, properly understood, it is not to be regarded as the multiplying of assumptions for the purposes of an argument, but rather as the postulation of causes to account adequately for the observed effects. Someone working in a formal discipline is generally not free to assume whatever he needs to arrive at some desired conclusion; but scientists are indeed free to assume or postulate those causes required to account for some phenomenon.

2. Neither, then, is the appeal to common sense unreflective or uncritical, for two reasons: first, we are free to re-evaluate what we include in common sense, as much as we can re-evaluate any theory; secondly, even so long as we count something as belonging in common sense, there remains ample room, at least on Reid's conception of science, to investigate its teleological or functional role.

3. Since the distinction between common sense and that which is not common sense is simply the distinction between that which we have by endowment and that which is the result of experience or training, then any means of drawing the latter distinction contributes towards our drawing the former. And in fact there are useful means of distinguishing what belongs to the human endowment: for instance, cross-cultural studies (including linguistic studies and appeals to the 'structure of all languages'); analogies drawn with animal behaviour generally; and observations of infants.

4. An appeal to common sense need not be 'little more than an appeal to mob authority', since to recognize that there is such a thing serves at least as a reminder, perhaps in the face of scepticism, that reasoning has to start from somewhere. And once we acknowledge this, we are justified in looking for something which has a reasonable claim to having the appropriate status – and here any appeal to the mere fact of common sense would have no force, since we would need to give reasons for including something within it.

5. Furthermore, an appeal to common sense need not be redundant, if we suppose, as in the case of other natural abilities, that we can be more or less sure and steady in our holding to it, and that it is good for an individual to allow his insight to be corrected, or guided, by the judgement of others. It is a reasonable assumption of the common sense school that we act more efficiently and securely to the extent that we have some explicit grasp of the principles on which we act. So an interlocutor may share in my adherence to a principle of common sense only implicitly, but in making my appeal I gain his firmer adherence, and a more secure sharing, when he comes to recognize and assent to the principle explicitly as well.

6. To this final objection (*viz* that common sense blurs together the descriptive and the normative), a defender of the common sense school

might respond that the descriptive and the normative are rightly and appropriately brought together in the case of the human mind, since the mind has 'active powers'. Thus it would be part of the experience of a mind to be aware of and consent to those principles by which it brings about changes in the world. (It is a mistake, of course, to presume that non-rational or inanimate beings act as they do by being aware of principles governing their behaviour.[18] But we could not make this mistake, unless there were some correct application of it.) And as regards the problem of the 'truth-value gap', it would presumably suffice for a philosopher of common sense simply to retort, at this point, that there is no legitimate alternative: that we cannot reasonably doubt that the principles by which we must inevitably act are also justified principles. It is a matter of common sense that common sense is reliable. And here is an instance in which a circularity would not be vicious, but rather a pleasing confirmation, and something to be expected. Reid strains this point, of course: he muses that 'evidence, which is the voucher for all truth, vouches for itself as well' (*IP* VI v, p. 632). This is not convincing, but if his view is correct, this kind of account should not be *convincing*.[19]

Clark University, Massachusetts

---

[18] See Reid's discussion in *AP* I v, 'Whether beings that have no will nor understanding may have active power', and I vi, 'Of the efficient causes of the phaenomena of nature'.

[19] Many thanks, for numerous helpful discussions, to fellow members of the 2000 NEH Reid Seminar at Brown University, under the able leadership of James Van Cleve. Thanks also to Maria Rosa Antognazza for her gracious hospitality during my visit to the Reid Archives in the University of Aberdeen, and to the Higgins School of the Humanities at Clark University for a grant to travel to the Archives.

II

REID ON FICTIONAL OBJECTS AND
THE WAY OF IDEAS

By Ryan Nichols

I argue that Reid adopts a form of Meinongianism about fictional objects because of, not in spite of, his common sense philosophy. According to 'the way of ideas', thoughts take representational states as their immediate intentional objects. In contrast, Reid endorses a direct theory of conception and a heady thesis of first-person privileged access to the contents of our thoughts. He claims that thoughts about centaurs are thoughts of non-existent objects, not thoughts about mental intermediaries, adverbial states or general concepts. In part this is because of the common sense semantics he adopts for fictional-object terms. I show that it is reasonable for Reid to endorse Meinongianism, given his epistemological priorities, for he took the way of ideas to imply that his view about first-person privileged access to our mental contents was false.

I. INTRODUCTION

Our criticisms of historical philosophers, when not of a constructive nature, typically fall into one of two classes. First, one might say of a historical theory that it is incoherent, which I take to indicate not mere inconsistency, but rather unmitigated inconsistency at the conceptual heart of a theory. On occasion, this type of criticism is said to apply not merely to a theory but to a historical philosopher's entire system, an accusation Catherine Wilson brings against Leibniz, for example.[1] Secondly, one might say that a historical theory is false, even though coherent. While we may have good reason to think that some of Reid's theories are false, one rarely sees criticisms alleging that they are incoherent, or that his philosophical system taken as a whole is. In part this is because Reid thinks systematically and keeps himself apprised of the logical relations that one position bears to others which he adopts. But if S.A. Grave is correct, then a large portion of Reid's work is incoherent. Grave rhetorically asks

> What does Reid mean when he says that a centaur is the direct object of the conception of a centaur and that there are no centaurs, that the circle does not exist and

[1] C. Wilson, 'The Illusory Nature of Leibniz' System', in R. Gennaro and C. Huenemann (eds), *New Essays on the Rationalists* (Oxford UP, 1999), pp. 372–88.

is the direct object of the conception of it? One would like to be quite sure that Reid himself knew even vaguely. He goes on to speak of our conception of objects that do not exist as if he had said something perfectly straightforward, as though there was no appearance of self-contradiction in it which needed to be explained away.[2]

Grave thinks that either Reid fails to understand his own theory of conception, or (less provocatively) Reid's theory of conception as applied to fictional objects is incoherent.

The purpose of this paper is to demonstrate that Reid's analysis of the mind's ability to conceive of fictional objects coheres with his other philosophical commitments. This necessitates (a) showing that, to put it anachronistically, Reid is a Meinongian. Reid believes that we can conceive of and attach predicates to non-existent objects – objects that are not names, general concepts, properties or mental *ficta*. Part of the interest in this thesis lies in the way in which I expect many will react to it: 'Reid, standard-bearer of the common sense tradition, champion of empirical methods in philosophy, a Meinongian? Surely not.' This is why I shall (b) show that endorsing Meinongianism accords with Reid's philosophical goals, once we fully appreciate the nature of his rejection of the way of ideas. In addition to illuminating what Reid himself regarded as a keystone of his response to the way of ideas, and showing that he is not the prosaic common sense philosopher we often think he is, a further purpose of this project arises from a desire to defend Reid against Grave's allegation.

II. DEFLATIONISM, INFLATIONISM AND MEINONGIANISM

Richard Cartwright has presented a clever argument which we can use to elucidate negative existential claims.[3] Where 'p' refers to a person's belief *that unicorns do not exist*, the following paradoxical argument results:

1. p is about unicorns
2. Unicorns must exist in some sense in order for p to be about them
3. If unicorns exist in any sense, p is false
4. Therefore p is false.

Cartwright identifies possible responses to the argument, on the basis of which premise we deny. There are inflationist, deflationist and Meinongian responses to this argument. Each position must choose between conflicting inclinations. On the one hand, we seem to have the ability to predicate properties of fictional creatures ('Pegasus is white'), and to individuate them

² S.A. Grave, *The Scottish Philosophy of Common Sense* (Oxford: Clarendon Press, 1960), p. 36.
³ R. Cartwright, 'Negative Existentials', *Journal of Philosophy*, 57 (1960), pp. 629–39.

(Pegasus is distinct from his offspring). On the other hand, unicorns and winged horses do not exist, and to predicate anything of them seems to require maintaining that they have some type of intentional or mental existence.

Inflationists claim that to predicate anything at all of unicorns, even in negative existential claims, unicorns must have some measure of existence; this is to affirm (2). They also claim that *p* is about unicorns. They thus deny (3), and argue that unicorns 'subsist' or have some other mode of existence. What is lost by the inflationist in increasing our ontological commitments is gained by being able to explain our linguistic ability to individuate and say things about unicorns. But spelling out what these different modes of existence are has always been an intractable problem.

Deflationists argue instead that there is, properly speaking, no type of existence we can attribute to unicorns. They might argue that the inflationist equivocates with 'exist' by believing that unicorns do not exist, and by denying (3). Deflationists hold that *p* is not about unicorns, but about something else entirely. Most commonly, *p* is thought to be about a mental representation, e.g., one's idea of a unicorn. Alternatively one might say that *p* is about a property of the speaker affirming *p*. In either case the deflationist seeks to keep our ontology parsimonious, at the expense of premise (1) and at the expense of the kind of privileged access to our mental states that Reid associates with a common sense semantics for *p*. For Reid would argue that the deflationist position implies that people who think they are talking about unicorns when uttering propositions about unicorns do not know what they are talking about. Deflationism necessitates an explanatory artifice to account for the common tendency to predicate properties of fictional objects in these ways.

While Cartwright does not identify the third option with Meinong, James Van Cleve does.[4] The third option, *Meinongianism*, is to deny (2). (I concur with Van Cleve that contrary to popular belief, this, not inflationism, is Meinong's mature position.) This is perhaps the most surprising of the three options, because most people think that to predicate a property of any object, it must exist under some description – whether physically, mentally or in a third realm. This is why Meinong seems scarcely coherent when writing that 'There are objects of which it is true that there are no such objects'.[5] The Meinongian does not need equivocal senses of 'exist', as the

[4] J. Van Cleve, 'If Meinong is Wrong, is McTaggart Right?', *Philosophical Topics*, 24 (1996), pp. 231–54.

[5] Meinong, 'A Theory of Objects', in R. Chisholm (ed.), *Realism and the Background of Phenomenology* (Glencoe: Free Press, 1960), pp. 76–117, at p. 83. This is a translation of his 'Über Gegenstandstheorie', in *Untersuchungen zur Gegenstandstheorie und Psychologie* (Leipzig: Barth, 1904).

inflationist does, and so can affirm (3). But unlike the deflationist, the Meinongian does not forsake privileged access to our mental states by denying (1).

Inflationism allegedly sacrifices ontology for epistemology, while deflationism allegedly sacrifices epistemology for ontology. It is not clear just how the advocate of the third position understands the stakes of the debate. As a result, one might well deem the Meinongian position implausible. I shall defend the plausibility neither of Meinongianism nor of the controversial assumption that denying (1) impugns a notable variety of privileged access. Instead I shall argue that this Meinongian position is actually Reid's position, and I shall explain why Reid adopts it. With this taxonomy, we can look at how Reid describes our apprehension of fictional objects.

III. WHY REID IS A MEINONGIAN

When we 'barely conceive any object', says Reid, 'the ingredients of that conception must either be things with which we were before acquainted by some other original power of the mind, or they must be parts or attributes of such things'.[6] Reid is aware that this doctrine is not new. He explains his accord with Locke on the matter, and then argues that Hume's missing shade of blue is a red herring (*IP* IV i, p. 367b). The key difference between Reid and Locke is that for Locke, sensations (and for Hume, impressions) provide us with all our ingredients for conceptions. Reid holds that we can be acquainted with objects directly, not through sensations, in virtue of the ability of objects to cause concepts in us formally. Strictly speaking, sensations, though physically necessary, are not sufficient for the production of our concepts of bodies. That Reid endorses a direct, non-representational theory of cognition serves as an assumption for the present study. I shall say something more about this at the conclusion of this paper.

I shall first consider Reid's affirmation of (1) and (3). Reid's affirmation of (3), that if unicorns exist in any sense, *p* is false, is not nearly as explicit as his affirmation of (1), but it does not have to be. There are difficulties in showing that Reid affirms (3). First, there are difficulties of interpretation. Secondly, it does not seem that Reid has a conceptual repertoire imbued with various concepts of existence, which is needed to articulate (3). The only distinction with which he seems familiar in this context is the crude formal/objective distinction as presented by Descartes: Reid shows no awareness of Avicenna or Aquinas on this topic. Rather than being a difficulty standing in the way of showing that Reid affirms premise (3), this is actually a telling difficulty for

---

[6] Reid, *Essays on the Intellectual Powers of Man* (hereafter *IP*), in W. Hamilton (ed.), *The Works of Thomas Reid* (Bristol: Thoemmes, 1994), IV i, p. 367a.

showing that he denies it. For I doubt that Reid ever seriously considered reasons for which one would deny it. His plain-spoken philosophical vocabulary, which lies on top of his common sense methodology, militates against any attempt to find distinctions between uses of 'existence' in his work. But doing just that would be required to show that Reid denies (3). The only option within his purview is to claim that our thoughts of unicorns are thoughts of other thoughts, i.e., of unicorns objectively in thought. It will become apparent presently, in my consideration of Reid's affirmation of (1), that he rejects this option.

Reid's affirmation of (1), that p is about unicorns, is more detailed, because (1) is of considerably more philosophical importance than (3). Reid affirms that our thoughts of fictional objects are of non-existent objects and not of something else. He says (*IP* IV iii, p. 373a) 'I conceive a centaur. This conception is an operation of the mind, of which I am conscious, and to which I can attend. The sole object of it is a centaur, an animal which, I believe, never existed. I can see no contradiction in this.' The object of the act of conception is a non-existent fiction, an imaginary creature with the head and torso of a human and the body of a horse.

Reid continues 'The philosopher says, I cannot conceive a centaur without having an idea of it in my mind.... Perhaps he will say, that the idea is an image of the animal, and is the immediate object of my conception, and that the animal is the mediate or remote object.' To this, Reid first responds by arguing that upon inspection of the content of his thought, there appears to be only one object of conception, not two. Secondly, the single object of conception 'is not the image of an animal – it is an animal. I know what it is to conceive an image of an animal, and what it is to conceive an animal; and I can distinguish the one of these from the other without any danger of mistake' (pp. 373a–b). This marks a gratuitously simplistic semantics for fictional-object terms, one that I hesitate to attribute to any advocate of the ideal theory (I shall follow Reid in referring to the way of ideas as 'the ideal theory', for convenience). Leaving Reid's abilities as a historian of philosophy to one side, this comment marks an unequivocal affirmation of premise (1), that a belief that unicorns do not exist is about unicorns, and thus marks a corresponding denial of the deflationist position.

Of course, Reid might affirm (1) and (3) without denying (2) if he had some other means of escaping the conclusion of the argument, but, as I shall now show, Reid explicitly denies (2). He remarks squarely that 'conception is often employed about objects that neither do, nor did, nor will exist' (*IP* IV i, p. 368a; cf. II xii, p. 292a). In fact, he sees the deflationary way out of the paradox as one of the ideal theory's most far-reaching philosophical errors. He claims that the ideal theory falsely assumes that 'in all the operations of understanding, there must be an object of thought, which really exists while we think of it; or, as some philosophers have expressed it, that which is not cannot be intelligible' (*IP* IV ii, p. 368b). These assertions imply the falsity of (2), and its truth is inconsistent with deflationism. The deflationist claims that my thought of a unicorn is about something else that does exist. But Reid is quite clear that such conceptions are not about anything that exists. So the deflationist move that switches the object of thought from something that does not exist, a unicorn, to something that does exist, an idea, is not open to Reid. In fact Reid makes the further claim, of his belief that we can think of items that do not exist in any way at all, that he knows 'no truth more evident to the common sense and to the experience of mankind' (*IP* IV i, pp. 368a–b).

Deflationism is committed to an ontology with mental representations, like ideas. Reid has given many reasons to think that ideas are not the direct objects of our other faculties. Perceptions do not take ideas as intentional objects, but rather take physical bodies and physical qualities as their intentional objects.[7] He says the same about memory-beliefs and about conceptions. To think that there is a mental entity lurking within an act of imagination, i.e., 'to infer from this that there is really an image in the mind, ... is to be misled by an analogical expression; as if, from the phrases of deliberating and balancing things in the mind, we should infer that there is really a balance existing in the mind' (*IP* IV ii, p. 373b). Reid's rejection of this kind of deflationism is of a piece with his desire to ferret out the ideal theory's philosophical corruptions.

We can directly conceive of creatures that have never existed, just as we can directly conceive of structures that no longer exist, or events that have passed. Indeed Reid claims (*IP* IV ii, p. 374a) that we can conceive of an object that will never exist, a circle:

> What is the idea of a circle? I answer, it is the conception of a circle. What is the immediate object of this conception? The immediate and the only object of it is a circle. But where is this circle? It is nowhere. If it was an individual, and had a real existence, it must have a place; but, being an universal, it has no existence, and therefore no place.

Reid gives no indication that he is attempting to be subtle here by employing finely grained senses of 'existence'.

As a result of Reid's affirmation of (1) and (3) and his denial of (2), I infer that Reid adopts what I have described as the Meinongian position. We can apply predicates to non-existent objects, which implies that existence is a

---

[7] I develop Reid's analysis of this process in my 'Learning and Conceptual Content in Reid's Theory of Perception', forthcoming in *British Journal for the History of Philosophy*.

property, in roughly the sense which this phrase is given in ontological arguments.[8] I shall proceed by examining possible interpretations which do not attribute this Meinongian position to Reid.

IV. TWO ALTERNATIVE INTERPRETATIONS

There are two noteworthy interpretations that might be put forward, as representing Reid's views on the non-existent better than the one I favour. Naturally, a host of contemporary ways of analysing negative existential claims may be used to salvage Reid's theory, but I am restricting my attention to interpretative options open to Reid. Both of these options are deflationist. The first is inspired by the way he construes sensations adverbially, while the second draws from his analysis of universals. Crucial to both attempts is showing that Reid links his analysis of fictional objects to his analysis of sensations or general concepts. I shall argue that he does not do so.

First, Reid's theory of sensation may be used here to ground an interpretation on which our conception of non-existent objects is adverbial in nature. An adverbial theory of *sensation* is a theory according to which sensory states are best analysed not as relations to sense-data (as on the ideal theory), nor as representational states, but as purely qualitative states, i.e., as ways in which we are aware. Paradigmatically, the sensory experience of seeing a red chair is more accurately redescribed as seeing the chair by sensing redly. Avoiding problems associated with representational theories of sensation is the principal reason for adopting an adverbial analysis.

There is abundant textual evidence for construing Reid's theory of sensations along these lines in both major works. Reid claims that a sensation 'can have no existence but when it is perceived, and can only be in a sentient being or mind'.[9] Furthermore, sensation does not have an intentional object – though the perceptual event, of which the sensation is a part, is directed at an object. He says that 'in sensation, there is no object distinct from that act of mind by which it is felt' (*IP* II xvi, p. 310a), and 'I can attend to what I feel, and the sensation is nothing else, nor has any other qualities

---

[8] For the sake of completeness I have attempted to determine whether, in his philosophy of religion, Reid commits himself to a view about existence sympathetic to the present interpretation. Unfortunately Reid does not discuss ontological arguments. He does say that necessary existence is 'an attribute belonging to the deity', but that is equivocal, as are his other statements in his discussion of God's nature: see E. Duncan (ed.), *Thomas Reid's Lectures on Natural Theology* (Univ. Press of America, 1981), p. 63.

[9] Reid, *An Inquiry into the Human Mind* (hereafter *Inq*), in *The Works of Thomas Reid*, ed. Hamilton (Bristol: Thoemmes, 1994), II ix, p. 114a (p. 43 in the new critical edition edited by Derek Brookes, Pennsylvania State UP, 1997).

than what I feel it to have. Its *esse* is *sentiri*, and nothing can be in it that is not felt.'[10] Sensations do not exist independently of being apprehended or felt.

If we believe that Reid adopts an adverbial theory of sensation, then the way seems open to extending this interpretation to non-existent objects. According to this analysis, one's apprehension of a unicorn would become not a matter of taking a fictional object as the intentional object of a thought, but rather as a manner of thinking. The primary advantage of an adverbial theory of the conception of non-existent objects lies in the way in which it moves such 'objects' into the mental realm. This move largely nullifies the perplexity of their ontological status. Reid no longer needs to deny (2). In order to escape the conclusion of our argument, the adverbial interpretation has Reid denying (1).

Despite the *prima facie* circumstantial case for this interpretation, it is not Reid's analysis. While Reid recognizes that the act of conceiving is a mental activity, for this interpretation to succeed it must be shown that conceiving of non-existent objects is not an intentional state that takes an object. However, first, there are no explicit textual sources for believing that Reid applies his doctrine of adverbial sensation to the objects of conception in general, nor any evidence that he applies this doctrine to non-existent objects of conception in particular. Since he is clear that pain is a state of the mind that does not take an object, we are warranted in expecting a similar measure of forthrightness about any application of an adverbial analysis to the conception of non-existent objects.

There are further reasons against endorsing this interpretation in addition to this textual point. The adverbial theory of conception must hold that conceptions, like sensations, do not have intentional objects. By taking this route, the adverbialist claims that *p* is not *about* anything, therefore *p* is not about unicorns. Two points show that this is implausible.

The first emerges from Reid's distinction between sensations and conceptions. According to Reid's adverbial analysis of sensation, sensory states are nothing over and above their qualitative properties. But according to Reid, what distinguishes conceptions from sensations is that once we remove all the phenomenal properties associated with a conception, something remains, *viz* the conceptual mental content. Reid's discussion of conception is not often lucid, but one point about which he is clear is that conceptual states take objects and are not merely phenomenal states. Given his distinction between conception and sensation, this interpretation of fictional objects is implausible.

[10] *Inq*, ed. Brookes, p. 258. This is drawn from an undated abstract of the *Inquiry* prepared by Reid for Hume's review. It is addressed to Reid's intermediary, 'The Revd Doctor Blair'.

The second reason against the adverbialist's attempt to replace the propositional content in conceptions with phenomenological content is straightforwardly philosophical. The notion that conceptual states are purely phenomenal is not obviously coherent, which is to say that Reid's distinction between sensory and conceptual states is a good one. We tend to give Chisholm and other advocates of adverbial theories of sensation some latitude in their creative descriptions of sensory states. Certain facets of a philosophical account of sensation will be elusive, which we may attribute to the ineffable qualities of phenomenological experience. But in the case of accounting for propositional contents, we are entitled to heighten our expectations. The adverbialist fails to meet these expectations because it is difficult to understand what it means to say that I conceive that-faith-is-the-lost-virtue-ly, or that-Iain-Banks'-science-fiction-novels-are-exquisitely-crafted-works-pregnant-with-frightening-alien-possibility-ly. Such states do not seem comprehensible. Thus denying that conceptions are about anything at all fails as a strategy for showing that Reid does not endorse a Meinongian position.

The second alternative interpretation draws upon Reid's description of what he refers to as 'general conceptions'. This strategy would also require two steps. The first would be to show that Reid endorses a non-Meinongian account of general concepts (which he also calls 'universals'). This could be either a form of inflationism, holding that universals exist in a third realm, or a form of deflationism, that there is no sense in which they exist or can be predicated of real particulars. The second step would involve showing that Reid applies what he says about general concepts to fictional individuals. I shall present reasons for thinking that what he says about universals tends to sound very much like what we have already observed him to say about fictional objects, and thus that this strategy cannot progress beyond the first step just described. His considered view on universals, though, is unclear.

Reid explains that we form the bulk of our general conceptions in three steps: first, we analyse an object's attributes and name them; then we observe one attribute's presence in many objects; thirdly, we combine 'into one whole a certain number of those attributes of which we have formed abstract notions, and [give] a name to that combination' (*IP* V iii, p. 394b). Reid repeatedly denies that these names designate anything that exists. He says that if a universal were to exist, 'then it would be an individual; but it is a thing that is conceived without regard to existence' (V iv, p. 398a). More forthrightly, he says 'universals have no real existence' (V vi, p. 407a). Or, if one would like to talk of them as 'existing', one must know that 'Their existence is nothing but predicability, or the capacity of being attributed to a subject. The name of predicables, which was given them in ancient philosophy, is that which most properly expresses their nature' (pp. 407a–b). This is because we do not attribute to universals 'an existence in time or place, but existence in some individual subject; and this existence means no more but that they are truly attributes of such a subject' (p. 407a).

It seems that these passages allow us to conclude that Reid is not an inflationist (or a realist) about universals. While he is struggling to find a way to articulate his view in common language, we know that, in whatever curious form universals do 'exist' for Reid, they do not exist independently of real particulars.

In fact these passages seem to point indecisively towards a Meinongian interpretation of Reid on universals, for it seems that he claims that they do not exist, even though we can talk about them. Keith Lehrer and Vann McGee see Reid as endorsing some type of view in this neighbourhood, even though they are not primarily concerned with making a textual case for this attribution: 'Reid himself was unequivocal. *Universals do not exist.* We conceive of universals – that is, according to Reid, we know the meanings of general terms – but when we conceive of universals, as when we conceive of centaurs, we are conceiving of something that does not exist.'[11] For Reid, the claim 'Universals do not exist' seems to mean that universals do not exist on any of the following three options: as ideas or mental entities, as Platonic entities in a third realm, or as exemplifications in particular things. Thus when Reid does discuss universals, he takes them to be something like Meinongian objects: items to which we can attach predicates, though they do not exist.

Nicholas Wolterstorff has also addressed this issue. However, he says just the opposite: 'it's clear that Reid, in spite of linguistic appearances, was not a nominalist: *there are universals*'.[12] Wolterstorff claims explicitly that Reid was not a Meinongian. However, his account of Meinongianism resembles a form of what I have been calling 'inflationism'. Wolterstorff (p. 74) says 'Reid was not a Meinongian; I see no evidence that he even so much as entertained the thought that the substances that exist might constitute a subset of those that have being'. That is true, for Reid clearly does not utilize concepts of *existence, being* and *subsistence* to explain fictional objects. But I have shown that Reid commits himself to another form of Meinongianism, no less worthy of the appellation. At different points in his career Meinong endorsed both the 'subsistence' theory Wolterstorff identifies as 'Meinongianism' and the 'non-existence, non-subsistence' view I have identified with that term. Though this point may be important for determining

---

[11] Lehrer and McGee, 'Particulars, Individual Qualities and Universals', in K. Mulligan (ed.), *Language, Truth and Ontology* (Dordrecht: Kluwer, 1992), pp. 37–47, at p. 41 (my italics).

[12] N. Wolterstorff, *Thomas Reid and the Story of Epistemology* (Cambridge UP, 2001), p. 73 (my italics).

priority issues with respect to the development of theories of fictional objects, settling the matter is wholly irrelevant to my interpretation of Reid.

Wolterstorff claims that because Reid thinks that there are universals that can be objects of conception, he cannot be a nominalist. Thus perhaps he could light upon Reid saying that 'Universals have no real existence', and argue that, since Reid modifies 'existence' with 'real', there must be a sense of 'existence' appropriately predicated of universals. This, however, is not sufficient to show that Reid is not a nominalist. He might adopt a form of nominalism and contend that universals exist only in the sense that there are particulars that share attributes. Evidently, though, Wolterstorff believes Reid does not endorse nominalism in this sense, since he says flatly that he 'was not a nominalist'. Hence, given the persuasive evidence that Reid does not think universals exist in any Platonic sense, the most charitable way to understand Wolterstorff is by reading him as claiming that universals exist in a mental realm of ideas. But if so, the texts do not significantly support his interpretation.

The principal barrier to understanding Reid's position, and the interpretations of his commentators on this topic, is that these uses of 'exist' and 'are' are equivocal. When two of Reid's foremost commentators, Lehrer and Wolterstorff, come to diametrically opposed interpretations, it is likely (i) that there is some serious discrepancy in the way they are using key terms, or (ii) that there is no clear truth about the matter, in this case what Reid's analysis of universals is (or both, as I suspect). I have produced evidence to think that some fundamental ambiguities run through Reid's discussion of universals, but in addition there is the further fact (which the disputants do not mention) that Reid himself indicates that he does not know what universals are. He remarks, for example, 'As to the manner of how we conceive universals, I confess my ignorance' (*IP* V vi, p. 407b). We need to recognize the strong possibility that he has no determinate view of universals. In fact, in a much more thorough study of Reid on universals than either of the two discussed thus far, Susan Castagnetto gets us no further. After her analysis she concludes 'But there is still something odd about maintaining that there are universals even though universals don't really exist'.[13] This, of course, sounds just like what Reid says about fictional objects, which brings us full circle.

We have more evidence for interpreting Reidian universals as Meinongian non-existents than we have for interpreting them as mental entities, Platonic entities or sets of real particulars. However, I remain

---

[13] S. Castagnetto, 'Reid's Answer to Abstract Ideas', *Journal of Philosophical Research*, 17 (1992), pp. 39–60, at p. 46.

sceptical about finding out just what Reid's position is. Whatever view about universals we conclude is the one Reid adopts, it is sure to be significantly underdetermined. This being the case, what he says about universals cannot be successfully used to decide what he says about fictional objects.

Earlier, I mentioned that if one seeks to use Reid's discussion of universals to refute my interpretation of him as a Meinongian about fictional objects, then one would have to show first that Reid endorses a non-Meinongian theory of universals; then that, for him, fictional objects have the same ontological status as universals. Even if we were to assume that Reid endorses an inflationist or deflationist view about universals, that would still only bring my interlocutor to the end of the first stage of the process. In order to vindicate this interpretation, one must then show that Reid believes that fictional particulars like Pegasus have the same status as universals. Reid, though, does not explicitly support this move.

There are philosophical reasons against this hypothesis. Suppose Reid endorses a deflationist, nominalist interpretation. Then 'centaur' and 'horse' might refer to classes of instantiated properties in roughly the same way. However, it is not clear that this makes any sense. 'Horse' refers to the set of instances of the property called 'horse'. But the property of being a centaur has no instances, so we cannot interpret Reid's use of fictional-object-kind terms as being relevantly similar to his use of general-concept terms.

More important, though, is that any non-Meinongian account of universals will fail to preserve Reid's common sense epistemic theses. He says that when I think of a centaur, the object of that act 'is a centaur, an animal which, I believe, never existed'. The ideal theory implies that this common sense commitment is incorrect, and that instead I am thinking of an *idea* of a centaur, in response to which Reid asks 'What then is this idea? Is it an animal, half horse and half man? No. Then I am certain it is not the thing I conceive' (*IP* IV ii, p. 373a). This common sense semantics would produce the very same result were we to suppose that fictional-object terms like 'centaur' refer either to mental representations of centaurs or to a set of property instances. For I know that an animal that is half horse and half man is not merely a set of property instantiations, just as I know that a horse or a man is not merely a set of property instantiations. They are, rather, subjects of predication.

I shall explore Reid's allegiance to these common sense epistemic views presently, in order to uncover the deeper reasons for which Reid adopts Meinongianism. Why, after all, is Reid drawn to these naïve common sense claims in the first place?

V. REJECTING THE IDEAL THEORY

Whether or not Meinongianism correctly captures the nature of fictional objects, we can see that Reid exercises good judgement and attends to the internal consistency of his system in arriving at this surprising conclusion. I shall explain Reid's central epistemological reasons for adopting Meinongianism, and I shall analyse how it arises from Reid's rejection of the ideal theory.

Reid writes to James Gregory 'The merit of what you are pleased to call *my philosophy*, lies, I think, chiefly in having called in question the common theory of ideas'.[14] Reid is not merely being self-effacing: he is being honest, and for the present discussion his dictum is especially *à propos*. Reid's arrival at Meinongianism follows from his examination of what he takes to be the two key commitments of the ideal theory:

> There are two prejudices which seem to me to have given rise to the theory of ideas in all the various forms in which it has appeared in the course of above two thousand years.... The *first* is – That, in all the operations of the understanding, there must be some immediate intercourse between the mind and its object, so that the one may act upon the other. The *second*, That, in all the operations of understanding, there must be an object of thought, which really exists while we think of it; or, as some philosophers have expressed it, that which is not cannot be intelligible (*IP* IV ii, p. 368b, cf. II viii, p. 274a).

To clarify Reid's attributions, we can say that the ideal theory is committed to the following two propositions:

(a) For all intentional states of the mind, their immediate objects are mental representations

(b) That which does not exist cannot be the object of intentional states of the mind.

In (a), which is a principle of cognitive contact, Reid attributes to the ideal theory the thesis that our mental states take representations as their immediate objects. I understand Reid's (b) to be equivalent to the statement that, since we are immediately aware of representational intermediaries, they must exist under some description. It does not matter for Reid's purposes whether these representations allegedly exist in mental form (as ideas) or in physical form (as brain states), for he explicitly rejects both ways of construing representations.

---

[14] Letter reprinted in Hamilton's edition, p. 88b. (The date of writing is not supplied.)

By insufficiently appreciating the force of these two commitments, Grave insinuates, in the *bon mot* quoted above (pp. 582–3), that Reid does not know the contours of his own account of fictional objects. Understanding Reid's analysis in the light of (a) and (b) will help us avoid Grave's error.[15]

Reid believes that, amongst the advocates of the ideal theory, Hume and Locke in particular are committed to (a) and (b). Furthermore, he thinks that any such commitments will render one's theory of cognition implausible.

Hume's assent to (b), for example, is obvious. Ideas and impressions must exist because, by conceiving them, we call them into existence.[16] Thesis (a) may be broken down into two parts, one that affirms the immediacy of representations, and another that affirms the representative features of mental intermediaries. Hume affirms both portions of (a). As to the immediacy of representations,

> The only existences, of which we are certain, are perceptions, which being immediately present to us by consciousness, command our strongest assent, and are the first foundation of all our conclusions.... as no beings are ever present to the mind but perceptions; it follows that we may observe a conjunction or a relation of cause and effect between different perceptions, but can never observe it between perceptions and objects (*Treatise*, p. 212; cf. p. 193).

He also affirms that ideas are representational. Hume explains that 'all our simple ideas in their first appearance are deriv'd from simple impressions, which are correspondent to them, and which they exactly represent' (*Treatise*, p. 4). Ideas are representational, though they can only represent impressions (*Treatise*, p. 241; cf. pp. 67, 188), not external objects.

By this admittedly brief case on behalf of Reid's attribution of (a) and (b) to Hume, I intend to show only that Reid does have some reason to think that his predecessors fit the mould he casts for them. (A sound case can be made for Locke's adoption of (a) and (b), although with Berkeley the situation is, for obvious reasons, not so obvious.)

I shall now turn to showing how Reid's Meinongianism stems from his repudiation of (a) and (b). Reid's empirical method in his analysis of the operation of our mental faculties leads him to conclude that (a) and (b) imply that we generally do not know what we are thinking about. This marks the failure of the ideal theory to account for what Reid takes to be an epistemological datum. Assume (a), and we can coax out of Reid the following argument:

[15] An added point of interest in this discussion is the fact that (a) resembles the central commitment of what some, Laurence BonJour, for example, identify as the predominant contemporary theory of cognition: see his 'Is Thought a Symbolic Process?', *Synthese*, 89 (1991), pp. 331–52, at p. 336.

[16] Hume, *A Treatise of Human Nature*, ed. P.H. Nidditch (Oxford UP, 1978), p. 67.

5. 'Centaurs' refers to non-existent creatures that are half men, half horses [premise]
6. Since nothing that does not exist can be the object of thought, S cannot think of centaurs [from (a) and (5)]
7. S believes that he can and does think of centaurs [premise].

Reid believes he speaks in the name of common sense when saying 'I conceive a centaur. This conception is an operation of the mind, of which I am conscious, and to which I can attend. The sole object of it is a centaur, an animal which, I believe, never existed' (*IP* IV ii, p. 373a). This and like-minded passages clearly warrant attributing (7) to Reid. It follows that

8. When S has a thought which he believes is about centaurs, S is mistaken in his identification of the content of his thought [from (6) and (7)].

Now Reid seeks to generalize the result achieved in (8). S fails to have privileged access to his mental contents, not only in cases in which S thinks about centaurs and other fictional objects, but in most other cases as well. Since (a) is a universal generalization,

9. S is mistaken in identifying the content of his thought t whenever S believes that t's content is about anything other than a mental representation [from (8) and (a)].

Reid draws the line here: common sense epistemic principles must hold sway over implications of the ideal theory.

10. It is obvious that S is not systematically mistaken about the contents of thoughts about things other than S's mental states [premise]
11. Therefore (a) is false [by *reductio* from (9) and (10)].

The contemporary flavour of the argument is obvious, for related concerns have been raised about externalist theories of content by a number of philosophers. Like Reid, current defenders of privileged access also take an epistemic principle roughly similar to (10) as philosophically non-negotiable.

The key step in this argument is the inference from (8) and (a) to (9). We are justified in attributing this step to Reid, in part on the basis of a passage (from which I have already quoted) where Reid describes what he takes to be the deleterious epistemic consequences of a commitment to (a). When thinking about a centaur,

> this one object which I conceive, is not the image of an animal – it is an animal. I know what it is to conceive an image of an animal, and what it is to conceive an animal; and I can distinguish the one of these from the other without any danger of mistake. The thing I conceive is a body of a certain figure and colour, having life and

spontaneous motion. The philosopher says, that the idea is an image of the animal; but that it has neither body, nor colour, nor life, nor spontaneous motion. This I am not able to comprehend (*IP* IV ii, p. 373a–b).

Reid also emphasizes epistemic considerations earlier in *Essays on the Intellectual Powers*. Speaking of a commitment to a representational theory of cognition, he says

> The necessary consequence of this seems to be, that there are two objects of this thought – the idea, which is in the mind, and the person represented by that idea; the first, the immediate object of the thought, the last, the object of the same thought, but not the immediate object. This is a hard saying; for it makes every thought of things external to have a double object. Every man is conscious of his thoughts, and yet, upon attentive reflection, he perceives no such duplicity in the object he thinks about (*IP* II ix, p. 278b; cf. IV ii, p. 369a–b).

I take this passage as a repudiation of (9). Together, these passages show that Reid presumes a heady view about the transparency of first-person access.

I shall now consider some possible responses from Hume, in order to improve our understanding of Reid's *modus operandi*. Hume would argue that instead of conceiving of something that is half horse, half man, we are actually conceiving of a mental representation of such a thing. He would affirm (5), but deny (7). He might do this by arguing for a semantics of fictional-object terms such that our dealings with centaurs come under two concepts – 'centaur', the use denoted in (5), and 'centaur$_2$', which refers to representations of centaurs. Indeed, Reid himself could be seen as engendering such a semantics when he says

> What is meant by conceiving a thing? we should very naturally answer, that it is having an image of it in the mind – and perhaps we could not explain the word better. This shews that conception, and the image of a thing in the mind, are synonymous expressions (*IP* IV i, p. 363a).

However, despite the fact that Reid allows imagination a role in conceiving, he is quick to observe that talk of images in the mind is strictly analogical. Common usage puts images into the mind, but, in truth,

> We know nothing that is properly in the mind but thought; and, when anything else is said to be in the mind, the expression must be figurative, and signify some kind of thought (p. 363a).

Furthermore, one might think this response amounts to the factual claim that we have two concepts for all non-existent terms. Reid would argue that this does not let Hume off the hook. For (a) and (b) impel Hume to posit equivocal concepts not just for non-existent objects like centaurs, but for all sorts of other non-existent objects, like formerly existent people, and for existent tables and chairs as well. Of course Hume does something quite like this in *Treatise* I iv 2, when he distinguishes between vulgar and philosophical views about the objects of perception. But Reid's common sense commitments prevent him from taking seriously this option, of affirming (5) and denying (7).

Secondly, Hume may simply deny outright that we do know what we are thinking about in cases in which the objects of our thoughts are allegedly things other than mental states, i.e., he may deny (10). We can defend this response by considering that often one perceives some object and believes that it is one thing, but discovers, on closer observation, that the object is something else. This is not merely true of perceptions. Fregean cases of referential opacity indicate that this can be true of what Reid calls 'conceptions' as well.

Reid would respond by arguing that, were Hume to say this, he would conflate two different mental operations. Reid holds that conception is crucially related to other mental faculties, but is not absorbed by them. This leads him to make a distinction between 'bare' and 'co-ordinated' conceptions ('co-ordinated' is my term). Reid calls some acts of conception 'bare' because that which is conceived need not be the object of any other mental faculty (*IP* IV i, p. 361a). A 'bare conception of a thing' is a conception that occurs 'without any judgement or belief about it' (p. 360a). He adds 'We may distinctly conceive a proposition, without judging it at all' (IV iii, p. 375a). It is thus possible that one merely conceives of something, whether a proposition, image, event, physical object or state of affairs. In contrast, co-ordinated conceptions are conceptions occurring in tandem with the use of other mental faculties. Since conception is a component of perception for Reid, when I perceive Durham Cathedral, for example, the event of conceiving of the cathedral is co-ordinated with the perceptual event of seeing the cathedral.

Reid grants that in co-ordinated conceptions I do on occasion erroneously identify their objects. However, the fact that my co-ordinated conception is generated by the interaction of my senses with physical objects explains the error in perceptual cases, and even in Hesperus/Phosphorus cases (since our conceptions in that case too are dependent on co-ordination with perceptual experiences). On the other hand, to suppose that I may incorrectly identify the objects of my own bare conceptual acts is a much stronger thesis. This is to say that I might be imagining my wife reading Cicero's *De Domo Sua* and be wrong about the content of my state of imagination. Reid's interlocutor here is claiming not simply that it is possible that I may erroneously omit from my imagistic conception of my wife that she was reading a certain work by Cicero. Reid can allow that my bare conceptions may well be incomplete in various respects. In order to deny (10), Hume must make the significantly stronger claim that I may be in error that I am conceiving of my wife at all, i.e., that it is possible that I am conceiving of my neighbour's wife instead. In contrast, Reid thinks that contents of propositional attitudes in bare conceptions are transparent. By describing bare conceptions as opaque, this response to Reid's argument repudiates one's ability to know the content of one's mental states, even when those states are produced by using only the faculty of bare conception.

My aim in this discussion of two possible objections to Reid's argument has been to give the argument some Reidian texture. The success of Reid's argument relies upon an intrepid, though tacit, presumption of first-person privileged access. Reid supposes that I can think of centaurs while knowing that they do not exist. Given Reid's understanding of this presumption, he tacitly affirms the following crude disjunction: either I am mistaken that my thoughts about centaurs are about centaurs (and thus I must deny a robust thesis of privileged access), or I am thinking about and attaching predicates to something that does not exist (and thus I must affirm a form of Meinongianism).

VI. THE METAPHILOSOPHY BEHIND REID'S MEINONGIANISM

This is the dilemma Reid faced. The theories in each disjunct represent extreme positions. Those who wish to reject the ideal theory's commitment to a representational theory of thought (in (a) above) have many other options. On the one hand, many would deny Reid's naïve thesis of privileged access. Merely claiming that some but not all content is internal would mark a step towards a middle ground. On the other hand, we could use any number of familiar tools in the philosophy of language to attempt to skirt the problems about predication which Reid takes so seriously. These tools include Fregean distinctions between levels of predicates, two-sense theories that distinguish between 'exists' as applied to individuals and to kinds, Wittgensteinian appeals to 'formal concepts', or intensional logics purporting to account for the truth-value and logical form of propositions about fictional objects (or perhaps combinations of these proposals). Defence of Meinongian commitments about negative existential claims can itself be accomplished in a considerably more straightforward manner than via Reid's circuitous epistemological route.

A related option has been developed in this context by Marian David, who uses work by Brentano and Chisholm to make some distinctions between senses of 'exists', and then argues that if Reid's theory is to be made plausible, he must be 'committed to a restricted sense of "to exist" in which it expresses a property like being-red, i.e., a property in virtue of which objects are distinguished from each other'.[17] Unfortunately Reid's uses of 'exists', 'real' and 'object' do not permit an interpretation on which those terms function in the way David and others wish they did. For David's recommendation comes at the expense of Reid's denial of (2) above – that unicorns must exist in some sense in order for p to be about them. David thus concludes (p. 599) by saying 'Reid *should have* said "name" or "singular term" when he said "object"' (my italics). For an unprejudiced ruling on Reid, we would need to appraise certain advantages of Meinongianism more fully than is possible here, but perhaps David is correct.

Nevertheless Reid's adoption of Meinongianism is understandable and rational, given his philosophical goals, as I hope to have shown. He is willing to accept the views about the semantics of fictional-object terms which I have described, views which are philosophically controversial, on the condition that doing so is necessary to preserve his staunch allegiance to non-negotiable epistemic principles. This underscores the epistemological nature of Reid's rejection of the ideal theory.

In fact, Reid adopts a direct theory of cognition for similar epistemological reasons. If John Haldane's work on Reid's theory of cognition[18] is correct, as I believe it is, then Reid seems to endorse a theory similar to Aquinas', according to which objects directly and formally cause our thoughts of them. In Reid's version of this theory, such causal powers must be attributed to existing objects only, and not to non-existent Meinongian objects, but how Reid can carry this off consistently is not obvious. Positing formal causes and the like may be thought to mark an extravagant metaphysics, but in the present day just such a possibility has been raised in this context. Laurence BonJour (p. 346), in describing his own rejection of contemporary representational theories of cognition, readies himself for an alternative theory that 'will have to involve metaphysics of a pretty hard-core kind'. BonJour seeks a non-representational theory of cognition, for reasons in part having to do with first-person access to our contents – the sort of concerns which exercise Reid. As this study shows, Reid is indeed prepared to do metaphysics of a 'pretty hard-core kind' to preserve his convictions about privileged access.

[17] M. David, 'Non-Existence and Reid's Conception of Conceiving', *Grazer Philosophische Studien*, 25–6 (1985–6), pp. 585–99, at p. 595.

[18] See his 'Reid, Scholasticism and Contemporary Philosophy of Mind', in E. Matthews and M. Dalgarno (eds), *The Philosophy of Thomas Reid* (Dordrecht: Kluwer, 1989), pp. 285–304, and 'Reid on the History of Ideas', *American Catholic Philosophical Quarterly*, 74 (2000), pp. 447–69.

Despite pervasive problems with Meinongianism, Reid none the less becomes a more interesting and better philosopher when read as endorsing this theory. Reid's Meinongianism may reap dividends elsewhere in his philosophical system: for example, it may be capable of servicing some problems about perceptual error that plague direct theories of perception like Reid's. In the philosophical context of this paper, I have shown that the only other textually plausible alternative reconstruction of Reid's analysis of fictional objects is Grave's, and by his lights Reid's view is incoherent. In contrast, I have argued that Reid's theory of fictional objects falls straight-forwardly out of his rejection of the ideal theory. While I share some of Grave's consternation, my misgivings about Reid's views arise not from the belief that Reid does not understand the contours of his own theory of non-existent objects, but from worries about what positions Reid was willing to accept in the name of a common sense epistemology.[19]

University of Aberdeen

---

[19] I have benefited from conversation and correspondence about these matters with Gideon Yaffe, George Pappas, Jim Van Cleve and William Taschek, and from discussions with fellow participants in the 2000 NEH seminar on Thomas Reid, at which I presented an earlier version of this paper.

12

RECONSIDERING REID'S GEOMETRY OF VISIBLES

By Gideon Yaffe

In his 'Inquiry', Reid claims, against Berkeley, that there is a science of the perspectival shapes of objects ('visible figures'): they are geometrically equivalent to shapes projected onto the surfaces of spheres. This claim should be understood as asserting that for every theorem regarding visible figures there is a corresponding theorem regarding spherical projections; the proof of the theorem regarding spherical projections can be used to construct a proof of the theorem regarding visible figures, and vice versa. I reconstruct Reid's argument for this claim, and expose its mathematical underpinnings: it is successful, and depends on no empirical assumptions to which he was not entitled about the workings of the human eye. I also argue that, although Reid may or may not have been aware of it, the geometry of spherical projections is not the only geometry of visible figure.

I. INTRODUCTION: A QUESTION FROM BERKELEY

Encounter with the perspectival shapes of objects – the elliptical shape of the round coin lying in one's palm, for instance – is a ubiquitous feature of visual experience. The fact of perspectival visual perception leads to an ontological question: are the perspectival shapes that we see 'real' features of objects? Or are they merely a useful illusion, or perhaps a shimmering world of appearances, that help us to understand the real shapes of things? Seventeenth- and eighteenth-century philosophers of perception were deeply occupied with questions of this nature, and Thomas Reid was no exception. However, Reid takes the question of the ontological status of perspectival shape to be vexed:

> If it should ... be asked, To what category of beings does visible figure ... belong? I can only, in answer, give some tokens, by which those who are better acquainted with the categories, may chance to find its place.[1]

But even if we think that there is no saying where to place the perspectival shapes of objects in the grand Aristotelian categories of being, we might still

---

[1] Reid, *Inquiry Into the Human Mind on the Principles of Common Sense* (hereafter *Inq*), ed. D. Brookes (Edinburgh UP, 1997), VI viii, p. 98.

think that there is some important difference in metaphysical status between perspectival and non-perspectival shapes. And we might think that we have evidence for thinking there is a difference, even if we cannot understand the metaphysical facts with the clarity needed to specify what the difference is. In fact this is what Bishop Berkeley believes. In *An Essay Towards a New Theory of Vision*, he remarks that 'visible extension and figures are not the object of geometry'.[2] This is not a mere curiosity, but indicates, Berkeley thinks, that even if there is no difference in 'degree of being' between the perspectival qualities encountered in visual experience and the qualities encountered in tactile experience – both, after all, are merely ideas – there is a distinction much like an ontological one: the objects of touch, and not of vision, are things about which it is possible to gain genuine knowledge.

If Berkeley is right about this, then there is reason to give perspectival shapes a demoted status. If they are not the sorts of things about which a science is possible, then perhaps they are nothing but *qualia*, raw feels about which nothing systematic or non-subjective can be said. Reid holds, however, that Berkeley is mistaken: the perspectival shapes of objects and their non-perspectival shapes are equally respectable; it is possible to produce a science of the second *and* of the first.[3] Reid argues, however, that perspectival shapes are mathematically equivalent not to shapes drawn on planes, but instead to shapes projected onto spheres.[4] Thus while there is an important difference between the sciences of perspectival and of non-perspectival shapes, the difference does not point to a difference in status. The study of the theorems governing the perspectival shapes, and the effort to prove those theorems, is what Reid calls 'the geometry of visibles'.

The primary aim of this paper is reconstruction and critical evaluation of Reid's rather obscure argument for the claim that perspectival shapes are mathematically equivalent to spherical projections. As I shall show, a large part of the reconstruction of the argument for this claim involves an elucidation of what the claim itself really amounts to. A view of the sort that

---

[2] Berkeley, *An Essay Towards a New Theory of Vision* (hereafter *NTV*), in his *Philosophical Works including the Works on Vision*, ed. M.R. Ayers (London: Everyman, 1975), §141.

[3] The Berkeleian arguments behind Reid's geometry of visibles are discussed in N. Daniels, *Thomas Reid's 'Inquiry': the Geometry of Visibles and the Case for Realism* (Stanford UP, 1989): see esp. ch. 3. I disagree with Daniels' interpretation of Reid's geometry of visibles in many significant respects, as will become clear below. However, with respect to the Berkeleian background to Reid's visible geometry, I believe that he is correct.

[4] This fact has led Daniels (e.g., p. 12) to credit Reid with the discovery of non-Euclidean geometry much earlier than Gauss, Riemann and Lobachevsky. But Reid, as I shall argue, does not hold that the 'visibles' do not satisfy all of Euclid's axioms, so he is really applying projective geometry to perspectival shape, rather than developing a genuinely non-Euclidean geometry. See Paul Wood, 'Reid, Parallel Lines, and the Geometry of Visibles', *Reid Studies*, 2 (1998), pp. 27–41, for an elaboration of this point.

Reid holds can be supported by appeal to commonplaces of visual experience. When one lies on one's back under the centre of a square ceiling, for instance, all four corners of the ceiling will appear as obtuse angles, and yet the sides of the ceiling will appear straight. What this means is that in one's visual experience one encounters a square the angles of which add up to more than 360°. Of course a shape with these properties could never be drawn on a plane, and so it follows that the square that appears to one in this example is not geometrically planar.[5] But examples of this sort do not establish the claim that perspectival shapes are in some way geometrically equivalent to shapes drawn on the surfaces of spheres. The square that one sees could be geometrically equivalent to a parabolic figure, for instance, or to a figure on any one of an infinite variety of regularly or irregularly curved surfaces. Reid's argument, as will be shown here, does not depend on the empirical support provided, perhaps, by examples of this nature, although the result that he reaches is consistent with them. The argument depends only on a number of natural and appealing mathematical analyses of ordinary concepts. What makes the argument obscure is that Reid does not explicitly identify the mathematical analyses that he is using, but instead presents his argument informally. I shall uncover the details of the mathematical structure that lies behind the informal argument. My claim is that when his arguments are supplemented with some mathematical apparatus, Reid is absolutely correct: the geometry of the visible and the geometry of the spherical are one and the same. Explaining what this means, and why it is true, is the object of this paper.

II. THE GEOMETRY OF VISIBLES

II.1. *The eye as a point*

Reid's argument depends on an association of the eye with a point in three-dimensional space. But which point in space is to be appropriately identified with the eye? The eye, after all, is a complex three-dimensional object, and so occupies an infinite number of points. Although we might justify the association of the eye with a single point in space by appeal to the need for simple idealizations in any model, there is a better justification available, arising from the need to limit our discussion to objects that are in focus.

---

[5] R.B. Angell, 'The Geometry of Visibles', *Noûs*, 8 (1974), pp. 87–117, offers a variety of examples in support of Reid's claim that the perspectival shapes are not Euclidean planar shapes. Angell also contrasts the empirical evidence for taking the visibles to be spheric with the evidence for taking them to be hyperbolic: see esp. pp. 95–101.

When an object is not in focus, rays of light emanating from the same point in space hit the retina in different places. This is the case, for instance, when the distance from the retina to the lens is too long or too short (see Fig. 1). However, if we assume that all of the points of the object are in focus, then associated with each point of the object is exactly one point on the retina.[6] In actuality, this one-to-one correspondence between points on the surface of an object and points on the retina is exhibited only very rarely: much of the visual field, even in those who do not require corrective lenses of any kind, is not in focus at any one instant. Further, given that one's retina, like any biological structure, is mathematically irregular (it is not, for instance, a perfect spherical section), the lens of the eye must distort in various complex ways in order to bring an object into focus, and the required distortions will vary from person to person (even holding fixed the location of the object with respect to the eye), depending on the exact shape of the individual retina. It is distortions of just the needed sort that are being accomplished by someone who keeps an object in focus as it moves closer.

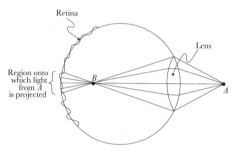

Figure 1: The distance from the lens to the retina is too long for point A to be in focus. If point B were on the retina, then A would be in focus.

To show that it is appropriate to identify the eye with a point, given that our discussion only concerns objects that are in focus, it is instructive to compare the eye with a pinhole camera, where the 'lens' is a hole the size of a single point, and the 'retina' is a flat screen onto which the light passing through the pinhole is projected. In the eye, by contrast, the retina is an irregularly curved surface, and the lens is a complex structure that fills an opening larger than a point. When we consider only objects that are in focus, however, the lens of the eye has in common with the pinhole the following property: both collect the rays emanating from a point and focus them onto a single point on the retina/screen. Therefore, given that the only relevant objects are those that are in focus, the lens of the eye is functionally equivalent to a single point in space.

Norman Daniels has claimed that Reid assumes, falsely, that the eye is a sphere, and that therefore the retina is a portion of a spherical surface, and

---

[6] As Berkeley puts the point (*NTV* §34): ' ... any radiating point is ... distinctly seen when the rays proceeding from it are, by the refractive power of the crystalline, accurately reunited in the retina or fund of the eye: but if they are reunited, either before they arrive at the retina, or after they have passed it, then there is confused vision'.

that Reid associates the eye in his geometry of visibles with the centre of this sphere.[7] In fact, given the justification just offered for treating the eye as a single point in space, no such assumption is required to reach the results which Reid wants. He need not make, and does not make, any empirically unjustified claims about the way in which the eye is actually constructed, in order to reach the geometrical results he is after. He is allowed to associate the eye with a single point in space because the lens of the eye collects light in just the way a single point in space collects it, if we limit our discussion to objects in focus.

II.2. *Visible figure and other 'visible' concepts*

Reid gives (*Inq* VI vii, p. 96) a recipe for determining the visible figure, or perspectival shape, of an object:

> Objects that lie in the same right line [i.e., straight line on a plane] drawn from the centre of the eye, have the same position, however different their distances from the eye may be: but objects which lie in different right lines drawn from the eye's centre, have a different position.... Having thus defined what we mean by the position of objects with regard to the eye, it is evident that, as the real figure of a body consists in the situation of its several parts with regard to one another, so its visible figure consists in the position of its several parts with regard to the eye; and, as he that hath a distinct conception of the situation of the parts of the body with regard to one another, must have a distinct conception of its real figure; so he that conceives distinctly the position of its several parts with regard to the eye, must have a distinct conception of its visible figure.

The visible figure of an object is the conjunction of the visible positions of each of the points occupied by the object's surface (it is difficult to define 'surface' for a three-dimensional object in mathematical terms, but an informal distinction between surface points and internal points can be assumed for present purposes). But what is the visible position of a point in space? Reid takes himself to have defined the notion in this passage; but in fact his definition is ambiguous between the following two claims:

---

[7] In support, Daniels quotes the following passage: 'I require no more knowledge in a blind man, in order to his being able to determine the visible figure of bodies, than that he can project the outline of a given body, upon a surface of a hollow sphere, whose centre is in the eye. This projection is the visible figure he wants; for it is the same figure with that which is projected upon the *tunica retina* in vision' (*Inq* VI vii, p. 95). However, as will become clear shortly, the projection of an object's non-perspectival shape onto *any surface*, whether or not it is spherical, will be a visible figure of the object. A projection onto a sphere with the eye at the centre and a projection onto the irregular surface of a retina are equally good visible figures of all of the same objects. Reid is claiming that in order to have a clear conception of an object's visible figure, one must be able to project the object's figure onto a surface, not that the surface must be exactly the same as the surface of a retina.

1. The visible position of a point in space is *the line* passing through both the eye and the point

2. The visible position of a point in space is *any point on the line* passing through both the eye and the point.

(It simplifies matters to think of the lines in both definitions as beginning at the eye and extending through the point in space, i.e., as vectors emanating from the eye, but nothing to be said depends on this simplification.) Both definitions respect the fact that each point on the line through the point and the eye occupies the same place in the visual field. Either definition would yield a definition of the term 'visible figure' which Reid uses in the passage: under (1), the visible figure is a set of lines; under (2) it is any one of an infinite number of different sets of points, depending on which of the infinite number of points on each of the relevant lines we select. However, we want our formal definition of visible figure to conform to the informal definition of visible figure as 'the shape that an object appears to have'. And so our formal definition should imply that various things that we take to be true of the perspectival shapes of objects are true under our formal definition. In particular, a formal definition of visible figure is unsatisfactory if either of the following is false:

(a) Each position within the visible figure of an object is occupied by one and only one point

(b) The visible figure of an object is 'path-connected': from any point in the visible figure to any other there is a path that passes only through points that are also within the visible figure of the object.

Given (a), definition (1) of visible position and the accompanying definition of visible figure are unsatisfactory: if the position of a point on the surface of an object is defined as a line, then each position is occupied by an infinite number of points. Definition (2) of visible position, however, suggests that the visible figure of an object should be defined as any collection of points constructed by selecting one point of equivalent visible position for each point on the surface of the object. However, under this definition, neither (a) nor (b) need be true. Since a line from the eye will often pierce the surface of a three-dimensional object in more than one place, if we include a point in the visible figure for each surface point, then the visible figure might include points that share visible position with one another. But the import of (a) is that where we see only one point, the visible figure should contain only one point.

In order to account for (b), a further restriction on the set of points that make up the visible figure is required. If any point sharing a visible position with a surface point of the object could be included in the visible figure of the object, then the visible figure could be a disconnected 'scattershot' of

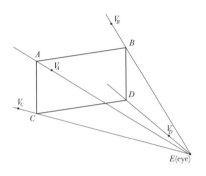

Figure 2: V_k has the same visible position as point k, for each k. But the set containing V_A, V_B, V_C and V_D might not be path-connected in the needed sense.

points in three-dimensional space. For instance, consider four lines each of which passes through the eye and one of the four vertices of a square (see Fig. 2). Now imagine selecting one point from each line but at wildly different distances from the eye (V_A, V_B, V_C and V_D in Fig. 2). If we selected a similarly disparate collection of points for each of the other lines from the eye through the other points of the square, we would end up with a collection of points no two of which were touching. But as indicated by (b), this is not what we want.

For these reasons, we should accept definition (2) of visible position, but we should think of the visible figure of an object as follows. A set VF of points in three-dimensional space is the visible figure of an object O relative to an eye E if and only if (1) for each point on the surface of O, there is a member of VF with the same visible position; (2) no two members of VF share a visible position; (3) the set of points is path-connected: for any two points in the set there is a path from the one to the other that passes only through other members of the set.

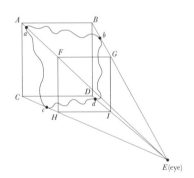

Figure 3: Squares $ABCD$ and $FGHI$ have all the same visible figures. Curves ab, ac, cd and bd lie on planes ABE, ACE, CDE and BDE, respectively.

Under this definition, the relation 'is the visible figure of' is many–many. That is, many different objects will have the same visible figure, and there will be many possible visible figures for any given object. In Fig. 3, squares $ABCD$ and $FGHI$ have all the same visible figures; any visible figure of the one is a visible figure of the other and *vice versa*. (In fact each is a visible figure of the other.) Further, the visible figure need not be a regular shape such as a square. The curvy lines connecting points a, b, c and d serve as the visible figure of either $ABCD$

or *FGHI.* The curve connecting *a* and *b*, for instance, lies on a plane that includes *A, B, F, G* and the eye, and so it appears to the eye to be a straight line that shares the visible positions of the points of *AB* and *FG.*

A visible figure is not an appearance, a sensation or any sort of mental state, nor would a complete characterization of the visible figure of an object need to appeal to any features of the mental life of the perceiver. A visible figure is just a set of points in three-dimensional space defined by reference to the position of an object and the position of an eye. Further, there need

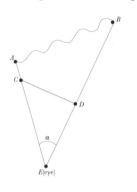

not be any entities occupying the points included in the visible figure of the object. To grasp the visible figure of a thing, we need not imagine that the points included in the visible figure are occupied by certain ghostly entities, nor, even less, that those points are occupied by physical things of the same sort as any ordinary physical object. The concept of a visible figure has no greater or lesser ontological significance than the concept of any other mathematically defined set of points.

Figure 4: The curve *AB* and the line *CD* have the same visible length equal to α.

Using the definition of visible figure, it is a short step to formal definitions of more specific visible figures, such as 'visible line segment' and 'visible triangle'. A visible line segment is a visible figure all of the points of which lie on a plane with the eye. A visible triangle is a visible figure which is equal to the union of three visible lines, *a*, *b* and *c* (the 'visible sides' of the visible triangle), where the intersection of *a* and *b*, *a* and *c*, and *b* and *c* each contains exactly one point; these three points of intersection are the three 'visible vertices' of the visible triangle. Given additional definitions of 'visible length' and 'visible angle', we can define notions such as 'visible equilateral triangle' and 'visible square'. Reid defines visible length in the same way as Berkeley:

> Apparent magnitude [i.e., 'visible length'] is measured by the angle which an object subtends at the eye. Supposing two right lines drawn from the eye to the extremities of the object, making an angle, of which the object is the subtense, the apparent magnitude is measured by this angle. This apparent magnitude is an object of sight, and not of touch. Bishop Berkeley calls it *visible magnitude.*[8]

(See Fig. 4 above for an illustration.) Given this definition, we would say that a visible equilateral triangle is a visible triangle all of whose visible sides have

---

[8] Reid, *Essays on the Intellectual Powers of Man* (hereafter *IP*), ed. B. Brody (MIT Press, 1969), II 14, p. 224.

the same visible length. A visible angle is what is sometimes referred to as a 'dihedral angle', or the angle between two planes that meet at a line. (Fold

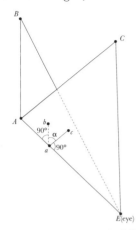

a piece of paper in half and hold it up so that the fold extends directly from your eye: the angle between the planes of the two halves of the paper is the visible angle.) In Fig. 5, to determine the visible angle *BAC*, one considers the angle between the plane which is defined by the eye, *A* and *C* ('plane *ACE*', for short), on the one hand, and plane *ABE*, on the other. This angle is equal to the planar angle between two lines each of which is perpendicular to the line connecting the eye and point *A* (line *AE*, the 'hinge' of the two planes), and of which one lies on the plane *ABE* and the other on the plane *ACE*.

Figure 5: α = visible angle *BAC*. α is the angle between planes *ABE* and *ACE*, which is equal to the planar angle at point *a* of lines *ab* and *ac*. *ab* lies on plane *ABE*, perpendicular to line *AE*, *ac* on plane *ACE*, perpendicular to *AE*.

Using these definitions, it is possible to prove that some, but only some, of the geometrical facts about planar figures are also true of their visible counterparts. For instance, it can be proved that all of the visible angles of a visible equilateral triangle are equal.

However, some facts about planar figures are not true of their visible counterparts. For instance, it is not the case that the visible angles of a visible triangle add up to 180°. Imagine the eye placed at the corner of a room where two walls and the ceiling meet. (See Fig. 6.) Now consider three

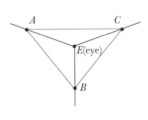

points each one foot from the corner of the room, and each on one of the three lines that meet in the room's corner (points *A*, *B* and *C* in Fig. 6). Now connect these three points with lines drawn on the two walls and the ceiling. The resulting figure is a visible triangle, but the angle between any two of the planes that meet at the room's corner is 90°. The result is that the three visible angles are each equal to 90°, and so the visible triangle's visible angles add up to 270°. But triangle *ABC* is also a planar tri-angle, in addition to being a visible triangle. So

Figure 6: Angles *AEB*, *AEC* and *BEC* are all equal to 90°, for a total of 270°.

although its visible angles add up to 270°, its planar angles add up to 180°. This is noteworthy only because it illustrates the discrepancy between the planar and visible features of single objects.

It is important that, suggestive as these results are, I have not shown (and it is not true) that visible figures lie on spheres. Given a fixed location of the eye, every object has an infinite number of visible figures that are planar. Given the definition of visible figure, we can construct a planar visible figure for every object as follows: for each point on the surface of the object, select exactly one point on a plane that intersects the line from the eye to the surface point; since there are an infinite number of such planes, there are an infinite number of planar visible figures for each object. Euclidean planar facts about these, such as that the angles of a triangle add up to 180°, do not hold true when the Euclidean concepts of an angle and a line are replaced by their visible counterparts, but this consequence does not show anything about the geometry of visible figures: visible angles, for instance, are simply different mathematical objects from planar angles, so there is no reason to expect them to behave in the same way. If a visible figure is in fact planar, then it obeys the laws of Euclidean geometry. And 'visible' theorems, such as, for instance, 'The visible angles of a visible equilateral triangle are equal', can be derived from the axioms of Euclidean geometry. In proving claims of this nature we need never deny any Euclidean axioms. I believe that Reid would deny none of this. But if not, then what does the claimed equivalence between the geometry of the visibles and spherical geometry amount to?

Imagine a function V that maps sentences of geometry which do not invoke any 'visible' concepts onto sentences in which each non-'visible' concept is replaced with its corresponding 'visible' concept. So, for instance, V maps the Pythagorean theorem, 'In any right triangle, the square of the length of the hypotenuse is equal to the sum of the squares of the lengths of the other two sides', to the visible Pythagorean theorem, 'In any visible right triangle, the square of the visible length of the visible hypotenuse is equal to the sum of the squares of the visible lengths of the other two visible sides' (a 'visible right triangle' has one visible right angle).[9] This mapping will not always preserve truth-value. While the Pythagorean theorem is true, the visible Pythagorean theorem is false: visible triangle ABC in Fig. 6 above presents a counter-example. I shall call a grammatical sentence of geometry G invoking no visible concepts 'proof-theoretically equivalent to its visible counterpart' $V(G)$ if and only if (1) the truth-value of G is the same as the truth-value of $V(G)$; and (2) if G is proved (or proved false) with a set of non-visible sentences P, then the set of visible counterparts of the sentences in P is a proof of $V(G)$, or a proof of its falsity.

---

[9] We do not transform arithmetical concepts like 'equals' into corresponding visible concepts. It is difficult to draw the distinction between the geometrical concepts (like the concept of an angle), which are transformed by this mapping, and the non-geometrical concepts (like the concepts of '+' and '='), which are not. I shall not tackle this problem here.

Reid's claim is that every theorem of spherical geometry – theorems that invoke the concepts (yet to be defined) of 'spherical length', 'spherical angle', etc. – is proof-theoretically equivalent to its visible counterpart.[10] Since it is also the case that for every theorem of visible geometry there is exactly one theorem of spherical geometry that has it as a visible counterpart, it follows that there are no theorems of visible geometry for which no proof-theoretically equivalent theorem of spherical geometry cannot be found. If this claim is true, then in order to prove a theorem of visible geometry, one needs only to prove the corresponding theorem of spherical geometry. Further, by proving a theorem of visible geometry, one can reconstruct a theorem and proof of spherical geometry by working backwards and replacing all of the 'visible' concepts with 'spherical' concepts in the theorem and proof. If this is true, then the truths of spherical geometry and the truths of visible geometry are equivalent, in an important sense.

I have shown already that theorems of planar geometry do not in general satisfy the conditions of proof-theoretical equivalence with theorems of visible geometry – the visible counterparts of many true theorems of planar geometry are false. But I have not yet shown that theorems of spherical geometry are proof-theoretically equivalent to theorems of visible geometry. The next section demonstrates why this must be so; it demonstrates, that is, that spherical geometry is truly a geometry of visibles.

II.3. *Reid's argument*

Reid's argument proceeds in three stages. He shows that any sentence about a 'spherical line' is proof-theoretically equivalent to its visible counterpart; then he shows that this is so for any sentence about a 'spherical angle' made by two 'spherical lines'; finally, he extends these results to sentences about 'spherical triangles'.

The first stage concerns spherical lines (*Inq* VI ix, p. 103):

> Supposing the eye placed in the centre of a sphere, every great circle of the sphere [i.e., circle drawn on the sphere concentric with it] will have the same appearance to the eye as if it was a straight line; for the curvature of the circle being turned directly toward the eye, is not perceived by it.

So far Reid is pointing out only that every great circle of a sphere centred at the eye is a visible line. Lying behind this claim is a definition of the concepts of 'spherical line' and 'spherical line segment': a spherical line is a great circle of a sphere; a spherical line segment is an arc of a great circle of

---

[10] Daniels (p. 10) claims that Reid's view is that 'the geometry of visibles is consistent if spherical geometry is'. This is to invoke only clause (1) in the definition of 'proof-theoretic equivalence' offered in the main text above. But, as will become clear, Reid takes the equivalence between the geometry of visibles and spherical geometry to be stronger than this.

a sphere. Reid goes on to note that not every visible line is an arc of a great circle centred at the eye (*Inq* VI ix, p. 103):

> ... any line which is drawn in the plane of a great circle of the sphere, whether it be in reality straight or curve, will appear straight to the eye.

For Reid, the question of whether or not a path-connected set of points is 'in reality straight or curve' depends on whether the Euclidean planar notions of 'straight' or 'curve' apply to it. And so the claim made so far is merely a trivial consequence of the definition of visible figure: every spherical line is a visible line, but not *vice versa*. This does not establish anything like proof-theoretic equivalence between sentences concerning spherical lines, or spherical line segments, and their visible counterparts, sentences in which the spherical concepts are replaced by corresponding visible concepts. Reid attempts to establish this, or at least to illustrate it, in the next paragraph:

> Every visible right line will appear to coincide with some great circle of the sphere; and the circumference of that great circle, even when it is produced until it returns into itself, will appear to be a continuation of the same visible right line, all the parts of it being visibly *in directum*.

I believe that Reid is here stating that there is a proof-theoretic equivalence between a particular theorem of spherical geometry and its visible counterpart. The theorem he has in mind is 'A spherical line has a constant spherical slope'. That this must be what Reid is saying can be shown by thinking about regular lines. In Euclidean geometry, the slope of a curve is the equation for the rate of change in position of the points of the curve with respect to one of the axes. It is a fact of Euclidean geometry that every regular line has a constant slope. Another way of putting this point is to say that the direction in which the line is heading is the same, no matter where on the line we are. All the parts of the line, that is, are '*in directum*' – standing on any point of the line, if we were to point in the direction the line is travelling at that point, we would point at the line itself.

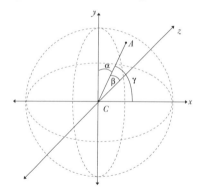

Figure 7: The spherical position of point A on the surface of the sphere centred at C is (γ, α, β), the angles of radius CA with respect to the x, y and z axes.

The 'spherical position' of a point is the three angles with respect to the x, y and z axes of a radius drawn to the point with the centre of the sphere at the origin (see Fig. 7). Any point on this radius (line CA in Fig. 7) has the same spherical position as any other point on this radius. A 'spherical curve' is any path-connected set of points each of which is equidistant from the origin. The 'spherical slope' of a spherical curve is the equation for the rate of change of spherical position in the points of the curve. The 'visible slope' of a visible curve, correspondingly, is the equation for the rate of change of visible position of the points of the curve.

What Reid is claiming in the passage just quoted is this: if a spherical curve has a constant spherical slope, then every visible figure of that spherical curve has a constant visible slope. He goes on (*Inq* VI ix, pp. 103–4) to explain why this must be true:

> For the eye, perceiving only the position of objects with regard to itself, and not their distance, will see those points in the same visible place which have the same position with regard to the eye, how different soever their distances from it may be. Now, since a plane passing through the eye and a given visible right line, will be the plane of some great circle of the sphere, every point of the visible right line will have the same position as some point of the great circle; therefore, they will both have the same visible place, and coincide to the eye; and the whole circumference of the great circle, continued even until it returns into itself, will appear to be a continuation of the same visible right line.
>
> Hence, it follows –
>
> That every visible right line, when it is continued *in directum*, as far as it may be continued, will be represented by a great circle of a sphere, in whose centre the eye is placed.

The first sentence of this passage is easily misunderstood. Reid deduces that the eye 'will see those points in the same visible place which have the same position with regard to the eye' from the fact that points lying on the same line with the eye have the same visible position, regardless of their distance from the eye. But this implies that Reid must be using the phrase 'position with regard to the eye' to mean something different from the term 'visible position', otherwise no deduction would be required; that is, if the terms are being used synonymously, then it is a tautology that the eye 'will see those points in the same visible place which have the same position with regard to the eye'. I suggest that Reid is using the term 'position with regard to the eye' to mean 'spherical position', in the sense just defined. When so understood, he can be taken to be making the following non-tautological claim: two points have the same visible position if and only if they have the same spherical position with respect to a sphere centred at the eye.[11] He

---

[11] This claim is easily proved. (a) If two points have the same visible position, then they lie on the same line drawn from the eye, and so on the same radius of a sphere drawn from the eye to the further point. But any two points on such a radius share the same spherical position. (b) If two points have the same spherical position, they lie on the same radius drawn from the eye to the farther of the two points. So they have the same visible position.

then uses this fact to show that any 'continuation' of the spherical line is a 'continuation' of the visible line, and *vice versa*. The slope of a curve at a point tells us in what direction – that is, towards what position – we must travel in order to continue the curve. And so Reid is claiming that whatever the spherical slope of the spherical line is at any given point, the visible line has the same visible slope, and *vice versa*. And thus it is shown that any theorem about spherical lines and their spherical slopes is proof-theoretically equivalent to the analogous theorem about visible lines and their visible slopes; after all, facts about lines and slopes, whether spherical or visible, are simply a function of the spherical or visible position of the points that make them up. So, given that spherical position and visible position are no different, theorems about the one and theorems about the other are true for the same reasons.

Before moving to the second stage of the argument, it is worth drawing attention to the way in which Reid phrases the conclusion of the first stage:

> every visible right line, when it is continued *in directum*, as far as it may be continued, will be represented by a great circle of a sphere, in whose centre the eye is placed.

In what sense is a great circle the 'representative' of a visible line? If Reid had said that the great circles were representatives of the non-perspectival figure of some curve, then he would be making the point (familiar from Berkeley, *NTV* §§139–48) that visible figures of an object are a 'sign' of the non-perspectival figure of the object; that is, they tell us what the non-perspectival figure of the object is. But this is not what he says. He says instead that the great circles are the representatives of *visible* lines. Great circles *are* visible lines, although not all visible lines are great circles, so in what sense are they the *representatives* of visible lines? We might understand this 'representation' talk like this: one thing is a representative of another when it can speak for the other. Perhaps what Reid means is that great circles 'speak for' visible lines in the sense defined by proof-theoretic equivalence. That is, sentences concerning them and invoking spherical concepts (spherical positions, spherical angles, etc.) are proof-theoretically equivalent to sentences invoking visible concepts instead. To put this another way, if you want to know whether or not a visible line has a particular visible feature, and why it does or does not, all you need to do is consider if the spherical line has the analogous spherical feature. The spherical will tell you about the visible.

In the second stage of the argument, concerning spherical angles, Reid writes (*Inq* VI ix, p. 104)

> the visible angle comprehended under two visible right lines, is equal to the spherical angle comprehended under the two great circles which are the representatives of these visible lines. For, since the visible lines appear to coincide with the great circles,

the visible angle comprehended under the former must be equal to the visible angle comprehended under the latter. But the visible angle comprehended under the two great circles, when seen from the centre, is of the same magnitude with the spherical angle which they really comprehend, as mathematicians know; therefore, the visible angle made by any two visible lines is equal to the spherical angle made by the two great circles of the sphere which are their representatives.

In this passage Reid invokes two different notions of an angle which I have yet to discuss. He writes of the angle that two intersecting curves 'really comprehend'; this is what I shall call the 'real angle' between two intersecting curves. And he writes of the 'spherical angle' between two different great circles of a sphere. How are these notions defined? I suggest that by the 'real angle' between two curves that intersect at point A (see Fig. 8), Reid means to refer to the planar angle made by lines tangent to the two curves at that point, each lying on the plane occupied by the corresponding curve. This is consistent with Reid's usage of the term 'real' to mean 'Euclidean' or 'planar'.[12] Imagine slicing a loaf of bread with two intersecting cuts. Now consider the curves on the surface of the bread made by the two cuts. Take the line tangent to the surface at the point of intersection and on the plane travelled by the knife. Do this for each cut, and consider the angle created by the two resulting lines. This is the real angle made by the two curves created by the two cuts.

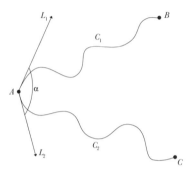

Figure 8: L_1 and L_2 are the tangents at point A to C_1 and C_2, respectively, and on their respective planes. α is the real angle made by C_1 and C_2, and is equal to the planar angle of L_1 and L_2.

    The real angle between two intersecting curves is called a 'spherical angle' if the curves are arcs of great circles of a sphere. So, for instance, imagine replacing the bread in the above example with a perfectly spherical tennis ball, and make sure that both cuts pass through the centre of the ball. The real angle at the point of intersection of the two resulting surface curves is a spherical angle. However, while this is a sufficient condition for being a spherical angle, it is not a necessary condition, because it could be that only

---

[12] If the curve is itself a straight line, then it will be used to calculate the real angle, since the tangent will not be well defined. So if both curves are straight lines, the real angle is just the planar angle between the two lines. To give a complete formal definition of 'real angle' we would also need to say how the real angle is to be calculated when the derivative of one or the other curve, at the point of intersection, is not defined and the curve is not a straight line. I leave this complexity aside.

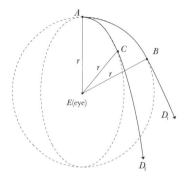

Figure 9: *A*, *B* and *C* lie on a sphere centred at E. Curve segments *AB* and *AC* are arcs of great circles of the sphere. Curves D_1 and D_2, of which *AB* and *AC* are segments, are not arcs of great circles.

a segment of each curve near the point of intersection is an arc of a great circle of a sphere. In Fig. 9, the segments *AB* and *AC* of curves D_1 and D_2, respectively, are arcs of great circles of a sphere centred at *E*. Beyond points *B* and *C*, D_1 and D_2 diverge from great circles of the sphere. But the real angle made by D_1 and D_2 at *A* is still a spherical angle. This yields the following set of necessary and sufficient conditions for a spherical angle: the real angle between curves D_1 and D_2 that intersect at point *A* is a spherical angle if and only if there exist segments of D_1 and D_2 both of which include *A*, and both of which are arcs of great circles of a sphere.

When we interpret in the way suggested Reid's talk of 'real' and 'spherical' angles in the difficult passage just quoted, then he appears to be trying to prove the following:

3.   If the real angle made by two visible lines is a spherical angle with respect to a sphere centred at the eye, then the visible angle made by the two visible lines is equal to the real angle made by the two visible lines.

This is provable, although it is unclear if Reid has the proof in mind. Here is the proof. Referring to Fig. 10, the real angle made by the curves *AB* and *AC*

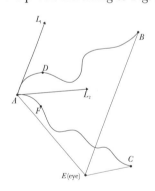

Figure 10: Curves *AB* and *AC* lie on planes *ABE* and *ACE*, respectively. L_1 and L_2 are tangents at point *A* to *AB* and *AC*, respectively. L_1 and L_2 lie on planes *ABE* and *ACE*, respectively.

at point *A* is the angle between lines L_1 and L_2. If this angle is a spherical angle, then there are points *D* and *F*, on *AB* and *AC* respectively, such that *AD* and *AF* are arcs of circles centred at *E*. This implies that L_1 and L_2 are both perpendicular to line *AE* – a tangent to a circle is always perpendicular to a radius of the circle. But since L_1 lies on plane *ABE*, and L_2 lies on plane *ACE*, the angle between L_1 and L_2 is equal to the dihedral angle between planes *ABE* and *ACE*. But, by definition, this is the visible angle at *A*. Q.E.D.

It is important to see that the converse of (3) is false: there are cases of curves in which the visible angle and the real angle are the same, but neither curve has a segment that lies on a sphere centred at the eye. This is possible because, first, although lines perpendicular to the

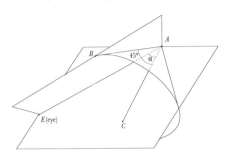

hinge between two planes make a planar angle equal to the dihedral angle between the planes, there are many other lines lying on the same planes that make a planar angle equal to the dihedral angle and that are not perpendicular to the hinge. In fact, as Fig. 11 illustrates, given two planes that intersect on a line *AE*, and given any line through point *A* on one of the planes (line *AC* in Fig. 11), it is possible to find a line on the other plane (line *AB* in Fig. 11), also passing through *A*, that makes a planar angle with the first equal to

Figure 11: The dihedral angle between planes *ABE* and *ACE* is 45°. The cone with axis *AC* is a 45° cone. The intersection of the cone and plane *ABE* is line *AB*. α is less than 90°, but the angle made by *AB* and *AC* equals 45°.

the dihedral angle between the planes. In Fig. 11, such a line was located by identifying the intersection between plane *ABE* and a 45° cone with *AC* as its axis.

What this implies is that the mere fact that the visible angle made by two curves is equal to the real angle made by those curves does not imply that the curves are circular near the point of intersection: the tangents at that point need not be perpendicular to the line of sight for the real and visible angles to be the same. But if the tangents are not perpendicular to the line of sight at that point, then the curves are not coincident with circles centred at the eye. What this means is that although sentences about spherical angles are proof-theoretically equivalent to sentences about visible angles, they are not the only sentences that are. There are many pairs of curves that are not spherical lines but make real angles equal to their visible angles. In fact, given any curve at all, it is possible to construct an intersecting curve that makes a real angle and a visible angle of equal magnitude: given the tangent at the point of intersection, using the procedure above, find a corresponding line on another plane through the eye and the intersection point that makes a real angle equal to the visible angle; then pick any curve to which that line is tangent at the point of intersection. What this implies is that the geometry of spherical angles is not the *only* geometry of visible angles.[13] It is not clear whether Reid appreciated this

[13] So Daniels (p. 11) is wrong to say 'Projection onto no other surface [besides a sphere] preserves the properties of visible figure'. There is an infinite number of such surfaces.

point, although he may have. When summarizing his claims about the geometry of visibles, he never, to my knowledge, says that the *only* geometry of the visible is spherical geometry.

What remains to be shown, although I am most of the way there already, is that theorems about spherical figures are proof-theoretically equivalent to theorems about visible figures. Reid argues the point only for visible triangles – he suggests that their 'representatives' are spherical triangles – although he makes the point, without offering an argument for it, regarding visible circles (see *Inq* VI ix, p. 104). But if the point applies to visible triangles, it is not difficult to extend it to all other visible figures as well. Reid offers his argument for extending the results shown so far to spherical and visible triangles in the following passage (p. 104):

> Hence it is evident, that every visible right-lined triangle will coincide in all its parts with some spherical triangle. The sides of the one will appear equal to the sides of the other, and the angles of the one to the angles of the other, each to each: and, therefore, the whole of the one triangle will appear equal to the whole of the other. In a word, to the eye they will be one and the same, and have the same mathematical properties. The properties, therefore, of visible right-lined triangles, are not the same with the properties of plain [*viz* planar] triangles, but are the same with those of spherical triangles.

The point here is quite simple: the parts of a triangle are just three line segments and three angles; the parts of a spherical triangle are three spherical line segments and three spherical angles; and the parts of a visible triangle are three visible line segments and three visible angles. Therefore anything that is said about a (planar, spherical or visible) triangle can be paraphrased into a sentence that makes no mention of triangles, but mentions only (planar, spherical or visible) sides of certain (planar, spherical or visible) lengths, and (planar, spherical or visible) angles of certain (planar, spherical or visible) magnitudes. But in the first two stages of the argument it was shown that any theorem regarding spherical lines or spherical angles was proof-theoretically equivalent to its visible counterpart. It follows that theorems about spherical triangles are proof-theoretically equivalent to the corresponding theorems about visible triangles. So spherical geometry is a geometry of the visible.

III. CONCLUSION: APPEARS–IS

It is important that nowhere does Reid's argument depend upon any claim to the effect that perceived objects are as they appear. He is not suggesting that all visible figures are in fact spherical. In fact, as pointed out earlier, this is false: a projection with respect to the eye of the surface-points of an object onto any of a variety of surfaces, planar, spherical, parabolic, or even highly irregular, is a visible figure for that object. This is important for Reid's overall philosophy of perception. Reid was, of course, a direct realist, and no direct realist can claim that any entity is by its very nature as it appears, without invoking something like ideas or sense-data – special entities that are so 'present to the mind' as to preclude mistake about their properties. There is no reason to think that Reid takes this to be true of visible figures. In fact, given that he takes himself to be discovering many facts about visible figures that are not obvious to the normally sighted, he must think that there is a great deal about visible figures that we do not know simply by seeing them.

Reid is claiming not that the visible is the spherical, but that *the geometry* of the visible is the same as *the geometry* of the spherical. What has been shown here is that this is true, and thus that Berkeley was wrong to base his view that visible figures are less 'real' than the non-perspectival shapes, or in some way lower on the metaphysical ladder, on the claim that they are not the objects of a genuine, objective science. Thus, and this would have been a point of particular importance to Reid, there is no reason to think that an encounter with the perspectival shape of an object is less an encounter with a real entity than an encounter with the object's non-perspectival shape. In both cases, we are encountering the object itself.[14]

University of Southern California

[14] For comments on drafts and helpful conversation, thanks are owed to Steven Janke, Paul Zeitz, James Van Cleve and the other participants in his 2000 Summer NEH seminar on Reid, particularly Ryan Nichols and Ed Slowik. Thanks also to Sue Chan for invaluable help in creating the figures.

INDEX

abstraction, 89, 96, 177
action, cause of, 124–5, 128, 130, 159
agency, 2–3, 110, 113, 130
    displayed in animals, 110, 113–15,
      127–8, 167–8
    a matter of experience, 15, 18–19
    presupposes will, 126, 168
    wrongly ascribed to nature, 15, 17–18,
      20–2, 116–17, 155
Ambrose, A., 131–2
analysis/system, 163
analytic/synthetic, 93, 96
Aquinas, 172, 187
argument from analogy, 15, 17
argument to best explanation, 103, 165
Aristotelianism, 69, 115, 154, 156, 189
Aristotle, 38, 65, 130, 164
Armstrong, D.M., 62–3, 68
Arnauld, A., 145
Arthur, A., 7
attention, 59–60, 83, 126–7, 129
attraction, 106–8, 116, 158
Austin, J.L., 8
Avicenna, 172

Bacon, F., 18, 103, 156
Bayle, P., 20
Beanblossom, R., 11, 88
Beattie, J., 5–6, 151, 153, 157–8, 164–5
behaviour, making sense of, 113–15,
    118–19, 121–5, 127, 130
belief-forming mechanism, 32–4, 38–9, 43,
    149, 161
beliefs, as causes of action, 159

beliefs, inescapable, 30–4, 36–7, 39, 56, 87,
    90, 111, 136–7, 150–1, 153, 159, 162
    justifying, 31, 34–5, 38–9, 41, 52, 56
Berkeley, G., 2, 49, 53–4, 57, 65, 70, 72,
    101, 109, 111–12, 139–40, 142, 144–5,
    154, 182, 190, 196, 202, 207
Blair, H., 5–6
Blumenfeld, D., 10
BonJour, L., 187
Boscovich theory, 100, 105–6, 109
Boswell, J., 6–7
Boyle, R., 71
brain events, 48, 55, 60, 62–3, 109, 181
brains in vats, 134, 147–8, 150
Brentano, F., 186
Brody, B., 11
Brookes, D., 25–6, 33–4
Brown, T., 30
Buridan's Ass, 125
by virtue of relation, 49–51, 56, 59, 61, 64,
    67

Campbell, G., 5–6
capacity, see *power*
Carnap, R., 166
Cartesian circle, 25–7, 159, 161–2
Cartwright, R., 170–1
Cassam, Q., 90–1, 95
Castagnetto, S., 179
causality, 2–4, 17–19, 96, 104–5, 108, 130
causation, agent, 130
cause, concept of, 85, 119
centaurs, 89, 169, 173, 178, 180, 183–4, 186
charity, principle of, 160

Chisholm, R., 8, 177, 186
Christianity, 101–2
Christie, A., 127
Churchland, P., 80–1
circles, 169, 174
coach, sound of, 49, 62–3
cogito, 93, 161
cognition, fallible, 39–40, 135, 167
cognitive faculties, truth-aimed?, 26–7, 38, 156–8, 161
coherentism, 42, 87
colours, 65, 70–2, 74–6, 78–9, 140
'common sense', ambiguity of, 151–2
common sense, 3, 28–31, 34, 53, 71, 85, 87, 93, 99, 110, 142, 151, 164–6, 174, 180, 182–4, 187–8
    and reason, 3, 28–9, 31, 33, 90, 141, 149
    as practical, 29, 42–3, 115
    first principles, 3, 19–20, 24, 28–38, 82–3, 86, 95, 100, 110–11, 141, 152, 156–8
    first principles, as axioms, 35–6, 38, 43, 149, 158
    first principles, as causes, 158–9
    first principles, as constitutive, 34, 36–8, 42–3
    first principles, as practical, 3, 128, 130, 166–8
    first principles, indispensable, 32, 34, 37, 43, 111, 140, 158, 165, 167–8
    first principles, justifying, 25, 31–6, 39, 84–8, 90, 94, 96, 139–40, 142, 146–7, 167–8
    first principles, scepticism about, 37
    problems about, 152–3, 166–8
    superior to argument, 141–3, 165–6
conception, 48–51, 53, 86, 88, 136, 172–3, 185
    adverbial theory of, 175–7
    bare/co-ordinated, 185
    dependent on learning, 57, 78–80, 88, 137, 172
    is of things not ideas, 173–4, 180–1, 183–4
consciousness, 46, 60, 86, 89, 91, 97
    reveals the mental, 82–9, 91–6, 129

constant conjunction, 3–4, 18–19, 22–3, 63, 116–17
content of belief, 50–2, 58–9, 62, 170–4, 176–7, 183, 185–6
contextualism, 148
control, 113–14, 116, 119, 122, 126–30
Cousin, V., 83–4, 93, 97
Cudworth, R., 20

Daniels, N., 25, 192–3
Darwinian theory, 38–40
David, M., 186–7
definition, 116–17
deliberation, 113–15, 117, 122–4, 126–7, 129, 174
    controlled, 122–3, 125–7, 129
Democritus, 65
demon argument, 26, 147–8
Dennett, D., 27, 39–40
DeRose, K., 32–5, 57, 148
Descartes, R., 25–6, 65, 70, 93, 95, 101, 110, 135, 139, 145, 152, 159–62, 172
desire, 114–15, 120–2, 124, 127–8
dispositions, 66–70, 116
    causal basis of, 67–71, 74–5, 77, 80
    conditional analysis of, 67, 69
    identity theory of, 68–9, 75
doubt, 26–7, 32–4, 37, 93, 159, 162
dreaming, 135, 138–9
dualism, 47–8, 100–1, 104–6, 109–11
Ducasse. C.J., 8
Duggan, T., 10–11

Einstein, A., 165
encyclopaedism, 153–7
Epicurus, 20, 65, 70
epistemology, as science, 24, 41–3, 83, 94–6
evidence, 26, 31, 33, 56, 82, 86, 88, 103, 106–8, 130, 135, 138–9, 142, 148–50, 163, 168
    need for, 2, 24–5, 33–4, 103, 106–8, 148, 154, 165, 167–8
evolutionary epistemology, see *Darwinian theory*
exertion, 14–15, 18–19, 22, 117, 119–20, 122–3

'exist', ambiguity of, 171–5, 177–9, 186–7
existence, a property, 174–5
explanation, 103–4
    limits of, 155–8
    personal/scientific, 155–6
eye, as a point, 191–3

fact/value distinction, see *is and ought*
faculties, reliability of, 25–8, 32–5, 37–41,
    138–9, 142, 147–50, 159, 185
Farquhar, J., 5
feelings, 46, 58–9, 146, 175–6
fictional objects, 86, 88–9, 169–88
final causes, 20, 26, 155–8
Fodor, J., 27, 39–40
foundationalism, 42, 96, 135–6, 160
fragility, 66–8
Fraser, A.C., 9
functional property, 27–8, 119, 121, 167

Galilei, G., 65, 70
general terms, 89–90, 94, 169–70, 174,
    177–80
generalization, 89–90, 94, 96, 177
Gerard, A., 5–6
God's mind as explanation, 20–1, 26, 38,
    155–6, 158, 163–5
Goldman, A., 27, 40–1
good sense, 28
Grave, S.A., 11, 110–11, 169–70, 182, 188
Gregory, D., 2, 4
    James, 7–9, 181
    John, 2, 4–7

Haack, S., 40–1
Haldane, J.J., 187
hands, 131–2, 134–5, 137–8, 140, 144,
    146–8
hardness, 49–50, 53, 55, 57–8, 77–8, 140,
    146
Harman, G., 41
Harré, R., 84
Hartley, D., 99–100
heat, 72, 77
Holbach, Baron d', 101

human nature, see *principles of our constitution*
Hume, D., 1–8, 14, 17–19, 21, 23, 26–8,
    30–1, 35, 51, 53–4, 70, 84–5, 88–9,
    94, 96, 98–9, 116–17, 122, 128,
    139–40, 142, 144–5, 152, 154–5,
    159–60, 162–4, 166, 172, 182, 184–6
Hutcheson, F., 128
hypotheses, 24, 103–8, 112, 142, 164–5

'ideal system', see *ideas, way of*
ideas, present to the mind, 28, 51, 72, 142,
    144–5, 173–4, 181–2, 184, 207
    presuppose impressions, 3–4, 111–12,
    162, 172, 182
    similar to things?, 51–4, 60, 71–2, 77,
    111–12, 142, 144–5, 161
    way of, 4, 28, 54, 57, 65, 70–2, 84, 86,
    101, 112, 143–5, 154, 162–6, 170,
    173–5, 180–8
    way of, leads to scepticism, 72, 163–5
imagination, 86, 88–9, 103, 138, 174,
    184–6
immaterial principles, 20, 22, 106–10, 112,
    117, 154
inertia, 106–8
infallibility, 32–3
instinctive faculties, 18–19, 25, 29–30, 39,
    111
instincts, 14, 114, 127, 166
intellectual representation, 91–2, 94–5
interaction problem, 18, 100–2, 108–9
intrinsic natures, 68–70, 75, 78–9, 81
intuition, 31, 85, 91, 161
irrational action, 40, 124–5
is and ought, 4, 35–7, 40–3, 153, 167–8

Jackson, F., 49, 70, 75
Jensen, H., 84
Johnson, S., 6–7, 17

Kames, Lord, 7, 9
Kant, I., 1–2, 4, 6, 8, 10, 36, 83–98, 127,
    143, 161, 166
knowledge, by perception, 33, 133, 135–6,
    138, 143, 148, 161

knowledge, sources of, 27, 136, 138, 143, 145–50, 154, 161
Kornblith, H., 41–2

language, common structure of, 17, 32, 71–2, 83–4, 89, 94, 124, 141, 162, 167
laws of nature, see *nature, laws of*
Le Clerc, J., 20
Lehrer, K., 8, 11, 33, 41–2, 83, 88–9, 97, 153, 178–9
Leibniz, G.W., 21, 169
Locke, J., 14, 65, 70–3, 77, 116, 139, 145, 156–7, 162, 172, 182
Lycan, W., 27

McDowell, J., 71
McGee, V., 178
McGinn, C., 71
MacIntyre, A., 153–4
Mackintosh, J., 30
Maffie, J., 24, 40
Malcolm, N., 131–2
Malebranche, N., 65, 70, 139, 145, 162
Malherbe, M., 86–7, 92
manifestation, 67–8, 116
materialism, 7, 99–106, 108–10, 112
matter, 100, 103
    powers of, 2, 17–21, 100–2, 105–11, 144, 158
Matthen, M., 40
Meinong, A., 171, 178
Meinongianism, 170–2, 174–5, 177–82, 186–8
memory, 26, 86, 136, 138, 143, 174
mental events, correlated with brain events, 100–6
mental operations, 47–8, 53, 60, 73, 83–7, 89, 92–3, 95–6, 116–17, 119, 126–7, 129, 138, 146, 160, 173, 183, 185
mental properties, 70–1, 83, 95
mental substance, 47, 94–5, 109–11
metaphysics, 27–8, 47, 56, 82–5, 88, 91, 96, 99, 187, 190, 207
methodology, 24–5, 82–5, 92–3, 95–7, 102, 108, 112, 132–3, 139–41, 173
Mettrie, J. de la, 154

Millikan, R., 27
mind, nature of, 82, 85–7, 92–7, 99, 101, 104–5, 109–12, 118, 146, 154, 157, 160, 162–4, 168
miracles, 21–2
Molyneux's problem, 80
monads, 21
monism, 101
Moore, G.E., 8, 10, 131–50
moral responsibility, 21–2, 29, 125, 128
moral sense, 128–9
motive, strongest, notion of, 122–6
    strongest, can be resisted, 124–5
motives, controlled, 114, 125–9
    evaluation of, 125–6
    influence of, 126–7
multiple realizability, 68
Murray, R.K., 1

naming, 89–90, 177
natural magic, 57, 77, 89
natural selection, 27, 38
naturalism, 24, 27–8, 40–3, 113–14, 129–30, 154, 166
    'providential', 25–8, 33, 38, 43
    epistemological, 24–5, 27–8, 40–3, 154
nature, laws of, 3, 18, 22, 26, 53, 74, 105–6, 117, 153, 155–8, 165
natures of things, 105, 155–8
necessary connection, 18–19, 22, 84–5, 96
necessary truth, 19, 30, 76
Newton's rules of reasoning, 24, 26, 99–112, 114, 154–6
Newton, I., 18, 99–100, 103, 106–7
nominalism, 178–9
non-existence, 169–79, 183–6, 188
normative, see *is and ought*
noumenal/phenomenal, 85–8, 90–4, 96

object of mental act, 45–6, 48–51, 55, 58–61, 64, 86–7, 89, 120–1, 137, 142, 173–7, 181, 184–5
objects of thought must exist, 181–2, 187
occasionalism, 101, 109
ordinary-language philosophy, 115, 131–2
Oswald, J., 6, 151, 153

Panglossian optimism, 40
Parmenides, 164
pencils, 142–3, 146
perception, 44, 47–8
    as evidence, 138–40, 142–3, 146, 148–50
    by a medium, 60–1
    direct object of, 59, 61, 64, 172, 174, 185, 207
    immediate object of, 50–5, 60, 72–3, 79, 142, 144–5
    not inferential, 50, 54, 136–7, 145–6, 148–9, 161
    original/acquired, 78–81, 137, 167
perceptual belief, dependent on sensation, 59
Peripatetics, 20, 65, 145
personal identity, 7
phenomenological qualities, see *qualia*
philosophy as science, 152–7, 159–60, 162, 164–7
Plantinga, A., 27–8, 38–9
Plato, 51
Platonism, 101, 178–9
pneumatology, 82, 153–4, 160, 162–4
'power', ambiguously applied, 17–18, 21–3, 116
power, 2–3, 9, 14–23, 47, 82, 99–100, 106, 110–11, 114–18, 120, 122–3, 127, 129–30, 138, 154–6, 168
    and constant conjunction, 18–19, 22
    as capacity not to act, 3, 21–2, 116–19, 122
    conception of, 14–15, 17–19, 21, 116
    distinct from causality, 3, 17–23, 116–17
    incompatible with necessity, 21–3
    not object of consciousness, 14, 116–19
    occult quality, 19
    presupposes intelligence, 20–2, 121
predicables, 177–8
prejudice, 31–2, 39, 42, 52, 95
presentational content, 50, 55, 57–8, 62
Price, R., 100, 102
Priest, G., 70–1
Priestley, J., 6–7, 10, 21, 98–112

'principle', sense of, 158
principles of our constitution, 18, 49, 53–4, 56, 65, 73, 77–9, 81, 137, 141, 149–50, 152, 155–64, 166–7
principles, nature of, 42–3
privileged access, 171–2, 183–6
proof, 134–6, 138–9
    out of place, 31, 35, 133, 135–7, 139–41, 143, 146

qualia, 49, 62–3, 176–7, 190
qualities, known by effects, 66–71, 74–8, 80–1, 167
    mind-independent, 47–8, 50, 54–9, 63, 65, 146, 189
    not immediately perceived, 59–61, 64
    occult, 66–9, 73–5, 77–8, 80–1, 96, 118
    perception of, 44, 47–54, 56–9, 62–3, 73–5, 79–81, 85, 140, 146
    primary/secondary, 47, 55, 57–8, 65–81, 189–90
quality terms ambiguous, 72, 75–6
quantum mechanics, 94
questions, internal/external, 132, 143
Quine, W.V.O., 27, 41–3

Raeburn, H., 8
rational action, 29, 115, 123–4, 126–8
rationality, 38–40
Raynal, G.-T., 15, 17
real angle, 203–5
realism, direct, 44–5, 47, 49–51, 59–64, 112, 172, 187–8, 207
    representative, 50–4, 57–8, 60
    scientific, 99, 101, 110
reason, 29, 136, 160–1, 166
    not the only judge of truth, 138, 161
reasonable creatures, 29
reasoning, 29–31, 34–5, 38–9, 41, 47, 53–4, 77, 90, 115, 136–8, 140–1, 146, 148–9, 157–61, 166–7
reflection, 46, 60, 64, 82–3, 85–6, 93, 96–7, 130, 135, 162, 164, 167, 171, 183–4
Reid, Thomas, life of, 1–8
relational access, see *relative notion*

relative notion, 50, 58, 66, 68–9, 73–81, 118–19, 123
reliabilism, 41, 149–50, 168
representationalism, 144–5, 174–5, 181–2, 184, 186–7
ridicule, 140
Robinson, D., 84
rules, regulative/constitutive, 36–8
Russell, B., 141–3, 146, 152
Ryle, G., 8

scepticism, 163
    external world, 26–7, 30, 32–4, 52–4, 72, 88, 90, 93, 112, 131–4, 138, 140–1, 143–5, 149
    Hume's, 3–6, 28, 30–1, 88, 152, 163–4
    hypocritical, 37
    Pyrrhonian, 164
Searle, J.R., 36–7
second-order property, 67–8
self, consciousness of, 87–8, 90–6, 110
self-evidence, 3, 29–32, 35–6, 38, 112, 139, 141–2, 146, 151
sensation, 44–8, 50–6, 58–9, 61–2, 70, 73–4, 77, 79, 137, 146
    adverbial theory of, 73, 175–7
    as mode of thought, 59–60, 63–4
    asymmetrically related to perception, 63
    distinct from perception, 73
    doxastic account of, 62–3
    inference from, 52–5
    is not belief, 56
    object of?, 45–6, 49, 55, 59, 64, 73, 89, 176–7
    referentially empty?, 46, 59, 64
    sign theory of, 44–5, 48–9, 55, 59–64, 79, 137
sensationalism, 54, 57–8
sensations, contingent, 76, 78–9
    not much noticed, 59–60, 137
sense-data, 50, 144–6, 207
shapes, real existence of, 189–90, 196, 207
Shelburne, Lord, 101
sign, natural, 63
Smart, J.J.C., 71

smells, 65, 74, 78–80
Smith, A., 5
Smith, N. Kemp, 164
soul, reality of, 17, 95, 101, 104–6, 112
spherical angle, 202–4, 206
    geometry, 199–200, 202, 205–7
    position, 200–2
    projection, 190–1, 199, 206
Steward, H., 95
Stewart, D., 5
Stich, S., 40
Strawson, G., 30, 89
    P.F., 88
Stroud, B., 131–2, 143
substance, 21
suggestion, 49, 53, 55, 57, 61, 63–4, 73–4, 77, 137, 146
    is not inference, 56
Sutton, T.J., 87, 90
Swinburne, R., 155
'system', definition of, 163

tabula rasa, 156–7
Taylor, R., 10
testimony, reliability of, 19, 39
thought, power of, 100
transcendental arguments, 87–8, 90–5
Turnbull, G., 2–3

unicorns, 170–4, 176, 187
universals, see *general terms*
utility, 123–4

Van Cleve, J., 171
Vernier, P., 30–1
visible angle, 196–8, 202–5
    figure, 193–6, 198, 201–2, 206–7
    line, 196, 198–202
    position, 193–6, 201–2
    triangle, 196–8, 206
visibles, geometry of, 189–207
volition, 15, 21, 115–17, 119–20, 122–3, 125–6, 129–30
    distinct from cognition, 129
    distinct from exertion, 15

volition, object of, 120–1
    requires exertion, 120–1
voluntary action, 14, 18, 111, 113–14, 128–9
vulgar beliefs, 20–3, 52, 66, 72, 117, 152,
    171, 174, 185

warrant, 27, 41, 148
Wigner, E., 94
will, 2–3, 8, 14, 114–21, 127–8
    distinct from action, 14–15
    free, 21, 23, 110–11, 130
    higher-order capacity, 126
    presupposes conception of power, 14,
        18, 115–18, 121
    presupposes intelligence, 3, 121
    reductionism about, 114–15, 119,
        121–2, 128–30
    weakness of, 115, 124
Wilson, C., 169
Winch, P., 10
Wittgenstein, L., 8, 84, 89
Wolterstorff, N., 29–30, 33–4, 48, 74–5,
    151–2, 178–9
Wood, P., 99, 104
Woozley, A.D., 8, 10–11

zombies, 36–7, 157